...on of Social Workers

Series ...o Campling

┌─────────┐
│ B A S W │
└─────────┘

Social work is at an important stage in its development. The profession is facing fresh challenges to work flexibly in fast-changing social and organisational environments. New requirements for training are also demanding a more critical and reflective, as well as more highly skilled, approach to practice.

The British Association of Social Workers has always been conscious of its role in setting guidelines for practice and in seeking to raise professional standards. The concept of the *Practical Social Work* series was conceived to fulfil a genuine professional need for a carefully planned, coherent series of texts that would stimulate and inform debate, thereby contributing to the development of practitioners' skills and professionalism.

Newly relaunched, the series continues to address the needs of all those who are looking to deepen and refresh their understanding and skills. It is designed for students and busy professionals alike. Each book marries practice issues and challenges with the latest theory and research in a compact and applied format. The authors represent a wide variety of experience both as educators and practitioners. Taken together, the books set a standard in their clarity, relevance and rigour.

A list of new and best-selling titles in this series follows overleaf. A comprehensive list of titles available in the series, and further details about individual books, can be found online at:
www.palgrave.com/socialworkpolicy/basw

Series standing order **ISBN 0–333–80313–2**

You can receive future titles in this series as they are published by placing a standing order. Please contact your bookseller or, in the case of difficulty, contact us at the address below with your name and address, the title of the series and the ISBN quoted above.

Customer Services Department, Macmillan Distribution Ltd, Houndmills, Basingstoke, Hampshire RG21 6XS, England

Practical social work series

New and best-selling titles

lena dominelli

anti-racist
social work

third edition

palgrave
macmillan

Published by
PALGRAVE MACMILLAN
Houndmills, Basingstoke, Hampshire RG21 6XS and
175 Fifth Avenue, New York, NY 10010
Companies and representatives throughout the world

PALGRAVE MACMILLAN is the global academic imprint of the Palgrave Macmillan division of St. Martin's Press, LLC and of Palgrave Macmillan Ltd. Macmillan® is a registered trademark in the United States, United Kingdom and other countries. Palgrave is a registered trademark in the European Union and other countries.

ISBN-13: 978–0–230–54301–0
ISBN-10: 0–230–54301–4

This book is printed on paper suitable for recycling and made from fully managed and sustained forest sources. Logging, pulping and manufacturing processes are expected to conform to the environmental regulations of the country of origin.

A catalogue record for this book is available from the British Library.

A catalog record for this book is available from the Library of Congress.

10 9 8 7 6 5 4 3 2 1
17 16 15 14 13 12 11 10 09 08

Printed and bound in China

To all of us, wherever we are,
toiling to bridge the gap
between racialised oppression
and racial equality to achieve
human fulfilment in its rich diversity

Contents

Figures

| Acknowledgements

Writing a book is not the easiest of tasks. Rewriting this one for the third edition has been difficult given crucial developments in racialised social relations, particularly in the law and order arena and a new focus on terrorist activities. These have shifted many of the debates around ethnicity, 'race', religion and culture, and have significant implications for perceptions of 'difference' from the dominant norm and how racism is both conceptualised and responded to. These have impacted upon all of us in diverse ways and complicated the building of relationships of trust amongst us.

Nonetheless, we remain bound together on this planet and carrying out a dialogue across differences is unavoidable if we are to live under conditions of equality. And so, I wish to thank the many people who have interacted with me and shared their experiences, often in lengthy discussions during the writing of this book. You are too numerous to mention by name, but I valued your input and narratives, particularly your questions that forced me to rethink what I was writing about, how I expressed it and what I ended up with. Thank you.

I also wish to thank colleagues at the University of Durham who freed me from teaching and other duties so that I could have thinking time to work on this book. And, I want to express my appreciation to my family, nuclear and extended, for their unending love and help with daily frustrations, computer problems and daily chores. They have also supported me through rough times.

Finally, Jo Campling, your commitment to anti-racist social work compelled me to embark on a third edition in trying times. You have been an inspiration to me over the years of our friendship and a stalwart promoter of the profession. I shall miss your dedication and support in future, but hope that you have gone to a better place and would have been pleased with the end-product.

Lena Dominelli

Introduction: anti-racist social work as contested terrain

Introduction

Racialising discourses continue to permeate social life in Europe. Rising acceptability of far-right nationalistic sentiments, demonising discourses about immigrants and asylum seekers and growing electoral confidence of narrow nationalist or quasi-fascist parties indicate the reality and increasing acceptability of racist social dynamics in this land mass (EUCM, 2005). These developments encourage the 'othering' of difference, exclusion of foreigners, rejection of Third World nationals as European settlers and promote a 'Fortress Europe' mentality and xenophobia. 'Othering' difference is central to racist dynamics and power relations (Dominelli, 2002b).

Anti-foreigner attitudes have hardened following the attacks on the World Trade Centre in New York in 2001, Madrid Bombings in 2004 and London Bombings in 2005 and given new twists to the racialisation of different cultures and ethnic groups. The United Kingdom is no exception to the advance of injustice through racialised politics. The far-right white supremacist British National Party (BNP) gained its first electoral success at local level when Derek Beackon won a by-election in Millwall Ward, Tower Hamlets (Isle of Dogs), London in 1993. By the 2006 local elections, it moved from a fringe party fielding a few candidates to contesting 363 seats. It was returned in 44, double its previous holdings (Wheeler, 2006); and polled 41 per cent of the vote in Barking and Dagenham compared to Labour's 34 per cent (M. Taylor, 2006).

Set against actions that renew racism are the struggles of minority ethnic groups for liberation, freedom to be themselves and acceptance as human beings. Alongside these are endeavours of peoples, black and white, to eradicate racial oppression, promote equal opportunities legislation and initiate individual and collective struggles for social justice and human rights. Western characterisations of racism define 'black' people as inferior; white people as superior. These terms are not comments about specific identities, but about positioning within racist dyads that affect every aspect of daily life, life chances and status in society. Racism's interaction with identity is not predetermined but dependent on how actors negotiate social relations to accept, accommodate or resist racism. Anti-racist endeavours in the twenty-first century are embedded in notions of social justice and human rights within full citizenship, often accompanied by demands that transcend national borders.

Despite legislative changes at European and national levels and gains in British anti-racist directions from the 1960s onward, the forms that racism takes and sites in which it is elaborated through social interactions continue to morph and develop, making the challenge of eradicating it one of constant vigilance, rethinking our understanding of its dynamics and unending action against racism in all its forms. Understanding the social contexts of human exchanges enable us to unpack the backdrops against which the specifics of racism evolve. These can be contradictory and make promoting racial justice hazardous and difficult. To surmount these, people have to prepare for the potential risks and resistances they will encounter. Risks impacting upon white people who work for racial justice differ from those black people endure every day of their lives. While white people's commitment to racial equality gets tested, black people face humiliation, disparagement, constant threats of violence, discrimination in employment, health, education and housing.

Racism involves ideologies, policies and practices about who and what is superior or inferior. It relies on credible narratives that establish racial hierarchies for ordering social relationships across groups that are racialised differently. The negative evaluation of racialised attributes is central to racism. 'Race' becomes an artefact ordered to achieve certain ends. I define 'race' as a social construct based on the politicisation of traits that vary over time and range from biological features such as skin colour, hair texture and eye colour, to social attributes that cover cultural elements like language and religion that are associated with a person's sense of being and belonging. Racist dynamics occur within binary dyads that inscribe positive values to characteristics deemed superior and negative ones to those thought inferior. Lighter skin colour, associated with Northern European ethnic groups, is inscribed as superior. Darker skin is less valued and linked to those from other parts of the world, including historically, Southern Europe (Douglas, 1983).

'Race' becomes a symbolic device created through social relations of racial differentiation in individual and group encounters among people who are ethnically and culturally different. Racism can be defined as a process of racial differentiation enacted in and through social interactions and exchanges embedded in daily routines or everyday life practices. Racism is a socially constructed phenomenon that varies in form over time and different locations. People use the idea of 'race' to constitute a reality of racial differentiation that establishes a hierarchy of value and meaning embedded in binary dyads linked to superior and inferior attributes. Its dynamics are not peculiar to the West. However, the focus of this book is on Western racism's impact on black and white peoples mainly in the United Kingdom. People use 'race', ethnicity and nation interchangeably. They are discrete: 'race' focuses on physical attributes or phenotypes like skin colour; ethnicity on origins associated with a specific cultural group; and nation with nationality within a nation-state (Ratcliffe, 1996).

Narratives are peoples' accounts of how they live and reasons for doing what they do. They configure and are configured by everyday life practices (ELPs), are created in and through space and time and maintained by social interactions. Understanding narratives provides insights into how varying discourses of 'race' and racism become practices that people create, accept (often unwittingly), reproduce or reject and is critical in transforming unequal social relations. Changing a narrative can alter how 'race' and racism are perceived and renewed or destroyed in and through everyday life practices, organisational structures and cultural norms. Analysing narratives can expose the dynamics and processes whereby racism is created, reinforced and eradicated (A. Taylor, 2006). Exercising agency in shaping discourses to achieve certain ends makes eradicating racism a contested activity. In racist social relations it privileges those with the luxury of choosing to ignore the injustices that racism inflicts. Practitioners constantly work with narratives created by: people who access services, employers and broader society. They are well-placed to develop new narratives that enact anti-racist practices aimed at creating a society where racism is no longer an issue (Hall, 1997). The task requires social workers to go beyond simply empowering people as individuals and engage in transformative change in everyday life practices; institutional arrangements; organisations; and society's cultural, political and economic frameworks.

About this edition

Social work as *professional work* has been remarkably absent from New Labour's remit. Today's climate for promoting anti-racist social work is bleak. The General Social Care Council (GSCC) does not deem it a separate *requirement* of assessment but one to be incorporated into values teaching and Islamophobia mars the social landscape with racial profiling and injustice (Amnesty, 2004). I aim not only to write a book that engages students, practitioners and educators in intellectual pursuits, but one that encourages readers to: think critically about existing practice; and include those who are racially excluded as equals. Besides raising awareness of complex issues, I invite action that promotes practising anti-oppres-sively. I refer to earlier literature to show that historical works can be current. The forms racism assumes today differ from those prevailing in the late 1970s or early 1980s when I conducted research for the first edition of *Anti-Racist Social Work*. In this, the third, I reflect on anti-racist social workers' concerns of the twenty-first century including Islamophobia and how to advance ethnically aware, less racially oppressive policies and practice.

Becoming anti-racist social workers encompasses a broad range of knowledge, skills and tasks embedded in anti-racist values that I consider in this book. Tasks that anti-racist practitioners can undertake include:

● developing a working knowledge of theories of racism that contextualise social work within the state apparatus and outside it;
● understanding the dynamics of overt and covert forms of racism;
● recognising how social processes and institutions legitimate racism within and outside social work structures and how these impact upon the profession; and

- relating these dynamics to everyday professional routines and everyday life practices.

Evidence for my analysis is drawn from conversations with black and white people interested in anti-racist social work; documentary analyses; content analyses of public discourses conducted in the media; and research undertaken by others and myself. Experiential evidence supplements empirical evidence and makes it possible to forge connections between personal lives and social problems and structures (Butler, 1990). Social work in the United Kingdom, especially England, provides the main context for my writings. This variant of the profession is embedded in wider arenas, nationally and internationally where existing discourses (re)articulate and (re)formulate national ones. I cover events in other countries to draw transnational comparisons and show the interdependent growth of social work as a global but locally rooted enterprise.

I structure this book around the idea that anti-racist social work remains relevant to eradicating racial oppression and worth pursuing. The struggle for it is not straightforward and occurs simultaneously at different levels within three interactive forms of racism – personal, institutional and cultural. I explore these terms in Chapter 1, examining definitions of racism, anti-racism and oppression. I look at the relevance of socio-economic, cultural and political contexts and discourses embedded within these to tease out the epistemological and ontological realities that impact upon particular positions and highlight the significance of agency and social interaction in (re)producing racial oppression. I position anti-racist social work within a continuum of practice ranging from racist to non-racist. I also cover arguments propounded by critics (left and right) of anti-racism as they raise concerns that anti-racists have to address.

In Chapter 2, I explore racialised identities and deconstruct the terms 'black' and 'white' to unpack the implications of totalising versions for social work practice. In Chapter 3, I examine how a profession that purports to promote welfare and ensure social justice becomes a site for racial oppression, regardless of the personal intentions of individual social workers.

In Chapter 4, I explore anti-racist social work with children and families by considering specific examples of practice. I examine contested areas like inter-racial adoptions, and the identities of multiple-heritage children. In Chapter 5, I focus on social work with adults and older people to unpack the links between ageism and racism. In Chapter 6, I argue for anti-racist empowering practice with offenders. In Chapter 7, I consider anti-racist social work with asylum seekers and refugees, and highlight how political discourses fan the flames of xenophobia.

In Chapter 8, I explore the use of community work strategies in anti-racist social work. I conclude in Chapter 9 with suggestions about: how anti-racist social work can empower both 'black' and 'white' people who access services (clients or service users); the skills that social workers need for such work; and different levels in which interventions are necessary.

1 | The shifting terrain of racist dynamics and anti-racism

Introduction

'Race' and racism are contentious terms. The existence of racist dynamics in social relations is not always acknowledged. In some European countries, the categorisation of people into different 'races' is rejected by appeals to a universalised notion of nationality; for example, a Frenchness that obliterates difference (Abye, 2001). In others, the word 'racist' is suppressed, for example, Switzerland. Some white people take umbrage at being seen as racist and refuse to engage in understanding the complex and intricate racist dynamics they unquestioningly accept in everyday life practices (ELPs). Others actively engage in forming alliances to eradicate it. These varied responses expose contested and constantly shifting terrains that (re)produce and (re)configure racism. In this chapter, I explore how 'race', racism, anti-racism and oppression shift in meaning and are embedded in ELPs to acquire potency. I argue that anti-racist initiatives can eradicate racism. Achieving this goal remains problematic and uncertain.

I place 'race' in quotes to indicate that the term is contested and socially constructed rather than biologically derived. People continue to utilise biological attributes in the social construction of particular ways of seeing and doing 'race' in the world. The word 'race' highlights the politicisation of biological traits alongside social ones and their evaluation in social interactions as either negative or positive to produce the racialisation of both black and white peoples.

Defining racism and unpacking racist dynamics

The 2001 Census gave the United Kingdom a minority ethnic population of 4.5 million or 7.6 per cent (ONS, 2002), an increase over the 4 per cent it comprised in 1981. Of these, 55 per cent were under 16 years old. Minority ethnic groups are more likely to: reside in low-income households; be unemployed; have health problems; and be victims of racially-motivated crimes than white ethnic groups (ONS, 2002).

The number of immigrants entering the United Kingdom has been restricted since the 1970s except for family reunification purposes; growth in these populations is occurring through births to those already here (ONS, 2002). The ONS (2002) claims that the minority ethnic population is growing more rapidly than the white one, revealing that ethnicity characterises only 'black people', not all peoples.

Definitions matter

How 'race', racism and anti-racism are defined matter. Words indicate understandings of reality, shape interactions within discourses that produce them, and expose specific conceptualisations of power relations and people's place in the world. They also influence actions taken. Words both reveal and construct ways of knowing, exposing the epistemological and ontological assumptions that underpin thoughts and behaviours. Questioning words and meanings is more than arguing about semantics.

Scientifically, *all* human beings belong to the same 'race' – *homo sapiens*, believed to have originated in Africa, a position alluded to by Charles Darwin (Kohn, 2006:38). The amount of melanin produced by melanocytes in skin determines skin colour. This is a biological process linked to the environments in which people live. In these, melanin interacts with sunlight to produce many skin shades amongst humans. Historically, the meaning of the term 'race' has varied. It once focused on a racialised hierarchy that encompassed the physical attributes of all 'races' – identified by skin colour and depicted in popular parlance as white, yellow, red and black (Gobineau, 1953). Definitions of 'race' propagated by Count Gobineau illustrate a biological theory that racialised skin colour. Later, it focused on allegedly different intelligence levels that favoured the white 'race' (Hernstein and Murray, 1994). 'Race' as a biological entity has acquired a new lease of life through genetic biology and socio-biology. These explain variations in human physicality and behaviour through genomes. *The politicisation of this biologically based process through the negative valuation of darker skin results in racism* and exposes its socially constructed basis.

The politicisation of biological attributes is evident everywhere. Under colonialism, European forms of racialisation focused on 'others', were extended across the planet, and became embedded in countries settled by Europeans. Spread through imperialist ventures, it redistributed world resources to those with desirable physical traits. The continued valuing of lighter skin amongst people of African origins in Jamaica is attributed to this (Williams, 2007). Other forms of racism hold sway in different socio-economic and cultural contexts. These debilitate and destroy humanity; for example, caste in India where a hierarchy establishes the Brahman, Kshatria, Vaisia and Sudra, above 'Untouchables' or Dalits who, traditionally, were deemed barely human. In Europe, racist discourses based on culture superseded biological ones in the 1980s (Barker, 1981). Cultural racism, reinvented through a 'war on terror', emphasises culture and religion amongst Muslims, giving Islamophobia a dyad that led George W. Bush to assert a 'clash of civilisations' between East and West (Ahmed, 2003).

Stuart Hall defines racism as 'a set of economic, political and ideological practices whereby a dominant group exercises hege-mony over subordinate groups' (1980:338). A hegemonic construc-tion of racism captures people's hearts and minds in an untheorised common sense that masks the dynamics that underpin it so that consent is obtained without conscious action. Foucault (1991) calls these dynamics the 'instruments of governmentality' or means whereby people control and discipline themselves. This is achieved through narratives that turn signifiers of 'race' like skin colour into artefacts of everyday life. These assign place and meaning to oneself and others through taken-for-granted processes of racialisation that establish binary dyads of superiority and inferiority. They become embedded in daily routines by processes that create and affirm racialising narratives at the personal, institutional and cultural levels. Permeating every aspect of social life these narratives consti-tute 'technologies of the self' that produce the 'self'. Their unartic-ulated assumptions underpin racism, make it a normal feature of everyday life practices, conceal its endemic presence in society and enable people to focus on the crude, irrational beliefs and actions of a few evil individuals. These dynamics allow white people to cast themselves as non-racist, take umbrage at being called racist, and become extremely defensive when accused of living in a racist society.

Oppression is a system of domination that denies individuals dignity, human rights, social resources and power. Discrimination is a small part of an oppressive system concerned primarily with *access* to social resources and power. Racism is a specific form of oppression that stereotypes and negatively values peoples' ethnic and cultural attributes. It interacts and intersects with other forms of oppression like classism, ageism, sexism and heterosexism. Some consider these 'isms' additive; others as existing in parallel universes with competing hierarchies of oppressions. Reframing these as created in and through interactive relationships with intersecting components nests racism within intersecting universes of oppression. In these, a person endures all forms simultaneously as each mediates and is mediated by the others.

'Race' and racism are constructed during interactions between black and white people. They have been and remain complex, emotive concepts covering a range of heterogeneous populations, black and white. Each has its own positioning in racist social relations. Racism has not been and is not simply a matter of 'black' versus 'white'. Undoing racism is not solely a matter for black people. Engaging white people in tackling racism, their role and privileging in racist frameworks is crucial to eradicating it (Frankenburg, 1997). Understanding particular expressions of racism in historical context is useful in deconstructing it for specific purposes.

From the first edition of this book, I argued that 'black' and 'white' were social constructs that facilitate our understanding of racist dynamics rooted in a binary framing of social relations that configured one group – 'black' people – in an 'object' position at the receiving end of racist dynamics, while 'white' people, as the authors of these relationships, located themselves as 'subjects' holding agency for initiating action. My focus on 'black'–'white' relations was not to deny the relevance of other forms of racism at the time, but to concentrate on one that I felt provided insights that would help social workers address others, albeit while taking account of the specifics that impacted upon each ethnic group (Dominelli, 1988:7). Thus, I indicated that those of 'white' ethnicities, like the Polish, Germans, Irish and Italians, were also at the receiving end of racist dynamics, but that the experiences of each group was different and merited study in its own right. I expressed the same view in relation to different ethnicities within populations of African and Asian descent and suggested that both 'blackness' and 'whiteness' had to be deconstructed to advance equality. The positions of all parties to an interaction have to be unpacked and understood.

In subsequent works, I highlighted how this positioning is affected by the responses and intentions of all parties to a relationship through the exercise of human agency whereby people mediate what happens in a particular context. Those cast as inferior do not always accept being so defined. They may: internalise their position by accepting it; accommodate it; or resist it. Those depicted as superior may accept, accommodate or resist it too. Outcomes are not predetermined, but negotiated in and through social interactions that can enact, re-create or disrupt these relationships. Whichever option participants in an interaction go for shapes the final outcome (Dominelli, 2002a). Black people who internalise white norms seek to emulate white people and their lifestyles. This includes protagonists like Pecola who prayed nightly for blue eyes to win approval in Morrison's *Bluest Eye*; black children who paint their skins white (Coard, 1971); black children demanding white foster parents; or black service users wanting white social workers. In outlining black people's development in his model of nigrescence, Cross (1992) defines this as the pre-encounter stage.

These experiences have been exacerbated by simplistic forms of racism awareness training in vogue during the 1980s. These fostered the idea that power lay only on one side of the oppressor–oppressed divide and did not focus on the subtle playing out of relations of subordination and domination in everyday life practices wherein localised resistance by oppressed people is enacted. Understanding connections between different aspects of racism requires sophisticated anti-racist analyses that address situations in systematic and holistic ways. An alternative to simplistic forms of racism awareness training was conscientisation (Freire, 1970).

practice tips *defining conscientisation*
Conscientisation is a process that engages people in: deconstructing their realities to better understand them and the complexities embedded within everyday life practices and professional routines; and unpacking the social

> processes and power relations that link personal behaviour to social relationships that perpetuate or maintain specific social positions and promote social inclusion for some and exclusion for others.

Conscientisation creates anti-racist insights into and for social work by revealing black people's experiences of racism as not simply about resisting being oppressed by white people, but carving out a dignified life in the interstices of the social spaces that they both shape and are shaped by when interacting with others. It also exposes how the normalisation of white people's worldviews enables them to: take its construction for granted; become detached from racialised situations; ignore the multiple dimensions in which whiteness is created; fail to recognise subjectivity of others; negate equality in and through action; and (re)create privileging specific to them.

Multidimensional racist dynamics

Forms of racism

Racism as the enactment of social relations that create a racialised binary dyad with superior and inferior elements carries implications for both those who oppress and are oppressed. Racism has three inter-related interactive components that are embedded in and negotiated through the minutiae of everyday life and professional practice: personal; institutional; and cultural (Dominelli, 1988). These three forms are interactive, have some overlapping elements that feed into and out of each other and in the process of being enacted, they racialise social relations to create racialised hierarchies of oppression that value some attributes by devaluing others. Moreover, these three forms establish white norms as the only gateways to a dignified life.

Institutional and cultural racism constitute structural racism because social resources and power are used to sustain them, whereas personal or individual racism is socially frowned upon, despite its reliance on structural racism to sustain it. Racism is a multidimensional form of oppression or more than discrimination. This analysis differs from Thompson's (2006) PCS (personal, cultural and structural) model in that it is holistic; sees the three types of racism as interlinked and interactional; and defines both institutional and cultural racism as structural (Figure 1.1). Focusing only on discrimination, therefore, does not address the structural nature of institutional racism, although it would make a social worker practising in an anti-discriminatory manner *personally less oppressive* than one who does not.

Figure 1.1   Dimensions of racism

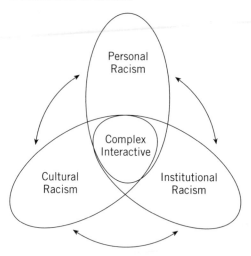

Personal (or individual) racism is practised by individuals as prejudices, negative attitudes and activities that deny certain categories of people dignity and equality. They draw on institutional and cultural racism for legitimacy. Personal racism as in-your-face hatred promoted by bigoted individuals is the form that most people think about when referring to racism in society. Personal racism may be institutionally condoned as revealed by the CRE's (2003c) report into the murder of Zahid Mubarek. His white killer, an avowed racist skinhead combined cultural and institutional racism in Feltham Young Offenders Institution with his own personal racism and that amongst white staff and white inmates to reinforce statements that disparaged black people and set up Mubarek as an object lacking humanity and expendable in extracting himself from custody (Dominelli, 2006b; Keith, 2006).

Institutional racism refers to the routines of professional practice and policies that determine eligibility and entitlements to social resources by excluding some people more than others. It pathologises excluded groups for their failure to succeed within the system; is missed in taken-for-granted everyday routines; is legitimated by public power and authority; and rations power and resources to people perceived as racially inferior. Institutional racism makes racially tolerant individuals act in racist ways, without being aware of it. It reinforces the controlling dimensions of social work, intensifies its policing functions with respect of minority ethnic groups and excludes them from playing prominent roles in creating and delivering mainstream services.

Macpherson (1999:321) defined institutional racism as the:

> collective failure of an organisation to provide an appropriate and professional service to people because of their colour, culture or ethnic origin. It can be seen or detected in processes, attitudes and behaviour which amount to discrimination through unwitting prejudice, ignorance, thoughtlessness, and racist stereotyping which disadvantage minority ethnic people.

British society is indebted to Lord Macpherson for raising institutional racism, an issue that had been denied for so long, and giving it a high profile. It rightly highlights its embodiment in professional practice including health. Minority ethnic doctors are located at the bottom of the labour hierarchy and in less popular specialisms, for example, geriatric medicine (Goldane, Davidson and Lambert 2004). Yet, the Macpherson definition muddles the different forms of racism in the latter part of the quote. Eradicating racism requires clarity in thought and in understanding its complex structural dynamics including the interconnections between its different elements to shift action in anti-racist directions. In its absence, individuals resort to seeing racism as the product of individual bigotry, removed through education that eliminates ignorance as Lord Scarman (1981) did in his inquiry earlier. Sadly, this is also the endpoint of Macpherson's definition.

Cultural racism consists of those social values, traditions, ideas and norms that guide social interactions between people, and groups and assign worth to some and devalue others. Embedded in culture, these elements – including language and religion that people use to compose a *collective* worldview – legitimate a person's or group's place in society and behaviours that cultural racism draws upon to provide the cement of popular racism that integrates, affirms and perpetuates institutional and personal racism within everyday expressions of racism. Institutional and cultural racism thus become the structural components of racism that feed into and out of personal racism and each other, to create complex connections between them. This connectedness complicates the eradication of racist dynamics and practices. Not understanding the linkages between them results in the structural components of racism working against white people's personal intentions of goodwill in promoting black people's welfare. Their connectedness also frustrates well-meaning initiatives that leave them feeling personally disempowered in and resentful of anti-racist projects.

In Britain, cultural racism normalises white Anglo-Saxon culture as superior; disparages black people's cultures by using white English culture as the norm used for judging these; and labels those deviating from its benchmarks 'deficient'. Hence, black lifestyles, child-rearing patterns, behavioural norms and ambition to improve their lot are undervalued or treated with contempt and disdain. Difference is deemed 'dangerous' and practices associated with it are rejected. This endorses the idea that those embedded in black cultures and organisational structures need 'rescuing', as is the case with black adolescents like Asian ones who are defined as experiencing cultural conflicts with parents (Ahmed, 1984) and African-origined children who are seen as subjected to inappropriate discipline and requiring increased surveillance and control. Gilroy refers to the latter as 'differential intensity' (Gilroy, 1982).

Culture, as a dynamic set of attributes claimed by one group of people, creates bonds of identification between people who may be different and unites those who share similar features. These identifiers are racialised, gendered and interactive. They include social values that shape a worldview and artefacts that compose it; for example, language, religion, traditions, rituals and social divisions. These identifiers are adapted to circumstances that emphasise some more than others for specific purposes. Cultures change over time from within or in encounters with those from different cultures. In a globalising world, a culture that comes into contact with another retains some of its heritage as continuities; others that change become discontinuities. Gilroy (2000:130) comments on the spread of African American culture across the globe:

> cultural commodities have been used to communicate a powerful ethical and political commentary on rights, justice and democracy that articulates but also transcends criticism of

modern racial typology and the ideologies of white supremacy. The living history of New World blacks has endowed this expressive tradition with flexibility and durability.

He also highlights how similarities and differences in these exchanges maintain traditions of black struggles for freedom in new contexts and inspire others.

Cultural identifiers shift relationships between the private and public domains and impact upon families. Gilroy (2000:189) argues that in the 'turbulent narratives' of rap music, conservative framings of a black family as a sanctuary for raising children coexist with intimate private spaces that fathers and mothers enjoy by depositing children with extended family. Competition for private personal and family space subjects children to paternal indifference, described in gender-neutral ways. Narrowed opportunities for public and private expressions of pleasure produce hedonistic lifestyles that become subversive spaces where black male agency is re-enacted in patriarchal terms that (re)create black women and children as both winners and losers. Celebrity status amongst African American male superstars may have given them power and control over their own lives. But, in the broader social framing of American society, black men's masculinities are subjugated ones that deny black men wholly self-defined agency (Connell, 1995). So, social privation impacts directly on the roles that black men, women and children can assume in their families.

Racialised power relations

Power relations and systemic inequalities are crucial to the (re)production of racist social dynamics that establish specific claims to social resources and identity. In racist social dynamics, power relations are formed during processes of racialisation and occur within a framework of interaction and negotiations that accept, accommodate or reject racialising assumptions. Those rejecting this framework may replace it with either new racialising assumptions giving them control or egalitarian ones. Rejection can either involve consensus or impose a specific worldview on others via coercive means as happened in the racialisation of territories and peoples under colonisation. Those exercising power dominate others by mechanisms of intimidation and control encapsulated in Figure 1.2 below

Figure 1.2   Racialised power relations

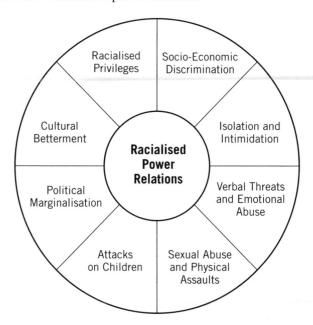

Source: Adapted from L. Dominelli (2002) *Anti-Oppressive Social Work Theory and Practice*. Basingstoke: Palgrave Macmillan, p. 80.

Racialisation as a socially constructed process

Identity is formed through social relationships embedded in complex interactions. It is a multi-faceted and fluid aspect of a person's sense of self – who s/he is deemed to be/wants to be. It is linked to being part of a wider group associated with a specific spatial territory or interest that has a logic of belonging and place to those embedded within it. Knowing who you are in a representational sense in specific social contexts is as crucial as knowing who others are and how they see you. Racialised identities have social processes that configure and represent identity attributes in certain ways.

For ten years, I asked social work students at Masters' and Batchelor's levels to write down three terms that describe them. Seldom was 'race' or ethnicity given, even in lectures on these topics. When they were asked to discuss identity traits with other students and compare notes with how others saw them, even if a black and a white student were involved, rarely was 'race' or ethnicity mentioned. At best, one or two students out of an entire cohort would self-define as British or European, even when discourses in the media had saturation coverage about 'immigrants', 'Europeanness' or defining 'Britishness'. 'Ethnicity' and 'race' were not meaningful descriptors to them. Their roles as (primarily white) students or parents and personal traits like honesty, reliability and friendliness were more significant and accounted for most of their descriptions. Black students were more likely to self-identify as black, but were not often represented. My observations across the United Kingdom suggest that racism is explored less frequently today than it was before the Central Council for Education and Training in Social Work (CCETSW) abolished Appendix 5 in *Paper 30* in 1994.

Current coverage of anti-racist theories and practice on placements is also inadequate. In placement visits as recent as 2006 when I last carried them out, practice teachers told me, 'We couldn't do much on the anti-racist front because we have no black clients', indicating that despite several decades of discussing anti-racist approaches to social work, white ethnicities were not considered part of ethnicised relationships by predominantly white groups. These were people committed to anti-racism, willing to learn and play their part in creating a non-oppressive world. Their responses show a lack of knowledge and skills for doing so, a skills deficit that CCETSW and now the GSCC have failed to address amongst white educators and practitioners constituting the majority of those teaching social work. They define tackling racism around the presence of black people – a problem of their absence; and neglect white people's ethnicities by their presence (Dominelli, 1991).

Problematising definitions of 'race' and ethnicity

Devolution affirms the United Kingdom as a multi-cultural, multi-ethnic and multi-national society where diverse peoples coexist. The exact racial composition of its population is unknown. Collecting identity data is problematic, but the Census gives an official terminology.

Case study   A formal classification of peoples

The 2001 Census improved on previous categorisations by having six categories of ethnic groups that operated on two levels. *Level 1* consists of: White; Mixed; Asian or Asian British; Black or Black British; Chinese; and Other. *Level 2* contains further differentiation, namely: Asian or Asian British; Black or Black British; Chinese; or Other Ethnic Group for the black category; and White British; White Irish; and Other White; for the white category. Level 1 draws upon a Black-White dyad with limited differentiation in the Black category to distinguish between those of African descent and other black people. Level 2 is more inclusive, covering Indians, Pakistanis, Black Caribbeans, Black Africans and those of multiethnic backgrounds, but is confusing.

These changes include some ethnic groups but exclude others, black and white, for example, Arab Britons or Black Irish. And is 'White British' sufficient to tell us about English, Scottish or Welsh peoples, let alone peoples of other white ethnicities holding British nationality, but differently positioned in racialised hierarchies in the United Kingdom? And where are those who associate with none of the above categories? The meaning of each category is unclear. Do respondents base their answers on place of birth, ethnicity, nationality or what? Where does religion fit in? British law recognises Sikhs, but not Muslims, as an *ethnic* group. Yet, Sikhism is based on a religious identity that encompasses several ethnicities and nationalities. Faith differences have long been associated with ethnicity, as Catholics of Irish origins in the United Kingdom can attest. These categorisations are problematic because how ethnicity is defined impacts directly on how 'race', racism and the social processes of racialisation are understood.

Recognising the inadequacy of the Census categorisation, the Labour Market Division (LMD) within the Office of National Statistics (ONS) refined it further. White became British and Other White; Black or Black British became Black Caribbean, Black African, Other Black; Asian or Asian British became identified as Indian, Pakistani, Bangladeshi or Other Asian; Chinese remained Chinese; Mixed became White and Black Caribbean, White and Black African, White and Asian, Other Mixed; and Other Ethnic

Group was unchanged. This differentiation revealed that people of Pakistani and Bangladeshi descent are the poorest groups and those of Chinese origins, numerically the smallest, but said nothing about those this classification excluded.

The LMD formulation remains risky for policy-making and is further complicated by the interchangeable use of the categories 'race', ethnicity, nationality and religion. Like is not compared with like and geographical, religious and ethnic groupings are mixed together. Like the original categorisation, the LMD one ignores the processes of racialisation that racialise not only ethnicity, but also class, gender, age, nationality, religion and other social divisions that produce disparities within each category, making this categorisation unusable except in crude generalisations. These various social divisions are significant in constituting reality and have to be understood because differences and similarities have to be deconstructed to progress the eradication of racism. All categorisations are problematic in that they exclude some people by including others and focus on specific features that ignore others, and so should be used with caution.

Minority ethnic groups live in spatially segregated areas: 98 per cent live in England. Of these; 48 per cent are in London and comprise 37 per cent of its population (ONS, 2002). For the first time, black people outnumber white people in two London boroughs: Newham – 60.6 per cent and Brent – 54.7 per cent (ONS, 2002). They are also concentrated in areas with established black populations including Birmingham, Leicester, Leeds, Liverpool, Bradford, Cardiff and Glasgow. Their numbers and spatial distribution affects their status in life and services they receive (Clark and Drinkwater, 2002). Patel and colleagues (2004) and Patel and Lim (2004) have identified Chinese elders as the most dispersed, isolated and lacking in relevant services because their concentration in catering as self-employed workers prevents them from developing community links and self-help organisations. Some minority ethnic groups have progressed since 1991; for example, gains in educational achievements amongst Indians have surpassed those of white people (ONS, 2002). Racialised gender relations render women's discrimination different from men's in each ethnic group. In education, women of Caribbean descent out-perform men of similar origins.

Despite differentiation in experiences, high levels of discrimination persist amongst minority ethnic groups (CRE, 2006b). Black

British people are under-represented in high-status employment positions and as recipients of welfare services (ONS, 2002). They are over-represented in: schools as poor achievers; criminal proceedings; and higher tariffs of the court sentencing system, especially custodial settings (Home Office, 2002a). Discretionary practices limit their access to influential positions in decision-making structures in local and central government, trade union organisations, the courts and prestigious jobs. Equal outcomes may be achieved if different inputs meet varied needs within a common objective of equality to redistribute posts.

Black people have limited access to influential positions in local and central government and other organisations; for example, demographics in the House of Commons show few black MPs. The first black MP was of Asian origins and elected in 1892. After a hiatus of nearly 100 years, four black candidates were elected to Parliament in 1987. This rose to 12 in 2001, reaching 18 by 2005. This increase is far short of the 55 needed for equal representation. To date, only two elected MPs, both black men, have become ministers: Paul Boatang, who has now left politics, was the first black Minister and worked in Health, the Home Office and Treasury. Keith Vaz, Minister for Europe until he criticised government policies, was dropped in 2001. The President of the Council and Leader of the House of Lords from 2003–7 was a black woman, Baroness Valerie Amos. She was earlier Secretary of State for International Development for a short period. Paul Boatang covered social work, which he termed social *care*, in his brief as Minister of Health and later for children in the Home Office. As Secretary of State for International Development, Valerie Amos covered international community work and social development. Black people's poor representation at the highest level in Parliament is also reflected in the welfare state as both recipients of services and as employees.

In local authorities, the number of black councillors remains small. In Sandwell in 1984, black people made up 11.5 per cent of the population. Four black people were local representatives and between 1 and 2 per cent of employees were black with few in the senior echelons (*Sunday Times*, 15 April 1984), a picture that has altered little. However, the British National Party (BNP) had gained 4 out of the 70 seats in the 2007 local elections. The vast diversity within any minority ethnic group makes it difficult to speak authoritatively about their experiences of racism. The conceptual tools for dealing adequately with these have yet to be developed, although there has been progress in unpacking racism's dualistic dynamics and complexities. Further analyses of differentiation require specific examination of a range of different elements like gender and ethnicity, age, religion, geographical location, language skills, specific contexts and other factors. Exploring each specifically would take debates further, but cannot be achieved in this short book. I use the terms 'black' people and 'white' people as symbolic devices to indicate one dimension of reality: that socially constructed interactive processes racialise both social and biological attributes to divide people into those *assumed* superior and entitled to privileges (white) and others cast as inferior and disadvantaged (black). I focus mainly on the dynamics of racism, processes whereby it is created and their significance both for black and white peoples' lives and for social work practice. Specific illustrations highlight particularities and differences in experiences.

Reflecting upon unitary identities

Words socially construct signifiers of specific identities. As representations, these change over time to reflect particular socio-economic and political realities. In the 1960s, 1970s and early 1980s, 'black' became a political term symbolising a unity amongst diverse ethnic groups to resist racist practices. This socially constructed unity relegated concerns linked to specific identities to the background, not to be forgotten, but to be addressed subsequently (Brixton Women, 1984). Forging a unitary identity when different ethnic groups were divided from each other initiated collective political action that highlighted the necessity of eradicating racism. In 1978, the Organisation of Women of Asian and African Descent (OWAAD) described joint struggles on 'stop sus' with liberation movements in Africa in their Newsletter *FOWAAD*. These organisations were allied to the trade union and women's movements and brought together diverse ethnic groups around a black movement. Their unity suppressed the uniqueness and heterogeneity of each separate identity for strategic reasons; ignored specificities in racial oppression; and neglected complaints related to particular groups. As each ally sustained daily life around specific identities, these arrangements created inclusion and exclusion simultaneously.

Tensions ultimately fractured these temporary and transient alliances. By the mid-1980s, their fragile unity became endangered and some, like OWAAD, dissolved. People of Asian origins rejected the label 'black' for failing to account for historical and cultural differences. Yet, 'Asian' is a poor descriptor as it masks heterogeneity between peoples of different cultures, religions and ethnicities originating in Asia. Americans use the term 'people of colour' and hyphenated appellations to address complexities. These also inadequately address heterogeneity; for example, Hispanic Americans come from a range of different countries, ethnic groups and cultural traditions, not just one.

Ethnic groups are divided by age, gender, class, disability and sexual orientation. As more than culture and geographic region are involved in identity formation, the issue of what to call different ethnic groups remains unresolved and divisions deepen within and across these groups. What is needed is a terminology that respects differences within an egalitarian framework and acknowledges commonalities. Achieving this is difficult when claims of ownership involve territorial integrity and belonging. In some situations, different interests generate conflict among groups that were once allies. People of Asian and Afro-Caribbean descent fought over questions of territorial ownership, belonging and gender relations in Perry Barr, Birmingham during 2005 (Phillips, 2005a). Asian and white youths battled on the streets of Bradford, Burnley and Oldham in 2001 (Cantle, 2002). Black-white relations are further complicated by white backlash, as indicated by Proposition 189 in California. Based on a moral panic around differentials in birth-rates across ethnicities, it sought to restrict the term 'American' to white Protestant Americans to allay fears that Hispanic Americans, increasing disproportionately, would overtake them numerically in the twenty-first century (Small, 1994).

Peoples' attributes are racialised in social interactions that create a binary dyad that divides people into superior (white) and inferior (black) beings to create relationships of domination and subordination. These racist dynamics racialise people differently, whether or not these are acknowledged. White people are racialised in ways that privilege whiteness; black people are disadvantaged by the same process. This dyad narrates people into the inclusionary category of 'us' and exclusionary one of 'them'. It racialises the 'them' and *de*-racialises the 'us' group. This enables the 'us' group to think it is outside the framework of racialised social relations and believe statements like '"Race" is an issue for black people'. Social workers do likewise when they claim 'Racism is not an issue for us because we have no black clients' without seeing it as problematic. Eradicating racism means locating both the 'them' and 'us' within the same framework of racialised beings and relations to uncover the simultaneous privileging of white people and disadvantaging of black people. *The racialisation of one and de-racialisation of the other is one movement.*

Discussions of racialised identities in liberal Western democracies have been fraught. The overriding cultural values of equality and tolerance make those privileged by racist discourses feel uncomfortable talking about gains that accrue to them and do not see themselves as racialised. The perception that 'race' applies only to those configured at the receiving end of racist dynamics enables white people to see themselves as *un*racialised beings operating within a neutral framework of social interaction. Not racialising themselves has been a major obstacle in 'deconstructing whiteness' (Frankenburg, 1997) or seeing heterogeneity within and between groups. An assumed homogeneity across the black–white binary divide renders invisible the specificities of racism's impact on different ethnic groups. This includes denying its influence on *dis*advantaged white ethnic groups from Eire, Southern, Central and Eastern Europe; and black ones from places like Africa, Jamaica, Bangladesh, China, Pakistan or Syria; and advantaged white English and white Protestant ethnic groups.

Those resisting these characterisations develop strategies to counter racist onslaughts on their identity and focus on affirming their achievements and place in the world (Graham, 2002). Cross (1992) calls this the internalisation-commitment stage of black identity development. White social workers should recognise acceptance, accommodation and resistance strategies and be aware of models that can assist black children develop attachments to a range of important others, assert and maintain the integrity of their identities and enhance their self-esteem (Robinson, 2002). Africentrism takes the history of African-origined peoples as a source of pride and highlights their substantial contributions to world achievements (Asante, 1987). Supporting black people in and through social work requires organisational change and transformations in professional practice, including co-working in egalitarian partnerships, employing black social workers in significant numbers and at all organisational levels, developing meaningful links with black communities and providing suitable services and options for black and white clients.

As a socially constructed system, the bases of racial oppression are arbitrary and defined for specific purposes. 'Race' becomes exclusionary by rationing or legitimating the receipt of social resources to those belonging to the valued racial group. In European societies, this is restricted to white European nationals by discourses that assume those from third countries in the Southern hemisphere migrate to abuse Europe's welfare systems instead of contributing to them. Empirical evidence reveals that the opposite occurs. Ethnic minority employees are employed to sustain welfare services. Doctors, nurses and social workers from overseas maintain the British health and social care systems (Patel et al., 2002).

Sensoy (2006) in commenting upon Asian Cultural Heritage Month in Canada highlights the majority group's failure to recognise its privileging and racialisation by reflecting that 'in Canada, without having to make any special proclamations, white heritage month is continuously being celebrated' because white privileging is invisible. Its invisibility pervades 'assumptions about the dominant white culture, its collective history and social relationships'. He wants Canadians to unpack this lack of awareness because Canada's 'social health depends on our sincere and sustained attention to our racial history'. The purpose of raising consciousness is not to cause:

> white children to be ashamed of who they are . . . [but] to develop conscious, critical habits of mind . . . [and] well-reasoned and compassionate solutions to social tensions and problems.
>
> (Sensoy, 2006:A17)

This message resonates with anti-racists in other countries where a dominant group exercises power over others rather than living with them in egalitarian social relations.

Racist social dynamics are configured around specific ethnic groups and racialise characteristics that differentiate one ethnic group from another within a negative evaluative framework. This creates racialised hierarchies of being and value that privilege certain groups over others, while drawing on a basic dichotomy of superiority and inferiority to produce specific outcomes. This includes privileging allegedly superior individuals or groups and disadvantaging those deemed inferior. The latter are stereotyped; cast as deficient, non-contributors to broader society; and distanced from the superior group through processes of 'othering'. Those configured as inferior experience this racialisation through exclusion, deprivation, discrimination, humiliation, scapegoating, disparagement and denial of their humanity.

The changing faces of racism

Islamophobia, a new variant on an old theme, indicates how racist dynamics are created anew as people interact with each other, switching between the biological and social realms, making racism an unstable social arrangement that alters over time and with changing social circumstances. Whilst science accorded biological racism legitimacy during the eighteenth and nineteenth centuries, politicians legitimate contemporary racism by utilising cultural features in distinguishing one 'race' from another (Barker, 1981). This includes politicising attributes like language, religion, dress and lifestyles. Since the attack on the World Trade Center in New York on 9 September 2001 (9/11), Islam has become a key signifier for darker skinned people wearing their traditional dress. In this, religious difference is used to characterise Muslims as inferior and dangerous – an idea captured by the term 'Islamic terrorist'. Fear and hatred of Muslims has been called Islamophobia, the specific form of racism used to attack Muslims. Ahmed (2003:8) defines Islamophobia as 'a generalized hatred or contempt of Islam and its civilization . . . [that is placing] pressure on the Muslim family and on social, political and even moral life'. This exacerbates conflict between people of different faiths and civilisations and destroys any sense of compassion or justice that could promote harmony between them (Ahmed, 2003).

Those who divide people on the basis of religion do so arbitrarily with scant regard for their realities. People originating from the Indian subcontinent, whether Sikh, Hindu or Muslim, are perceived as 'Islamacists'. Lumping people together to deny them a unique identity, human rights and place in society depicts racism in action. Such exclusion legitimates assaults against the person as occurred in southern England after the London Bombings of 7 July 2005 to a young man of dual heritage – white English and Ghanaian African, who was called a 'Paki' with 'Bin Laden as his brother' before being attacked by white English skinheads (personal communication). These reactions are an extension of the 'new racism' that Martin Barker (1981) identified when Margaret Thatcher spoke out against 'swamping British culture' with 'alien' ones. Her statement was enforced by the 1981 Nationality Act which introduced the concept of *patriality* – having at least one parent or grandparent born in the United Kingdom – to citizenship; removed the automatic right to citizenship of those born here, ending the 700 year-old tradition of *jus solis*; and gave credence to the view that black people did not belong in Britain (Gordon, 1985). Thatcher's comments reinforced Anglocentricity by focusing on white English culture as the British norm. The development of the new racism coincides with loss of empire, a settled, indigenous black population in the United Kingdom and the repatriation of black people on a voluntary basis (Kaufman, 1998). It also deepens the link between citizenship and immigration.

Blurring the boundaries between nationality and citizenship has entered official discourses. In Canada, the first black Governor-General, Michaelle Jean, born in Haiti, was pictured in the papers as spending 'Mother's Day in her Motherland', that is, Haiti (*The Province*, 14 May 2006) even though she is the official representative of all Canadians, taking the place of Queen Elisabeth II. This discourse suggests she has a 'motherland' other than Canada; is not truly committed to Canada; or symbolically blurs nation-state boundaries and affiliations, that is, officially sanctioned transnational relationships. The latter response would reflect life in multi-ethnic communities.

The white media adds to the depiction of black people as undeserving members of British society by conflating crime statistics with 'race' to hold black people responsible for high crime rates and economic decline. These statistics cast a long shadow over black people's lives, especially young black men of African-Caribbean, African and Arab descent (Hood et al., 2003; Braidwood, 2003). Racial profiling combines policing public spaces with closer surveillance of private ones making encountering the police during 'stop and search' more frequent and dangerous for black youths than white ones and engenders fear in black communities (Hearnden and Hough, 2004). Coupled with HIV/AIDS, gun culture and the drug economy, these depictions intensify fears shaping public spaces in black communities and mean that 'Daily life becomes a perpetual dress rehearsal for death' (Bauman quoted in Gilroy, 2000:196).

The racialisation of 'dangerous underclasses' promoted by New Right theorists like Charles Murray (1994) use social workers' unpopularity with the public on child protection, failed 'do-gooding', permissiveness on 'race', scroungers and 'law and order' to affirm the demand that welfare state services be withdrawn. They blame white social workers for helping undeserving people, of which black clients are one group, without containing and controlling social problems. Bureaucratic social work and culturally competent social work essentialise 'ethnicity' and redirect service delivery towards control and containment (Dominelli, 2003).

Discourses about white refugees and asylum seekers from Eastern Europe depict them in racist terms and illustrate how racism is reinvented for changing circumstances. Their plight highlights the powerful role of the media and government policies in constructing people as 'others' who do not 'belong' within a polity. Their discourses suggest that scarce social resources are abused by 'foreigners' who are cast as simply interested in living off the labour of others by consuming public services and spaces (Lavenex, 1999). Little note is taken of how policies and practice create specific positions for groups of people by limiting welfare entitlements or prohibiting waged employment, as occurs to asylum seekers in Britain. Meanwhile, immigrants' enormous contributions to society remain devalued.

Barriers to anti-racist approaches: wheel of avoidance strategies

Anti-racism is a state of mind, feeling, political commitment and action to eradicate racial oppression and transform unequal social relations between black and white people to egalitarian ones. White people can act on these matters without relying on tokenistic responses that dump responsibility for change on black people by building bridges and alliances across difference and creating a better society for all peoples regardless of 'race', ethnicity or culture. Anti-racist relations focus on issues directly linked to 'race' whilst paying attention to their intersection with other forms of oppression. Active engagement with one dimension of oppression to achieve a given purpose limits addressing the others despite working on complex oppressive relations.

Avoiding engaging with racist dynamics

Black people's rights to self-determination create difficulties for white social workers who do not appreciate the implications of black autonomy for practice and view with suspicion and trepidation black people who reserve areas of action for themselves. This can occur in contested child welfare issues like cross-country adoptions or transracial fostering (Tizard and Phoenix, 2002; Dalmage, 2003; Barn, Ladino and Rogers, 2006). Considering white ways of relating to children as superior can impede development of child care practices that enhance black children's lives.

White people's fears of being oppressed by black people in a worldview characterised by dichotomous understandings of power and oppression impede anti-racist action. Based on a zero-sum power game of winners and losers, these fears are real. They have to be tackled directly to transcend racial divides. White people enact eight strategies of avoidance that restrict their involvement in anti-racist behaviour: denial; omission; avoidance; decontextualisation; the colour-blind approach; patronising approaches; and exaggeration. More than one can be evident in any given situation and each interacts with the others. The wheel of avoidance strategies diagram depicts these (Figure 1.3).

Figure 1.3   Wheel of avoidance strategies

Source: L. Dominelli (1997) *Anti-Oppressive Social Work*. Basingstoke: Palgrave Macmillan, p. 73.

Avoidance strategies also enable white people to engage superficially with activities aimed at eliminating racism and limit black people's space for self-empowerment.

practice tips   strategies of avoidance

Understanding how strategies of avoidance operate enables social workers to counter racism and support anti-racist practice. I describe these below:

1. *Decontextualisation*. People decontextualise racism by conceptualising social relations in a vacuum devoid of power relations. They may accept its existence 'out there', e.g., South Africa under apartheid, but refuse to believe it permeates their everyday activities. A crucial feature of this strategy denies black people's individual experiences of racism. Or, it may ignore racism under the pretext of focusing exclusively on another form of oppression, e.g., sexism.

2. *Denial*: Denial strategies rest on people's rejection of racism, especially its cultural and institutional variants. They ignore evidence of widespread cultural and institutional racism but accept it as personal prejudices held by extremists.

3. *Omission*: Individuals subscribing to this view ignore the racial dimensions of social interactions, see 'race' as irrelevant in most situations and relate to others as if racism did not exist. Social workers' comment 'There is no racism here' to describe a district office in an area with a high proportion of black people living in it, without employing black workers or delivering services to black clients, reflects the failure to acknowledge institutional racism and has traces of denial.

4. *The 'colour-blind' approach*. This treats black people as if they were white people or accorded 'honorary' white status. The statement, 'I treat everyone the same' is a formulation negating a black person's specific experience of racism.

5. *The 'dumping' approach*. In this, white people hold black people responsible for creating and eradicating racism. It becomes a sophisticated form of 'victim' blaming, e.g., expecting black employees to tackle all matters relating to racism.

6. *The patronising approach*. This deems white ways superior but tolerates black people's approaches to things. Multiculturalism that does not address unequal power relations and structural inequalities exposes this strategy as a superficial acceptance of cultural diversity.

7. *Avoidance*. People are aware of racism in social interactions, but avoid opportunities to confront it. This might mean flinching at racist behaviour but keeping quiet about it, e.g., ignoring racist diatribes by colleagues or clients.

8. *Exaggeration*. This acknowledges racism in everyday life, accepts something must be done, but exaggerates or magnifies the value of minimal steps dealing with it (from the view of those at the receiving end), e.g., thinking that racism can be eradicated simply by introducing an 'equal opportunities' policy.

Racist dynamics permeate social work policies and practice

Social work practice is not exempted from personal, institutional and cultural racism in its policies, practices and theories. The presence of racism in social work was initially documented in 1978 by the Commission on Racial Equality (CRE) in *Multi-Racial Britain:*

The Social Services Response. Other reports followed and testimony from black people exposed the racist nature of their experiences. The identification of racism in the profession was followed by calls for anti-racist initiatives and black perspectives to promote racial equality (Ahmad, 1990). Anti-racist awareness training enjoyed popularity for a while, but was discredited for its simplistic approach to difficult problems. It made white people feel guilty as oppressors and without hope or strategies of action that would make them black peoples' allies in anti-racist struggles. Today, postmodernism legitimates individual, not collective struggles for freedom and thereby allows racist practices to continue oppressing black or minority ethnic peoples.

Racist, anti-racist, non-racist social action

The continuum of social action around racism in social work runs from racist to anti-racist to non-racist. Anti-racism is a stepping-stone between racist and non-racist social relations. Anti-racism bridges where we are at – embedded in racist social relations, to our goal of where we want to be – non-racist ones. Contemporary social relations are replete with racist framings that undermine black peoples' experiences as full citizens. Resistance to and countering racism are part of the anti-racist agenda. The non-racist reality being aspired to has to be created rather than assumed. Formed by eradicating racism, a non-racist environment can produce a context where 'race' is no longer relevant. If racism disappears, anti-racism is unnecessary. Erasing racist social relations has been complicated by the failure of previous anti-racist initiatives. These have been attacked by those supporting its objectives and those opposing them. Opponents consider it 'political correctness' perpetrated by those following fashion trends rather than seriously engaging in practices that meet people's need to be free from racial oppression. Others deny its existence despite a long line of official reports exposing racism. The most significant covered the murder of Stephen Lawrence (Macpherson, 1999); killing of Zahid Mubarek (Keith, 2006); and death of Anthony Walker (McVeigh and Hill, 2005). Supporters criticise anti-racists for not doing enough to eradicate racist practices; doing things badly; or being irrelevant (Gilroy, 2005).

Anti-racist social work

Anti-racist social work is a form of practice that takes as its starting point racialised social relations that depict 'black' people as inferior. It aims to eradicate racist social relations and dynamics from the profession and society. In realising this, white people tackle racist practices at the personal and collective levels; learn about black perspectives; and build alliances with black people by agreeing common objectives to eradicate racism and create egalitarian partnerships. Black people have their own expectations and demands for these alliances and engage with white people to achieve *mutually* acceptable ways forward (Bishop, 2001). They also address other forms of oppression that intersect with racist social relations; for example, sexism, classism. Focusing on racism alone can be a starting point for the journey.

Social workers assume that personal tolerance and commitment to professional ethics rooted in equality enable them to practice in non-oppressive ways. Black people's experiences of their interventions, numerous research projects and public inquiries demonstrate that this is not so (CRE, 2003c; MacKay, 2006). Anti-racists have analysed social work practice and developed alternatives like those discussed in Chapters 4 to 8. Answering questions as to how and why a profession dedicated to people's well-being oppresses black people has brought structural racism, defined as institutional and cultural racism, into the equation and exposed connections between it and personal racism that implicate personally tolerant individuals in racist practice. Devaluing black people's knowledge, skills and qualifications excludes them from competing for certain posts or over-qualifies them for those they hold (MacKay, 2006). Whether directly involved or not, white people's status as perpetrators and beneficiaries of racist social relations positions them differently to black people in anti-racist endeavours. In establishing egalitarian relations, white people will lose taken-for-granted forms of power and privileges. White people have an explicit choice to make about whether or not they work in anti-racist directions.

By casting diverse needs as competition for scarce resources, white social workers who sympathise with the hardships poverty imposes on white clients can feel unable to pursue claims for help and also undermine anti-racist endeavours. Emecheta (1983), speaking as a black woman, describes how easily her white social worker ignores the racial dimension in their interaction and when hearing white clients making racist remarks. Cohen (1985) reveals the difficulties white anti-racist youth workers face in raising consciousness about racism amongst racist white lads in a run-down working-class estate. Tenants associations expose similar dynamics (Ledwith, 2005). A white social worker working with asylum-seekers and refugees in southern England spoke of dilemmas in providing them with services when poor white people had none (Dominelli, 2004a). Their comments revealed a failure to understand that asylum-seekers and refugees had fewer rights or resources to access than white service users and exposes social workers' inability to rise beyond individual interventions to formulate collective strategies that enhance the well-being and quality of life in *both* groups. The picture is complicated by other changes. Neither the reproduction of racist practices nor their elimination are static, one-off events. Privatisation, globalisation, legislative changes, dwindling resources and bureaucratisation of practice through the new managerialism and neo-liberalism make its context a constantly shifting and developing one (Dominelli, 1996, 2004b). New understandings of racist dynamics and grass-roots demands for human-rights and citizenship-based practice contribute to the constant evolution of anti-racist and anti-oppressive practice.

Defining poor people as 'deserving' or 'undeserving' sustains individualised forms of practice that cast black people as 'undeserving' and ignores their life contexts. While having poverty and inadequate resources in common, poor white people's views that black people get unfair shares of social resources draw on decontextualised depictions of black people that ignore the impact of racism, a structural inequality, on their experiences of hardship and poverty. Forming alliances to address the problem of scarcity to meet both their needs is crucial if one group's options are not to destroy another's. In a citizenship-based democracy, each individual has a right to good services. The question is *how* to achieve this. Having social and community workers engaging people in both individual and collective actions can help.

putting it into practice

- Consider how you might understand racism as a complex and contested concept.
- Consider the significance of structural racism as an issue for social work practice.
- Consider how social workers might practice in oppressive ways and what they can do to become anti-oppressive practitioners.
- How can you make a contribution to eradicating racist social work practices?

Further reading

Anderson, M. and Hill-Collins, P. (eds) (2004) *Race, Class and Gender: An Anthology*. Belmont, CA: Wadsworth Publishing.

Asante, M. and Karenga, M. (eds) (2006) *Handbook of Black Studies*. London: Sage.

2 | Racialised identities

Introduction

Identity creates communities of affinity that emphasise features held in common to produce a homogeneous, unitary version that forges a unified community and submerges differences. Traditional definitions of identity (see Jenkins, 1996) are characterised by unity, treated as immutable and fixed. This 'holds' specific groups together while submerged differences bubble away under the surface. A hegemonic, unitary identity is established in opposition to difference to give shared meanings about who people in a specific group are, what they can be and what they can do in the world to those it encompasses. A socially constructed process of racialisation places these homogeneous categories within a binary dyad of superiority and inferiority that underpins racist dynamics by affirming a superior 'race'. In this chapter, I consider the impact of ethnicity, nationality, culture and other social attributes of racialised identities in majority and minority communities and how these impact on social work practice.

Identity formation involves power relations

Identity formation draws upon attributes based on mythical pasts and current realities. People may reclaim earlier identities or forge new and different ones. In creating new ones, the past may be trawled for suitable role models or features that can be adopted or adapted to meet present purposes. Continuities between past and present are emphasised in such situations. Discontinuities between two historical points can lead to the formulation of new defining characteristics. Identity formation is a political act produced through negotiated social interactions involving power relations that (re)create and (re)distribute power amongst participants. It involves both individual and collective action and can result from both peaceful and/or conflictual encounters.

Processes of separating or differentiating oneself from others deemed different are involved in identity formation, making exclusion an integral aspect of its development. Such separation would not be problematic were it to be conducted within an egalitarian framework. As it involves judging others negatively, identity formation establishes oppressive relationships whereby a person who self-defines as a superior 'subject' relates to the other as an inferior 'object' in a subordinate position. In creating the 'subject' as norm, the 'object' as different becomes deviant and labelled unacceptable.

The processes of forming identities create signifiers that become symbolically meaningful to and significant for specific individuals or groups. Identity is formed across a range of social divisions including gender, ethnicity, age, class, disability and sexual orientation. Other attributes like social status, position, income, religion, language and other cultural features impact upon identity formation and are social resources used in people's negotiations around identity. These social resources include a sense of belonging and entitlement to space in the public arena. Differentially allocated in dyads around various attributes that impugn different values, these affirm those that are superior and worthy of such resources, and whose entitlement cannot be questioned, while excluding others as undeserving.

Dyadic orderings become *givens* embedded in taken-for-granted assumptions of everyday life practices including power relations. Those in the dominant group take these resources as given; those in subordinate groups create social resources through their personal skills and charismatic powers. These power dynamics become crucial for women, who are cast as subordinate within ethnic and racial groups. Their bodies often embody the 'nation' associated with a specific ethnic or 'racial' group (Anthias, 2001; Anthias and Yuval-Davis, 1993). Severe controls can be imposed on a woman's right to self-expression in the interests of collective group survival. Spaces for subverting these constraints exist within the private sphere, often hidden from public eyes. The wearing of feminine clothing or make-up under a burkha, for example, indicates women's resilience and willingness to subvert pre-defined controls on their behaviour (Shakib, 2002). Women, relegated to the private sphere as carers of others – children, husbands and dependent relatives – see this as fair even if engaged in waged work (Baxter, 2000).

The household, workplace, civil society and state become spatial locations where specific obligations, responsibilities and rights associated with certain identities are configured and enacted. Whether in the workplace, community or home these spaces are interrelated and create boundaries that mediate and curtail individual and group behaviour within spheres that are policed for compliance. Social and physical surveillance, a crucial element in policing these boundaries, is performed in the public and private domains by the 'self', others and technological means.

The divide between public and private lives facilitates state involvement in identity formation. The state in implicated in identity formation processes by policies that legitimate or de-legitimate certain identities, especially those that occupy public space. These vary over time and amplify difficulties encountered by those defined as having 'deviant' identities. This has occurred in the construction of single parent women as housing-queue jumpers, young people as demonic troublemakers, asylum-seekers as welfare scroungers, and black men as dangerous criminals, for instance. Discourses around deviant identities are unitary. They focus on one aspect of identity, exclude some features, amplify others and portray people as uni-dimensional characters who are unworthy of public concern and undeserving of public resources. As members of society, social workers can reproduce these stereotypes by not thinking about such assumptions or how cultural and institutional racism is implicated in the routines of professional practice (RPP), or they may challenge them.

People can and do negotiate unitary or essentialist selves if it suits their objectives, to acquire a sense of belonging or receive approbation from others, according to their circumstances and purposes. People may wish to hang onto past signifiers of identity and bequeath them to future generations. Continuities in identity attributes are evident amongst diasporic populations: for example, Jewish people seeking a homeland; African-origined people surviving slavery in the New World; and settled groups with lengthy histories, for example the British monarchy as the unifying symbol of the British nation and protector of its peoples' rights. Cultures also adapt and change in response to encounters with those from other cultures. Jewish people in Britain will share characteristics with those in Israel or Ethiopia, but have distinguishing ones as British Jews. African-origined Americans' experiences of oppression will differ from those of Black Britons and their responses to these will vary. Maori people in New Zealand/Aotearoa have defined their own identity and demanded rights of self-determination and equality in deciding the fate of New Zealand/Aotearoa as agreed in the Treaty of Waitangi. Their solutions differ from First Nations peoples in Canada, but both have secured the right to indigenous child welfare practices to repair damage to the sense of self, family structures, politics and culture induced by colonial experiences (Tait-Rolleston and Pehi-Barlow, 2001; Thomas and Green, 2007).

The state ignores people's complex identities in the interests of unity. For example, when white working-class interests conflict with black working-class ones, the latter are subsumed and white people's concerns take precedence. Stuart Hall argues that unity negates the impact of 'race' when analysts 'ignore capitalist dynamics, for capitalism reproduces the working-class in a racially stratified and internally antagonistic form' (Hall et al., 1978:346). Black feminists have demonstrated that white feminists discount the specificities of their experiences under the notion of universal sisterhood (Anthias and Yuval-Davis, 1993). Begum (1993) and Hill-Collins (2000) have identified how white women's right to family life is not questioned as it has been for black women forced to undergo sterilisation and abortions as they were deemed 'unfit mothers'. While sharing some agendas with white women, black women have different ones.

Traditional social relations have rigid, normative definitions of identity to restrict the permeation of cultural boundaries by others, unlike contemporary ones where a fusion of cultures is commonplace, for example, the currency of Western pop music throughout the world; Indian Bollywood's popularity in the West; American rap music's adoption by singers of Arab descent in France. Fusion questions adherence to traditional cultural norms; undermines and rejects established worldviews; and creates new customs, values and art-forms, including those that resist oppression in processes that reformulate identity traits. These developments acquire new adherents; become mainstreamed and, in time, lose their radicalness. This process illustrates the dynamic, constantly changing nature of identities and cultures.

Traditional cultures have universalising tendencies that obliterate differences, if only to create unity for specific strategic purposes. These may lose meaning over time and be reformed or subjected to critique and challenge. Universalistic views of identity contribute to assimilating and integrating others into a unitary version of society (Lorenz, 2006). The American 'melting pot' provided an assimilationist vision for building a nation-state and contrasted with the 'mosaic' that featured in Canada or 'multiculturalism' favoured in the United Kingdom. The relevance of monolithic views of culture and identity were challenged by postmodernists who posited instead, hybrid identities, hyphenated identities or dual heritage identities (Modood et al., 1997).

Postmodern discourses and insights on 'race' challenge essentialist or totalising discourses of identity, including those popularised through social work practice and are relevant in developing anti-racist social work. Their tendency to fragment identity ignores historical realities whereby unitary identities were deliberately created around assumed homogeneities for particular purposes with positive and negative consequences. The nation-state created around *presumed* shared characteristics required the imposition of unity or shared aspects of identity on reluctant social groups. In forming the United Kingdom, Welsh and Scottish differences were submerged to create 'British' as a construct dominated by English peoples. In the Canadian nation-state, First Nations peoples were stripped of their identity – language, culture, religion, history and resources including land in the place called 'Turtle Island' (Canada); and French culture in Quebec and other parts of the territory was subjugated to impose Britishness as the basis of national identity. Similar occurrences have been documented in the formation of nation-states throughout the world and advanced the position of some people at the expense of others. Postmodern solutions to the complexities of identity remain problematic. Their characterisations carry a degree of homogeneity as those inhabiting smaller social spaces attempt to establish common bonds amongst those encompassed by each definition. Without these commonalities, identity formation is epitomised by the fractured self.

People have migrated across the world for centuries, often inter-marrying with those in other lands, so the number of ethnicities encompassed within the identity of a given individual may be more than one even if only one is emphasised. Multiple identities, at times called transnational identities for those settling in two or more countries for different periods, for example, Jamaicans with links and family in the United Kingdom, Canada and the United States, are becoming more common (Gouldbourne, 1999; Small,

2007). Conceptualising identities as developed through exchanges with others allows the multi-dimensionality and fluidity of identity to be better expressed. The unitary image of transnational individuals is being recast as those involved reject singular definitions that deny part of their heritage (Alibhai Brown, 2001a). One dual heritage person I interviewed said:

> I don't think of myself as black or white. I am both. I resent being made to choose between [one or the other] like social workers want me to. I am both.

Postmodern formulations of identity ignore tactical alliances around identity attributes for purposes other than nation-building. For example, women joining the women's liberation movement formed tactical alliances that ignored differences to have their voices as women heard and extend their influence across the world. As the movement grew and encompassed different groups of women, the relegation of difference was challenged by those who saw tactical alliances that assumed homogeneity were not working in a movement purporting to create equality amongst diverse populations. Differences not acknowledged, valued or deemed meaningful for the movement, excluded women. This lesson was conveyed by black womanists struggling for equality in the United States in a white middle-class dominated feminist movement (Hill-Collins, 2000). Valuing difference is not enough. Commonalities have to be celebrated too.

Identity and organisational change

Identity has become a basis of social organisation. In identity politics, individuals organise collectively through identity traits to improve life circumstances. Women, black people and disabled people have formed social movements to pursue rights and entitlements within a social justice framework. Their demands have produced organisational change including legislation to secure human rights and citizenship. These groups challenge power relations that disparage difference and value alternative forms of knowledge. The power of the group to do things for itself becomes realised with such actions. Identity-based groups can create networks that provide support and social capital to stretch limited resources during times of hardship. Networking extends the social resources at their disposal.

Identity-based groups can be disempowering if a false unity is enforced and difference obliterated or ignored. False-equality traps (Barker, 1986) are created when groups establish egalitarian relations by assuming that members work together on the same basis: equality is *presumed* rather than created as an actual status. Women-only groups assumed this when they formed unity around their oppression as women without distinguishing how their experiences of gender had been tempered by class, 'race' or other social divisions (Hill-Collins, 2000; Dominelli, 2002b).

'Othering' difference

Othering processes occur in a binary dyad that generates a 'self' in relation to an 'other'. They become exclusionary by dividing people into insiders who are included and outsiders who are not. Dyads rooted in inequality assume that one part of the dyad is superior, the other inferior. Inter-dyadic difference is associated with those in the 'other' category while constructing each part of the binary as the same. Outsiders are dehumanised or denied a personhood rooted in agency. This is reserved for those deemed superior. With superiority comes privilege, including the power arbitrarily to configure others and act as subjects in an interaction that uses unitary or totalising views of identity to create standards for judging those classified as 'other' as deviant and deficient for differing from dominant norms. As the superior hegemonic group, those in the 'self' depict themselves as worthy of social resources while formulating exclusion for 'others'. People value those like them who share the category 'self', but exclude and devalue those in the 'other' to make 'othering' processes exclusionary. These become accepted as normal unquestioned elements in everyday life, embedded in daily routines. Ascribing negativity to difference makes relationships problematic. If diversity were valued, positively celebrated, promoted or encouraged, oppressive dynamics could be undermined more readily. Suppressed internal divisions allow resistance to a dominant group's exclusionary social relations to occur from within.

Adherents of biological racism racialise a biological attribute like skin colour by casting one colour as superior and the others as inferior by comparison and claiming it encapsulates all features of a person's entire identity. Racialised identities are created around binary dyads of superiority and inferiority and rooted in 'othering' dynamics formed in the same processes of interaction that (re)produce racist practices and policies. Racialised identities are unitary, essentialised and applied to everyone in a specific category. 'Othering' dynamics produce power relations that racialise each person, regardless of racial grouping. Its impact depends on whether an individual or group belongs to a 'superior' majority group or an 'inferior' minority one. In racialised configurations, identity becomes a social problem only for those configured as inferior. In the West, this construction legitimates discourses in which 'whiteness' is not an issue in deconstructing racist practices. It problematises only those subsumed under the category 'black', taken to mean people situated as racialised objects in racist discourses; white people, as 'subjects', are exempt from racialisation.

Othering, as a dynamic, multi-dimensional process, can focus on any number of characteristics. It amplifies differences and assigns value to each social division associated with that attribute. For example, in racialised identities, skin colour is linked to 'race' while economic positioning is linked to class. A black middle-class person will hold a higher social status than a black working-class person because class signifies lower status in situations where other signifiers of identity hold similar value. A white working-class person has higher status than a black working-class person when 'race' becomes the key signifier of difference between them in a dyad constructed around a racist framework that assumes white is superior to black when other attributes are valued similarly. Socially constructed discourses about identity alter over time, highlighting different aspects of identity as context varies and changes its key definers. In today's racialised discourses, cultural practices including religion supplement biological determinants of identity. These fluid dynamics change identities and (re)establish stability to unify groups. The dominance of religious discourses over biological ones regained ascendancy as Islamophobia engulfed people observing the Islamic faith, regardless of ethnicity or nationality. After 11 September 2001, Muslims in the West have been redefined as terrorists rather than citizens. Religion and ethnicity have become politicised, culturalised and biologised to yield various forms of racialised profiling that work to their detriment.

Unitary identities permeate social work practice, education and theories

Social work educators treated identity and culture as unitary until postmodern theorists critiqued this as essentialist, unitary and immutable, even when socially constructed (Ramazanoglu, 1989). While these critics ignore the strategic essentialism of unitary identities in transient alliances for given purposes (Dominelli, 2004b), a strategically essentialist identity does not preclude other understandings of identity or challenges to it. People may endorse a commonly accepted view of themselves and groups they associate with while holding other notions of who they are. For example, an individual may live as a black, gay British man while accepting an overall identity as a black British person of African-Caribbean origins. He may identify as a British athlete without further differentiation at another point in time; for example, if competing in the Olympics for the United Kingdom. Increasing numbers of people holding multiple ethnicities and nationalities within their personae indicate the difficulty in maintaining one clear-cut, uniquely defining identity (Alibhai Brown, 2001).

Legislation that created CCETSW in the 1970s had unitary notions of identity embedded within its regulations. These were promoted as 'human growth and development' including attachment theories that centred virtually exclusively on a white middle-class mother–child relationship (Bowlby, 1983). Positing a linear and undifferentiated view of identity formation, with everyone in the United Kingdom following the same evolution, these assumed that identity differences were irrelevant to practice. Commonwealth immigrants were expected to become little English men and women through appropriate education and interventions (Levy, 2004). CCETSW, policymakers, practitioners and academics thought that they would eventually adjust to the (white) British way of life and leave their cultural traditions behind. Universalistic responses and services were thought fit for all; 'immigrants' were to take those they were given (Binnema and Hutchings, 2005).

Whether in the Certificate of Qualification in Social Work (CQSW) or Diploma in Social Work (DipSW), CCETSW failed to develop models of learning and teaching that exposed fractured and multi-faceted identities alongside their unifying dimensions. Unitary notions of identity have resurfaced under the guidance of the General Social Care Council (GSCC) which has resumed the requirement to teach human growth and development with scant reference to difference, anti-oppressive approaches or valuing of diversity, and its implications for theory and practice in qualifying social work at Batchelor or fast-tracked Masters levels. This is reflected in curricula where human growth and development are taught as if there were only one standard way for people to develop through the life-course from birth to death. Bowlby (1983) and Erickson (1959) are alive in today's curricula (Ingleby, 2006). Examining variations in identity and valuing differentiated diversities within any identity formation is left to those who teach it and their individual commitment to deconstructing these.

My trawl of courses on human growth and development on the Internet in 2006 revealed that the epistemological base and political philosophies underpinning understandings of identity remain largely unitary. Attachment theory à la Bowlby, with its universalistic and unitary notions of identity, continues to be taught despite struggles to recognise and celebrate diversity. Exploring how key conceptual frameworks like those encapsulated by 'attachment theory' can be applied in an ethnically diverse population is left for individual workers to establish (see Ingleby, 2006). Even in the early 1990s when anti-racism was an explicitly assessable requirement, identity was cast in unitary terms with little recognition of the significance of power relations in valuing ethnicities differently or of the heterogeneity within each ethnicity. Public policy on the welfare state makes unitary assumptions about citizens (Dominelli, 1991; Lister, 1997). Immigration legislation treats the 'other' as 'different', but assimilable if they remain in the United Kingdom (Freeman, 1992) by becoming 'registered' if Commonwealth citizens, or 'naturalised' if they were not, provided that they meet the requirements of living in the United Kingdom for a specified period, under the appropriate conditions of entry.

Social workers practice within fixed and unitary notions of identity in a hierarchy of worth that privileges white people. Identity in social work is constructed around roles, many of which are linked to familialist ideologies that spell out specific ones for each family member. These emphasise the white middle-class nuclear family made up of a mother, father and two children, a somewhat anachronistic model in a number of countries, including the United Kingdom, with high rates of single-parent women and divorced parents (ONS, 2002). This also ignores other family formations, for example, extended families, and encourages dependency amongst women and children, as the expectation is that men, as adult breadwinners, will provide financially.

Practitioners' tendency to treat ethnicity as a homogeneous identity remains current in culturally competent social work claiming ethnic sensitivity; for example, Lum (2000) and Winkelman (2005). European intercultural approaches also fall into the trap of unitariness and focus on education around cultural differences as the key way of ending racism, an approach unlikely to achieve its goal of promoting racial equality (Dominelli, 2006b). Even when acknowledging that different ethnicities exist, they assume sameness amongst those within an ethnicity. Social workers who regard children of dual heritage as 'black' ignore their actual position of having both a black and a white parent and what it means to them as individuals.

Unitary understandings of identity are not a 'bad' thing in and of themselves. There are occasions when human survival has depended on people acting together through a unified identity, that is, what brought them together rather than what separated them. The formation of nation-states; retention of specific ethnic identities under slavery or colonisation; and development of new identities that challenged oppression are such moments. These moments are not cast in stone. Identities change as people's needs and ideas about identity alter. Strategic essentialism explains the discontinuities that exist alongside continuities that maintain identity over time.

Unitary approaches to identity are not limited to curriculum matters. CCETSW failed to reflect the composition of British society within its own structures, another failing replicated by the GSCC. In 1986, CCETSW had one black member on its governing Council. This rose to two by 1995 despite the Black Perspectives Committee, which included black members at lower levels of the organisation, developing anti-racist teaching materials. The highest level reached by a black person in CCETSW, Deputy Director, was assumed by a white man in 1995. The first head of the GSCC was a white woman; her replacement is a white man. Black people are located in lower level posts.

Neither staff nor students on courses reflect the make-up of the British population today although there are a few black professors in social work and the numbers of black students on courses have risen. Excluding those with a 'white' and a 'black' (Asian, Caribbean or African) parent, who constituted 3 per cent of the 2004–5 cohort, black students comprised 22 per cent of social work courses – 10 per cent of African descent and 5 per cent of Caribbean origins. The smallest ethnic group was of Chinese descent with 3 people (0.06 per cent). Black students are unevenly spread spatially and ethnically. Many are in the 'new' post-1992 universities located in areas of higher minority ethnic distributions. Amongst white people, those of English origins made up 62 per cent of the cohort; those of Irish, Scots and Welsh ancestry were 1.6 per cent, 1.0 per cent and 0.9 per cent respectively (GSCC, 2006).

Assimilationist theories and discourses rooted in unitary concep-tualisations of identity have dominated cultural understandings of difference in British social work education from the 1970s to today. Liberal approaches to knowledge replicate unitary notions about identity by espousing equality amongst people deemed the same. Unitary racialised identities link different educational approaches as indicated in the literature from *Race and Social Work* (Coombe and Little, 1986) to *Cultural Awareness, Sensitivity and Competence* (Winkelman, 2005). These portray black people, not racist configurations of their places in society, as problematic. Referring to a European ethnic group, Orphanides (1986:84) states:

> the majority of first-generation Cypriots – more women than men – have had little opportunity to mix with the mainstream society and learn the English language . . . children with non-English speaking parents begin school at a disadvantage, which may impair their educational performance.

A textual analysis of this quote locates the problem within the Cypriot community's refusal to assimilate by learning English or change its employment and cultural traditions. Today's framings of immigrants echo this refrain which has become enshrined in policy; for example, Sure Start. David Blunkett as Home Secretary failed to address racism within the broader society when demanding that immigrants acquiring British citizenship learn English. Fluency in English is crucial for anyone living in the United Kingdom to engage fully in the public arena. Seeing its lack as the sole cause of racial inequalities continues to locate difficulties within an 'immigrant' individual or community and is unacceptable. Blunkett assumes that all 'immigrants' do not know English; many are fluent speakers. People can and do learn more than one language; they may speak English and know English culture before arrival (see Abye, 2007). Those born in the United Kingdom are settlers with English as their mother tongue. Also, the issue is not of concern only to immigrants. Monolingual English-speakers born in the United Kingdom can advance social interactions in a multicultural society by learning other languages.

Configuring black people as 'reluctant settlers' for not learning English or assimilating is linked to their burdening social services and feeds off a history of racist media hysteria unsupported by objective statistics. 'Immigrants' actively choose Britain to improve their lot and contribute to the economy. Most are of working age, do not require social services at this stage in their lives and contribute to their maintenance as welfare sector employees (Patel et al., 2004). Without their input, the welfare state, especially health services would collapse (Patel et al., 2004). Chronic understaffing has attracted qualified social workers from South Africa, India, Canada and Zimbabwe to Britain (Batty, 2003), causing serious shortages of professionals in the country of origin; for example, the decimation of Zimbabwean social services (Devo, 2006).

Unequal relationships between black and white people, unrecognised in classic social work texts, reaffirm white supremacy by decontextualising 'race' and obscuring power differentials that privilege white professionals and service users, not black ones. Despite attempts to place whiteness under the microscope it remains ignored (see Winkelman, 2005). Lack of progress in deconstructing whiteness reveals that those in power neither justify their use of power nor spontaneously challenge it. Racist structures mystify black people's positionality and configure them as having the same problems with racism as white people when they do not. White people's right to be in Britain is not questioned; they belong here. Black people are configured as guests admitted on a host's sufferance. This motif is evident in practice frameworks utilised by (white) social workers across Europe. When a host–guest relationship underpins black–white interactions, it reinforces the power of the former over the latter.

Legislation that denies immigrants' settlement rights and refuses to acknowledge that black people have entered the United Kingdom as *settlers*, even if constituted as transnational diasporic populations, reinforces racist dynamics by situating them outside a framework of equality. For example, British citizens of African-Caribbean origins in transnational families have deep connections to the United Kingdom, United States and Canada that underpin significant relationships within families and between countries (Gouldbourne, 1999). Support networks, remittances to relatives in the Caribbean (Small, 2007), frequent visits back and forth as a result of cheap flights and Internet communications enable people to maintain continuities in identities across time and space while adapting to locality-specific environments that are reflected in changes in identity (Williams, 2007).

That identity issues encompass the whole of social life was understood by white practitioners who deprived aboriginal peoples of their status and cultural traditions including religion, language and education, to turn them into (white) English men and women as occurred in the United States, Canada, New Zealand and Australia. Writing about First Nations' people in Canadian residential homes, Haig-Brown says:

> Their education must consist not merely of the training of the mind, but of a weaning from the habits and feelings of their ancestors, and the acquirements of the language, arts and customs of civilised life.
>
> (1988:29)

Their entire social and cultural life had to be undermined, destroyed and replaced by an Anglo-Saxon one. Resistance to these abuses of their human rights was deemed a lack of adaptability. Configuring black people as unable to adapt to change reinforces their being seen as risky and 'dangerous' to leave alone, necessitating either strict surveillance by white people including the police, or being rescued by them.

The list of traits that white practitioners expound to pathologise black worldviews and lifestyles is substantial and rooted in identity stereotypes. Alongside this, white people assume passivity in black people's relationship with the external world. These stereotypes include: Asian women as passive and sexually repressed; Asian girls as 'caught between two cultures'; West Indians as sexually promiscuous, matriarchal and unable to maintain nuclear family forms; Chinese students as unable to express anger as a result of 'Chinese insistence on politeness and reverence'. Black people who stand up for themselves or demand their rights are labelled as 'having a chip on their shoulder' or 'aggressive' and 'high risk' rather than 'assertive' (Lum, 2000).

In not adjusting to the British way of life, black children and their families rather than racism are blamed for excluding black people from Britishness. For example, a child missing school is seen as failing 'to come to terms with limited abilities and employment opportunities' (Cheetham, 1972:53). There is no suggestion that racism limits their horizons by inflicting psychological and material damage on them. Racist policies and practices are camouflaged as the searchlight focuses on the qualities of black people. This attitude persists over truancy. Black children, especially boys, overrepresented in truancy statistics are blamed for not adjusting (Flood-Page et al., 2000). No one suggests that the system may be failing to meet their needs and those of white working-class children. Education welfare workers operate within a one-size-fits-all education system deemed to meet the divergent needs of different groups of children, despite research showing the contrary is needed (Modood et al., 1997).

Narratives of belonging and ownership of place and space

Narratives of place and space are intricately tied into issues of identity and location by discourses within which people situate themselves, configure and are configured by others. They reveal the extent to which people accept or reject those with whom they share these spaces; form narratives about inclusion and exclusion; and establish normative discourses or benchmarks for judging others. Racialised narratives of place and space expose the contested nature of social relations of belonging and are articulated around who belongs, who does not and shades in between. Racialised narratives are fractured along other social divisions like gender, class, age, disability.

Discourses configure people's location in society and sense of belonging or being accepted as part of it (or not). I term these *narratives of place and space*. Narratives elaborate themes about one's individual and collective place in the world and how people act in and upon it. Expressed as narratives of place and space, these become narratives of inclusion and exclusion. Inclusionary ones focus on belonging and acceptance; exclusionary narratives on the reverse. Assumptions that underpin these narratives can be explicit or implied as taken-for-granted nostrums that do not have to be articulated or justified.

I undertook a discourse analysis of coverage about settlers, (im)migrants, asylum seekers and refugees in several broadsheet newspapers from May 2005 to June 2006 to arrive at popular narratives of belonging, place and space. These revealed themes or *narratives of place and space* based on binary dyads of non-belonging and rejection (exclusion) or belonging and acceptance (inclusion) as citizens of a given location. Discourses made by nationals usually focused on privileging, possession or ownership of a specific space as theirs. Discourses by non-nationals were articulated in response and often challenged exclusive definitions of their place in society. Figure 2.1 below depicts the typology revealed by these. Several discourses could coexist together.

Figure 2.1 Narratives of place and space

Those who 'belong' in a given territory simply assume 'This land is ours' discourses. Embedded in the everyday life practices of those with power to self-define racially, this does not have to be acknowledged or specified. Those in a dominant group can take 'race' and ethnicity for granted in the unspoken spaces they inhabit. As the norm, they do not perceive themselves as racialised.

---

practice tips   *understanding narratives of place and space*

Narratives of place and space are about positionality and help social workers to better comprehend inter-community relationships. I describe these narratives below:

1. *You don't belong here.* These stories focus on a 'numbers game' that limits those entitled to come, deports those already here and emphasises the unique characteristics of the dominant local culture over immigrant ones. Voiced by nationals, these exclude non-nationals. The *besieged native* was part of these discourses. Their ultimate goal was to make (im)migrants feel unwelcome or go back to their place of origins and could favour segregation or deportation.

2. *Become like us.* Assumed by nationals, this position urged (im)migrants, refugees and asylum seekers to adopt local customs and lose their original ones. It was the typical assimilationist position.

3. *We're human beings too.* These were articulated largely by non-nationals – (im)migrants, refugees and asylum seekers, who sought to connect on the basis of a common humanity and establish entitlement through notions of equality, human rights, social justice. Their claims were supported by some nationals, particularly those endorsing integration or a multiculturalism that tolerates others, often within patronising contexts.

4. *You can't get along without us.* The 'indispensable to the economy' theme was stated by settled non-nationals and newcomers and supported by some nationals. They showed how local economies would grind to a halt without (im)migrants and demanded integration on the hegemonic group's terms. They urged interdependence to facilitate integration or pluralistic coexistence.

5. *This is our land too.* Articulated by (im)migrants, refugees and asylum seekers who either were or had been non-nationals. Those narrating

→

these defined themselves as settlers who intended to stay. They rested their claims on past and current contributions to a country's socio-economic and political life and already being located within it. These narratives often promoted existence in parallel universes or separate developments.

6. *Let's share this land.* Made by nationals, settled non-nationals and would-be-entrants, these narratives emphasised the possibility of living in harmony in a society enriched by diversity, inclusivity and social cohesion. They supported pluralistic coexistence within interdependent and intersecting universes whereby each contributed to others in mutual exchanges based on equality.

Narrative 1 was articulated by those speaking from a position of superiority and ownership wishing to set the terms for accepting or tolerating newcomers. Narratives 2 to 6 reveal different forms of resistance to exclusionary narratives.

Britain's unitary identity under English dominance is breaking up. Besides challenges raised by those with origins outside the United Kingdom, the four key nations – English, Scots, Welsh and (Northern) Irish are more aware of their unique identities and reclaiming their language heritages, especially the Celtic ones as Welsh in Wales and Gaelic languages in Scotland and Northern Ireland gain ground in processes facilitated by devolution. In this reclamation, expressions of anti-English racism can be heard in Scotland and Wales, and anti-Scottish and anti-Welsh racism in England. These highlight how racism *covers more than black–white relations, and is based on* narratives of non-belonging created around discourses of ownership of a particular geographic area.

Racialised power relations in configuring responses to 'difference'

Racialised hierarchies configured around continuities facilitate the (re)racialisation of a specific group to transcend boundaries of location and time. Those based on discontinuities create spaces for resistance or (re)formulate and (re)create them on other bases. Racist dynamics are configured on a number of different social divisions including gender, class, age, disability, sexual orientation, religion, culture and language which can be added to or reduced, depending on the purpose of their interaction and the actual *contexts* within which identity is being formed. Each social division is racialised through complex interactions that produce a racialised entity, whether a person, group, territory or virtual space, making the experience of racialisation a holistic one. Racialisation affects everyone, including those in the so-called superior group. Everyone is racialised, but differently. The specifics depend on an individual's or group's position in a racialised hierarchy of being, actual contexts, who is doing the racialising and why. So, 'race' matters to all.

Black peoples' experience of racism has been one of being rejected for who they are – equal human beings with their own contributions to human development; and subjected to onslaughts that require them to emulate white (middle-class) men while retaining their distance (Fanon, 1968). In the West, this assumes a white supremacy that privileges white people (see Murray, 1994) and locates black people in a continuum of subjugated non-belonging with assimilation at one end of a racist spectrum and deportation at the other. In between are integration, multiculturalism and segregation.

Assimilation strategies articulated around 'You don't belong here' or 'Become like us' discourses require black people to accept white norms as the standards for measuring organisation and behaviour. These benchmarks privilege the dominant group's characteristics above all others and espouse equality on the basis of sameness. Assimilationist approaches racialise biological phenotypes and fix or essentialise 'race' in the process. Their physical basis means these features can be ignored but not altered; for example, skin colour. Thus, assimilation does not concede equality, no matter how successfully black people conform to expectations, and privileges a dominant group's characteristics above all others. Integration allows for coexistence despite difference. It draws heavily on assimilationist dynamics that essentialise 'race' or treat identity as fixed and unitary. Integrationist narratives focus on 'Become like us' and 'We're human beings too'. Integration leaves space for retaining different 'races' and cultures as separate, but parallel, entities while bestowing a modicum of acceptability.

Multiculturalism acknowledges difference, favours cultural diversity, facilitates the discovery of different lifestyles and is underpinned by a variety of narratives – 'We're human beings too', 'You can't get along without us', 'This is our land too'. While acknowledging cultural difference, proponents assume parity amongst cultures that interact in contexts devoid of structural inequalities and ignore power relations. Decontextualised multiculturalism is presented as a neutral state of affairs that enables people to live and let live. Multiculturalists configure cultures as coexisting in separate spaces of parallel universes not intersecting universes of convergences and divergences marked by power differentials within which negotiations about culture occur. Multiculturalism is incapable of tackling power dynamics encapsulated in and (re)created by racist social relations or addressing structural racism. It is useful in encouraging interactions amongst diverse peoples as individuals and contributing to reducing personal racism. Some people consider multiculturalism a useless descriptor incapable of responding effectively to diversity. Brendan Fernandes argues for:

> freedom of choice without feeling constrained by one's own background or origin and without losing one's sense of social responsibility ... [S]ocial individualism comes closest to describing this concept [and so] we cannot talk about a multicultural society, just a multinational one.
>
> (BBC News, 2002:10)

Segregationists ascribe to 'You don't belong here' narratives that cast black people as 'dangerous' and subject to strict and coercive forms of social control to keep them in their place. Repatriation schemes are segregation by displacement to another locale. Segregationists promote social relations that allow black people to develop separately in inferior spaces – cultural and religious domains linked to a private life excluded from a superior public one reserved for white people. Under apartheid, these private spaces upheld social divisions and curtailed black peoples' socio-economic growth by denying them opportunities to establish holistic independent developments. Segregation exacts terrible costs as stories of black people in apartheid South Africa and indigenous people in Canada, the United States, Australia and New Zealand make clear. White people collectively have not actively promoted egalitarian coexistence; black people have not acquiesced to object status. They resisted subordination overtly and covertly in the routines of everyday life and liberation struggles (Gilroy, 1987; Essed, 1991).

'The let's share this land equally' narratives represent this aspirational goal.

Racialised identities in popular discourses

Ethnicised narratives of place and space are strongly embedded within popular culture and contribute to and draw upon cultural, institutional and personal forms of racism. Social workers participate in these as members of a given society and students bring them into course dynamics. Understanding popular configurations of 'race' provides useful insights for teaching the specifics of racist dynamics as is indicated by a Survey of Multicultural Britain conducted by the BBC in 2002. It revealed that 60 per cent of black and Asian respondents had endured verbal racial abuse and 20 per cent physical abuse. A third of black people and a third of Asians had personally experienced racial discrimination at school, college or university and a similar proportion at work. Comparable figures for white people were 1 per cent and 3 per cent respectively. Ethnicity as skin colour is racialised and turned into abuse at collective and individual levels with narratives of not belonging as C. Leung reveals:

> My family are originally from Hong Kong, but I was born in Scotland. Being Chinese-looking means that I often hear the word 'Chinky' directed at me, and I get upset by it, as I can't understand why anyone would think of me as any less of a human being because of my colour. As a child I was subjected to a lot of racism, but not in my teens, so I thought that it had disappeared. I have noticed that in the last year things have been getting worse again.
>
> (BBC News, 2002:4)

Narratives that give the message, 'You don't belong here', are damaging. In commenting upon racism's long-term effect on the psyche, Sonny stated:

> Some Brits and institutions are racist. Racism is very damaging. My whole family were subject to racist abuse over the years, living as the lone Asian family in a white-dominated area. At school, I had to resort to violence to defend myself. I

felt alone and mentally wounded by the soul destroying hatred. I am still recovering from the consequences of racist hate.

(BBC News, 2002:2)

Another variation of the 'You don't belong here' theme casts minority ethnic groups as exotic specimens. As a colour-blind approach, it decontextualises and ignores the specifics of a situation, and exoticises and devalues black people as Pam Hunt does:

I grew up in rural Somerset in the late 40s and 50s. The first time I saw a coloured face was at boarding school ... I don't think anyone . . . even thought about it. We were all friends if we were of the same age . . . I remember desperately hoping that a friend from Tobago would ask me to . . . stay in the summer holidays. Never happened . . . I cannot say whether Britain is racist, some people are . . . many are not. I . . . feel that those who come here should make some effort to integrate themselves into our society by learning the language and so on.

(BBC News, 2002:6)

This narrative rests on a common racist stereotype that sees black people as having deficits to be made good through immersion in (white) British culture. A middle-class person from Tobago would have spoken English and been integrated into English culture and language through colonialism and education in the colony prior to arrival (see Abye, 2007). The narrative is one way. It does not see the interaction as a mutual exchange and dumps responsibility to do something about racism on the black person. The expectation is that the black person would adapt to British life and contribute to the white person's pleasure without reciprocity.

Marc McGrath continues the theme of immigrants not belonging in Britain, but reverses the tale to focus on the exclusion of white people. He says:

[W]e have seen an influx of people wishing to settle here for a better life. The Great British public have accepted this for the last 50 years, but it's come to a point where we have become strangers in our own major cities. Recently we have seen a small rise in nationalism, not racism. There is a difference. It is a backlash against an uninformed government (Conservative and Labour) who ... do not live in Peckham or Birmingham, where the native is a minority, so of course to them multi-culturalism works.

(BBC News, 2002:9)

This narrative recounts the 'besieged local' or 'overwhelmed (white British) native' theme. In it, the majority white population, 'inundated in its own land', is excluded at home. This narrative resonates with BNP ideologies. One black Briton, Khalid Miah, showed compassion for those making racist remarks:

I was born and bred in Birmingham and in my 20 years of life had not experienced any form of racism except quite recently, when at university a child made a racist remark. I was saddened, not at the child, but at what he had been subjected to that led him to make such a comment.

(BBC News, 2002:5)

Dual heritage couples face racist responses. During the nineteenth and early twentieth centuries the term 'mixed marriages' included Southern Europeans (Douglas, 1983). In 2002, John Kirk high-lighted education as key to bridging racial divides:

I am married to a Chinese scholar and have a Chinese stepson. They have been subject to racism on the street, in school and at work. Racism in Britain is due to ignorance and fear. Both can be reduced by education.

(BBC News, 2002:5)

Richard Blackwell exposes the fluidity of racist constructs and shows that a person is configured differently depending on context. The net effect is the same – exclusion:

My girlfriend was born in France and her father is black and her mother is white. The poor girl can't win. In France she's black, in Africa she's white and in the UK she's French.

(BBC News, 2002:5)

Regardless of ethnicity, respondents quoted above focus on personal racism without differentiating between or recognising racism's different forms. Some argue that Britain is the least racist country they know. They do so while situating themselves within discourses about 'foreigners' abusing welfare services. Paul B who has lived in several Third World countries over the past 20 years claims:

> I have observed from a resident's point of view (not a two-week holiday) the attitudes of these countries to their own regional variances, and outsiders . . . I believe that Britain is the least racist society I have experienced. As a final thought, if the UK is so awful why are people, in their droves, crossing several supposedly more civilised countries in order to get here?
>
> (BBC News, 2002:7)

This seemingly enlightened contribution externalises racism – it occurs, and is much worse 'out there', not in the United Kingdom. It endorses dominant discourses that have this country 'swamped' by (im)migrants and arrogance about the superiority of (white) British culture. Mark complains that (im)migrants enter the United Kingdom to abuse welfare because it is a 'soft touch' for 'medical treatment and handouts' (BBC News, 2002:9). This refrain was echoed by Marget Hodge on their being prioritised for 'social' housing.

Nelson, claiming he has not experienced racism, says the United Kingdom is less racist than other countries. He also feels compassion for Britons (unfairly) branded 'racists':

> I have lived in SE Asia most of my life and . . . London for . . . 7 years . . . My experience of London is very positive . . . not racist at all. Of course, there may be some exceptions. If you want to know what racism is, try Hong Kong for starters!!! That'll open your eyes to real racism. It's sad that the English are not allowed to embrace their culture without being accused of racist behaviour.
>
> (BBC News, 2002:6)

The concern that Britain does not lose its original identity is reflected in Andy's comments. These are laced with denials of being racist and discourses of 'you don't belong here', while playing the 'numbers game' in calling for immigration controls and seeing immigrants as scroungers rather than contributors to society:

> I do believe that other cultures can mix with ours and it has to enrich . . . and modernise our society . . . there is a level of tolerance in society especially when it comes to immigrants who the British public have to pay for . . . the older generation would say that we fought a war to protect and preserve our culture and when it is demolished by large minorities of other ethnic backgrounds it is then that people become less tolerant. I do not consider myself to be a racist but I do agree that Britain is a small country and in order to keep stability within the economy we can not afford to let these people through.
>
> (BBC News, 2002:7–8)

He also excludes black people from the body politic while continuing to see himself as inclusive and tolerant. For Andy, geography becomes a definer of identity. His view fails to notice that immigrants also create new identities and cultural forms that include everyone – diversity within unity (Dominelli, 2002a). The theme of 'blending in' or integrating and not drawing attention to oneself appears in what 'Anon' says. It fits with assimilationist discourses, forms part of a survival strategy for inclusion and buys into white narratives that 'black people are here on sufferance':

> I am an Asian living and working in the UK for the last seven years. I have never experienced any racism . . . [and] British people [are] very tolerant and fair . . . I have found Britain not racist . . . I have made every effort to blend in with British people and they have now accepted me as one of them.
>
> (BBC News, 2002:10)

People's rejection of others has been linked to their unwillingness to wed across racial divides. A 1955 survey of white British people's attitudes revealed that 83 per cent of white respondents would mind if a relative married a black person. It dropped to 22 per cent by 1996 (Bennett and Reese, 1999:1). This is taken to indicate a greater acceptance of black people in Britain, yet nearly a quarter of the white British population continue to reject them. This has implications for all types of racism, particularly personal racism that feeds into and off its institutional and cultural forms. Their views impact substantially on inter-community relations.

Assif focuses on the 'This is our land too' narrative by talking about positive contributions immigrants make to the economy. Without these, the 'whole foundation of this country would collapse'. For whites, he demands:

> history lessons on UK industry's dependence on immigrant labour . . . build[ing] up industries, employing others, looking after families here and in . . . countries of origins even if arriv[ing] with only a suitcase
>
> (BBC News, 2002:9)

Some white anti-racists had more nuanced views. They sought connections based on similarity, accepting difference and getting on in 'Let's share this land' narratives. Marc also rejected racists:

> I think some people have the view that every immigrant is an illegal immigrant who swam over the Channel to get here . . . Most people do it legally. I know lots of people of a different race and we all get on fine . . . only a small minority . . . are racists . . . of all the 'minority' groups in Britain, racists are the unwanted ones.
>
> (BBC News, 2002:3)

Cutelli is concerned that anti-racist endeavours will fail because:

> A system for social inclusion and exclusion will always arise in any situation. Therefore, attempts at racial integration are likely to continue to be fruitless.
>
> (BBC News, 2002:8)

Either/or narratives demand that minority ethnic groups do not set up ethnic enclaves but adopt elements of British culture. They assume that white British ethnic culture is superior, unitary and non-changing. But this culture, like others, is constantly changing and adapting to local circumstances and social interactions between people.

Having the space to be different individually and collectively is integral to citizenship. Citizenship offers the social protections of the group to the individual in return for loyalty. For Richard Hammond, citizenship is about 'language, shared values and a love of the land'. 'Britishness', he feels, has been eroded in contemporary discourses and simply means 'residing in Britain' (BBC News, 2002).

---

putting it into practice

- Consider how your identity impacts upon other people and how theirs impact on you.
- Which narratives of place and space do you, your relatives or friends use?
- Which narratives of place and space have you heard social workers use?
- How could social workers help include different ethnic groups in British society?

---

further reading

Owusu-Bempah, J. (1997) 'Race' in Davies, M. (ed.) *The Blackwell Companion to Social Work*. Oxford: Blackwell Publishers.

Banks, N. (1999) White *Counsellors, Black Clients: Theory, Research and Practice*. Aldershot: Ashgate.

3 | Deconstructing racist policies and practices in social work

Social work is committed to people's well-being. Ironically, practitioners undermine this objective by oppressing service users, reproducing racist policies and practices in their work in myriad ways. In this chapter, I consider how racism is perpetrated in and through social work policies and practices that ignore racialised identities to produce 'colour-blind' social work interventions. I identify and explore a range of strategies whereby practitioners decontextualise social work practice by practising oppressively and ignoring racialised relationships. In this, I highlight how the dynamics of racial oppression are embedded in social work policies and practices and reinforced through taken-for-granted assumptions that privilege white people.

Social work training and education reflect similar failings. I consider these in the context of the struggle to include anti-racist practice in social work curricula in the field and academy and explore assertions that its capacity to tackle racist practices has been diluted by moves towards anti-oppressive practice (Williams, 2003). When focusing on this dimension of the debate, I suggest that social workers examine:

- the multiple dimensions of oppression;
- its intersection with various social divisions;
- its impact on individuals or group relationships according to negotiated social positioning in these; and
- how not to become trapped in binary discourses about hierarchies of oppression.

Racial inequalities in the British welfare state

Social workers are believed tolerant of difference and deviancy, so it is surprising that they are considered oppressive by both clients and the general public (Phillips, 1993). Bagley and Young (1982) claimed that social workers were seven times more racially tolerant than the general populace. Their analysis examined personal racism without considering how its structural components, institutional and cultural racism, produce racist interventions. A focus on personal behaviour neglects links between eradicating racist policies and practices and transforming the socio-economic and political structures that support racism. Concentrating attention on the personally racist few condones the view that anti-racist struggles are not major organisational issues, but activities a few individuals conduct during leisure hours as Phillips (1993) suggests.

Racial inequality is the physical manifestation of racism in social relations. Its impact can be measured as discrimination in jobs, housing, personal social services and education. Numerous reports have exposed such discrimination over the years (Billig, 1997; ONS, 2002). Black people continue to: live in run-down inner cities and overcrowded dwellings (ONS, 2002); lose out on welfare resources like the personal social services, social security, community care; education; health services (Fernando, 1999; Barnes et al., 2000); and be over-represented in schools for educationally subnormal pupils, criminal proceedings and truancy (Flood-Page, 1999).

Few black people have become directors of social services or chief probation officers. In London, a handful of black men occupied director's posts by the mid-1980s; most were gone ten years later. The 2005 reorganisation produced a few black men and women as directors for children or adult services, usually linked to sectors like education and housing. Daphne Obang, Director of Social Services and Housing at Bracknell Forest Council and Chair of the Association of Directors of Social Services' Inclusivity Group, was one of these. Several black women breached top managerial ranks in probation in December 2004: Carol Bernard as Regional Offender Manager of Wales, having previously been the Chief Officer for Nottingham; and Anne Scott as General Secretary of the National Black Police Officers Association. Other top appointments include: Mike Fuller as the first black Chief Constable appointed to the post in Kent in 2003; Linda Dobbs as the first Black High Court Judge, reaching this post in 2004, and Constance Briscoe, one of the first black women appointed to the judiciary, number amongst the top ten women on the Bench; and Brian

Anderson as the first black Prison Director taking this position at Doncaster Prison in 2007. Black leaders of trade unions are in similar short supply, Bill Morris being a notable exception.

Racism damages those it oppresses socially, economically and politically. Racist constructs of black people can be internalised by black people if their social mobility is thwarted by structural impediments, disenfranchisement and exacerbated feelings of worthlessness. Internalised racism makes it easier for white people to pathologise, victimise and blame black people; and damages those who oppress others. The profession devalues black people's contributions despite equal opportunities policies and increasing numbers of employees by dumping responsibility for eradicating racism on them and not supporting their progression up the career ladder.

---

practice tips *enhancing work with black people*

Social workers can improve situations for black co-workers and service users by:

- enhancing black people's (families') strengths;
- promoting well-being within black families and communities;
- placing black children with foster and adoptive parents able to meet their identity and other needs, e.g., schooling, schools for black children;
- creating and providing services that treat black service users as equals;
- employing and promoting black workers as equals; and
- working to eradicate racism.

Institutionalised racism in wider social structures and personal racism integrate racist practices to social work. Immigration policies affirm institutional racism by denying black people living and working in Britain and paying taxes, 'recourse to public funds' if they are (im)migrants. Linked to conditional admittance to the country, this exclusion refuses employment benefits to those on work permits (Bloch, 2000); denies child benefit to children living overseas; disallows income support payments to women with husbands on prolonged trips abroad to fulfil extended family obligations. Social workers become implicated in these controls as post-entry immigration officers when checking eligibility for services.

And, they engage in *discourses about deficits*; use white benchmarks to judge social behaviour; undermine diversity; and ignore structural inequalities. A major motif in New Right discourses in the United States and Britain is racialising the welfare state. The 'dependency culture' concept is racialised, patriarchally gendered and blames black women and children for being poor and not financially supported by men (see Murray, 1994). These have shifted the balance of care discourses towards those purchasing services from private providers instead of state funded facilities for all.

A globalised economy intensifies pressure on the state to become globally competitive and cut welfare expenditures for individual citizens. Opening up welfare services to the market enhances profit-making opportunities through service provision and increases competition for public resources amongst excluded groups who are not players in the marketplace. Ensuing inequalities are deepened by GATS (General Agreement on Trades and Services) as it backs private, for-profit providers in health, social services and education. Social workers become trapped in managing these dynamics. Excluding black people from welfare benefits is rooted in notions of: abusing welfare by accessing benefits illegally; non-contributor status if born overseas; temporary residence in the country; and family-based welfare to provide their care. These myths monitor black people's access to services and feed surveillance; for example, passport checks to demonstrate entitlement to public facilities. These practices and the attitudes embedded in them:

- make racism acceptable;
- exacerbate black peoples' feelings of vulnerability, a condition compounded by the rising number of racist attacks on them;
- endorse laissez-faire attitudes and practices that produce poor service provision and delivery for black people entitled to it; and
- affirm black peoples' responsibility for meeting their own welfare needs.

These reactions fragment community cohesion and reinforce divisions within and between communities. The Denham, Clarke and Cantle Inquiries into the 'race' riots of 2001 in the northern English towns of Bradford, Burnley and Oldham respectively identified lack of community cohesion; social exclusion; unequal access to services and welfare benefits; limited interaction between black and white communities and families; and a sense of alienation and not belonging as key ingredients leading to the riots (Cantle, 2002; Clarke, 2002; Denham, 2002; Cantle et al., 2006). Social workers can play key roles in building social cohesion and promoting developments across racial divides.

Black people's visibility makes them easier targets for surveillance mechanisms that enforce entitlement regimes and efficiency scrutiny. These controls can deny settled black people's human rights and entitlements because they are treated as 'immigrants' rather than 'citizens'. Withdrawing some benefits from asylum seekers and refugees exacerbates these trends, reinforces their portrayal as scroungers and legitimates the rationing of resources to curtail welfare expenditures while residualising welfare services for all British people. These developments put social workers in invidious positions adjudicating competing claims for resources. I interviewed one working with asylum seekers, who said:

> I am uncomfortable when I give asylum seekers services I cannot give local residents who need them. They both need them. But because resources are scarce I can only give them to one – asylum seekers.

---

practice tips international resources

The United Nations' Universal Declaration of Human Rights (UDHR) has been signed by most countries giving its provisions a legitimacy that transcends any one culture. Treating people with dignity is central to it. Social workers can utilise the UDHR to prevent the humiliation of a person through violent or demeaning acts. This response is consistent with social work ethics, now endorsed internationally by the International Association of Schools of Social Work (IASSW) and International Federation of Social Workers (IFSW), organisations that represent the profession internationally. These instruments have been critiqued as Western-oriented. The argument has limited merit; practitioners should proceed with caution. Westerners have no monopoly on dignity and this value should not be conceded as relevant only to white people. Eastern philosophers have long argued for human rights and dignity (see *Journal of Buddhist Ethics*).

The Race Relations (Amendment) Act 2000 (RRA, 2000)

Government intervenes in the personal social services through policies and legislation that occupy a contradictory position on 'race'. It reproduces racist dynamics while promoting laws on equal opportunities, including the Race Relations (Amendment) Act of 2000, making 'incitement to racial hatred' and religious intolerance offences in 2004 and 2006, respectively. The Racial and Religious Hatred Act 2006 introduced a new offence to cover racially aggravated assault by building on legislation from 1998.

The Race Relations (Amendment) Act 2000 strengthened Race Relations Acts passed in 1965, 1968 and 1976. It demands government departments take seriously the responsibility to promote community cohesion and social inclusivity. Public organisations that provide personal social services are now responsible for equality in employment, housing, training, education and provision of goods and services.

---

practice tips   Race Relations (Amendment) Act (RRA) 2000

The general duty covered by the Race Relations (Amendment) Act 2000 has three requirements that social workers can use to work in anti-racist ways. These are the:

- elimination of unlawful racial discrimination;
- promotion of equal opportunities; and
- promotion of good race relations.

Originally, enforced by the Commission for Racial Equality (CRE), this structure changed in 2007 when the Commission for Equality and Human Rights (CEHR), headed by Trevor Phillips, replaced the CRE. The CEHR is responsible for monitoring all forms of inequality including gender and disability, each of which had its own Commission. This development constitutes the United Kingdom's response to Article 13 of the Treaty of Amsterdam. In it, the European Union required all nations to pass national legislation to outlaw discrimination on the grounds of 'race', gender, age, disability, sexual orientation and religion by 2006. Interestingly, the CEHR's prime focus will be discrimination, not oppression. A key determiner of inequality – class, is not covered.

Enforcement of existing human rights and equalities legislation is limited. Kamal Butt's murder in Nottingham after the 7/7 bombings indicate that equal rights discourses and policies have limited preventative force. The CEHR's capacity to create anti-racist environments is debatable. The state as a commissioner of services and major employer can frustrate its purposes. It employs substantial numbers of workers and pays for services (directly and indirectly), but cost considerations undermine claims to equality. Resource availability rather than human need shapes the services ultimately available (Dominelli, 2004a). Competing claims result in a complex interplay of forces that implicate the state in configuring racist social relations. Tackling these requires multi-level analyses and responses, and innovative approaches to working within a climate of inadequate resourcing.

Racist differentiation: sectarianism, religion and Irish peoples

The formation of European nation-states drew upon nationalist sentiments that were racist from the start, creating the 'other' as an object lacking dignity or worth and to be despised. In the United Kingdom, this has impacted not only upon peoples originating outside the Kingdom, but also Scots, Welsh and Irish ones. They were denied cultural attributes, languages, national aspirations and value as different peoples for the greater good of the England-based British Empire. Differences amongst these groups were negated by treaties that located power in London and gave the English way of life – albeit a specific version of it, hegemony. Outright suppression of, and military action against, those who resisted was typical. Religion and language were key battlegrounds, giving cultural racism a long history. People of Irish descent have experienced colonising practices that ignored their linguistic and religious heritage – practices that social workers continue when intervening in their lives as either settlers or (im)migrants without assessing their relevance to specific situations.

Catholicism was reviled, and the Act of Settlement of 1701 denied Catholics, whether English, Scottish or Irish, positions of state power and authority. Religious divisions remain manifest in Northern Ireland and major cities with large Irish communities. In Ulster, this religious prejudice produced a form of racism called sectarianism. Associated with violence, this religious-based racism has been largely invisible in social work (Mac an Ghail, 2000). People of Irish origins remain the largest ethnic minority group in the United Kingdom, but receive little recognition of specific religious or language needs when receiving social services. Before the Good Friday Agreement, they were over-represented in custodial settings (Borland et al., 1995). Configurations of anti-Irish racism have altered over time as resistance to British rule has become more entrenched and explicit. Terrorist tactics on both sides of the Catholic–Protestant divide have changed the experiences of racism for people of Irish descent, whether born in Eire, Northern Ireland or the British mainland. Social workers became implicated in these hostilities: in support of the British state; as mediators in war-torn communities; or as supporters of Irish struggles for liberation.

Fletchman-Smith (1984) argues that taking whiteness for granted is a privilege of being in the dominant group. The neglect of the significance of racialised identities for Irish service users indicates a unitary and essentialised approach to whiteness. Their experiences highlight the importance of: deconstructing whiteness; not seeing white people as a heterogeneous group; and unpacking racialised hierarchies of oppression within categories. Focusing on one aspect of identity is not enough. Other social divisions, including class, gender and religion, distinguish experiences of racism within an ethnic group. Dominant white groups have a choice about taking racism seriously. Their lives do not normally depend on their responses. Black people are aware of the colour of their skin every moment of their waking lives and cannot/are not allowed to forget (Riley, 1985).

Skin colour and cultural attributes of difference encompassing culture, religion, language and cuisine have been racialised and utilised to cast Catholic Southern Europeans as inferior to Northern Europeans. The Home Office devised a category of 'dark European' to deal with 'coloured' groups within the white mix for the Single Market Act 1986. Racial differentiation occurs within these groups; for example, the experience of Northern Italians is different from Southern Italians, not least because Northern Italian racism is levelled against Southerners as 'terroni' or peasants (Scarpino, 1992). I have also known of dark-skinned Sicilians being taken for Arabs in the United Kingdom. Germans have argued that only those German by blood can claim German nationality, to exclude Germanic-speaking peoples in Central Europe from being defined as ethnically German (Alba et al., 1995). Racism operates within and across white ethnic groups and nationalities.

Racism impedes social work's capacity to promote well-being

Besides working within societal frameworks that endorse racist approaches to social issues, social workers have structural arrangements that reduce capacity to undertake anti-racist social work. These cover apolitical professional stances that enforce neutral positions on contemporary social issues; emphasise social control over caring; prioritise rationing welfare resources over meeting needs; foster negative stances on ethnicity and diversity; and perceive black clients as undeserving of services.

Foucault (1983) argues that power relations are multi-dimensional and fluid because power is created in and through social interactions. This is rejected by the apolitical stance white social workers adopt in allocating resources and results in differentiated power relations and differential access being ignored. Everyone living in a particular place is assumed to be at the same starting point. Social workers negotiating access to resources may also experience moments of powerlessness or empowerment. They may have more sources of power than clients, for example, legislative-based power; power as gatekeepers distributing resources; expert power and knowledge; but feel disempowered vis-à-vis managers and policymakers. The power of the powerless and powerlessness of the powerful is central to these dynamics (Dominelli, 1986).

Uncritical approaches to cases and universality of treatment have facilitated practices that intensify the racist burdens carried by black people discriminated against by other parts of the welfare state and immigration controls. Racist practices are evident in service delivery that uses racism as a form of social control to keep black people in their place; excludes them from accessing services; enforces a universalistic approach to services that assumes everyone is the same, has the same needs, and can make do with the same response(s); and ignores overt racist practices created through racist dynamics. A status hierarchy privileging white people accords white, upper-class Anglo-Saxon men more social resources than working-class men and women, black or white. White social workers' failure to acknowledge subtle and covert forms of racism that permeate practice has contributed to black people's experiences of racism.

Universality of treatment as homogeneity undermines equality

White social workers who assume that black peoples' needs are the same as white peoples' engage in 'colour-blind' practice. The dynamics involved do not ignore the colour of someone's skin, but discount its relevance to service provision. Different attributes, while recognised, are thought immaterial and/or inferior to white ones. The colour-blind approach privileges white people by disregarding the impact of 'race' and racism upon life circumstances. Expressed as 'universality of treatment' this approach *assumes equality* rather than achieving it, and treats all individuals and groups as if they were 'all the same'. People are reduced to the lowest common denominator without regard to the actual social position they occupy individually or collectively. Little account is taken of black people's lower socio-economic position; different cultural traditions; familial organisations and obligations; attitudes towards life, society and social institutions; the variety and heterogeneity in their midst; and the systemic racism they endure daily. Pressure is exerted on black people to conform to white standards or stereotypes of their position. The treatment of those from one group as 'all the same' is also reflected in terminologies that acknowledge difference, but treat it as homogeneous and unitary, for example, the black family, the black community. There may be acknowledgement that a Jamaican's experiences differ from a Nigerian's, but those of all Jamaicans or all Nigerians are assumed similar. Social divisions like gender, class and religion are neglected in these constructs of ethnicity.

White social workers' training, professional ethics and service delivery view the British population as mainly homogeneous except for a few insignificant traits. The expectation that treating everyone the same ensures equality amongst individuals is deemed reasonable. Conceptually, it links the 'new racism' to white supremacy. Its underlying premises do not need spelling out; the 'race' being considered is obvious. There is no negotiation around differences to determine what is best. As universalism in practice, colour-blind approaches ignore structural inequalities that limit opportunities and social resources for black people. It is normative and demands that individuals and groups conform to the socially acceptable or 'desirable' behaviours specified by the dominant group. Its standards promote white middle-class values and lifestyles at the expense of those advocated by black people and are embedded in social work institutions in the field and academy through policy and practice.

The universality principle prevents white social workers from seeing the significance of bringing black clients to the same socio-economic starting line as white clients and inhibits their ability to explain the need to do so. Identifying and explaining gaps in black and white working-class peoples' access to power and resources are essential in stemming a backlash from poor, white working-class individuals disadvantaged by class. Class disadvantage impacts upon both groups but only black ones are underprivileged by 'race', making black people's encounters with class different. If equal on other social divisions, racism accounts for disparities in their experiences of discrimination or oppression. Recognising class-based commonalities and differences and the points they emanate from is crucial in promoting racial equality, understanding the differentiated nature of multi-dimensional deprivation; and becoming allies.

Not eradicating racist social relations denies black people appropriate services, for example, white probation officers not offering recommendations that might lessen the severity of a sentence results in black offenders being over-represented in prisons (Coid, Petruchevitch and Bebbington, 2002; Weatherburn, Fitzgerald and Hua, 2003); black elders 'making do' with culturally insensitive home care services. Systemic racism becomes a rationing device as occurred when Bangladeshi families in Tower Hamlets were excluded from council housing on the grounds that they made themselves intentionally homeless by leaving Bangladesh (*The Guardian*, 28 April 1987). Such sources of inequality need to be addressed if racism is not to label black people as undeserving and legitimate their exclusion from scarce social resources. The rationing aspect of racism feeds off social workers' duties as gate-keepers of public resources controlling demand. Classifying claimants as 'deserving' or 'undeserving' excludes disproportionately more black clients as they are more readily classified as undeserving by practitioners and more easily refused services when resources are scarce. Low incomes and the lack of social resources are key reasons for accessing public services. Being unable to respond to identified need poses an ethical challenge for social workers.

With dwindling resources, social workers operate in a state of siege. Paying tribute to client self-determination, endorsing needs-led assessments, empowering clients, or adjudicating amongst competing claims presented by different client groups give rise to ethical dilemmas. Which to choose? Bath aids for a black elder; a day nursery place for a black child; or respite care for white carers? Excluding claims for services by deeming these inappropriate popularises self-fulfilling excuses for doing nothing in difficult circumstances, as in 'black people can look after their own', and facilitates decision-making that affirms racist dynamics. Decisions based on these stereotypes are unfair and reinforce social exclusion. These exclusions lead black people to despair or create their own resources and autonomous spaces (Gilroy, 1987).

Becoming ethnically sensitive is a complicated first step in becoming anti-racist. Each ethnic group, including practitioners' own, is diverse. Assumptions about the whole cannot be applied to a specific situation without investigating its relevance in that case. Social workers keen to appreciate the different meanings ascribed to certain cultural practices by individuals may find they differ from those advocated by those speaking collectively on behalf of a specific group. Becoming ethnically sensitive is not about tolerating dehumanising or violent behaviour as 'culturally appropriate' in unfamiliar cultures. The challenge for practitioners is to investigate a situation, reflect critically upon what is needed and intervene without disparaging service users, and draw upon a wide range of resources in doing so.

No culture is monolithic and norms are contested in both minority and majority cultures. Rights are processual and contextual, so a situation must be carefully and sensitively investigated to ascertain what is going on and how a social worker can work with and promote well-being from the client's vantage point. This does not imply that a client is always right – it is a matter for mutual negotiation. Saying 'no' should not be confused as racism (Ahmed, 1984), nor 'yes' as automatically non-racist. Sometimes 'no' is the appropriate answer. A social worker would not say 'yes' to a white parent wanting to care for a white child without a thorough investigation. Black children deserve similar levels of care (DfES, 2006). Dialoguing with those requiring services, asking questions and ascertaining who the actual client is, produces better-informed practice and develops social workers' confidence in their professional judgments. Acting as proficient, critically reflective practitioners ensures that practitioners do not use instruments unthinkingly or simply apply a 'checklist' for anti-racist practice as this might restrict capacity in responding appropriately to a specific situation. A white social worker suspecting the abuse of a black child is more likely to ensure sensitive and appropriate interventions by reacting to the particularities of a case. Anti-oppressive values rooted in human rights, social justice and citizenship facilitate good practice. They are not substitutes for careful assessments of a situation.

---

practice tips   enhancing practice

Anti-racist practice is enhanced if practitioners are frank about the:

- limitations of what is achievable in a case;
- constraints they operate within, whether derived from legislation, resources available or information at their disposal; and
- engage service users in creating practice relevant to their particular situation.

Shifting educational frameworks

Traditional texts fail to explore holistic approaches that embed client and worker in contextualised relationships. Cheetham (1982) identifies organisational change in improving situations but treats 'race' as relevant only for people who access services and excludes white social workers' own racialised ethnicities from change processes. She also ignores the need to change racist immigration policies or reverse cuts in state-funded welfare provisions, trends that have intensified under neo-liberalism. A residence test that prohibits groups of (im)migrants from accessing welfare benefits is politically determined and part of the structural context. Denuding policies of context is serious as it obscures the political nature and impact of social forces on human action and exacerbates conflict.

Classic texts that ignored the significance of 'race' and ethnicity perpetuated the idea that racism is not relevant in or for practice, for example, *Social Work Practice: Model and Method* (Pincus and Minahan, 1973); *Towards a Socialist Welfare Work* (Bolger et al., 1981); *Women, the Family and Social Work* (Brook and Davis, 1985). Some analysed 'race' and racism in social work within assimilation positions, for example, Cheetham (1972). Others like Husband (1980) highlighted racism in social work, without locating it within a historical context or examining how 'race' intersects with gender, sexual orientation, religion, language and other factors. Ely and Denny (1987) theorised and classified different developments, including multicultural and black perspectives. Multiculturalism, a key component in social work texts that claimed anti-discrimination in their approach, was promoted as a way of eliminating racism, for example, Khan's (1979), *Support and Stress: Minority Families in Britain*. These spoke from a superior voice by pathologising the development of alternative lifestyles and services. A current example of society's failure to integrate black young people into communities where they live or resist racism is available at www.blink.org.uk. Recent texts contain the idea of equality in a pluralistic consensus and assume all cultures have equal power in a society; see, for example, Winkelman (2005). He focuses on ethnic awareness and cultural competence within a framework that sees ethnic identity as unitary and similar for all those in a group. Others have a chapter or two on 'race' and racism; for example, *Anti-Discriminatory Practice* (Thompson, 2006) and *Social Work: Current Issues, Themes and Dilemmas* (Adams et al., 2002).

---

practice tips   limitations of literature

From an anti-racist perspective, much social work literature remains problematic and needs to be read critically. It can:

- ignore racial diversity;
- treat racism in tokenistic ways or consider only on a limited aspect of it;
- focus on individual attitudes, preferences and prejudices – personal racism, to the exclusion of its structural forms;
- downplay the significance of social divisions like class and gender on the experience of 'race' and racism;

- minimise black peoples' experiences of discrimination and oppression;
- pathologise black family practices, including resistance to oppression.

With this confusion, dealing adequately with 'race' and racism in and through social work practice remains a task yet to be completed.

Anti-racist social work is contested

Ignoring the significance of 'race' is detrimental to forming helping relationships because whether acknowledged or not, people's implicit understandings of the issues impact on what they do and the relationships they form (Gitterman and Schaeffer, 1972:286). This holds whether or not those involved are 'black' or 'white'. For white people, ignoring 'race' perpetuates unacknowledged privileging; for black people, it confirms disadvantaged positions. The downplaying of racist dynamics is evident in casework, groupwork and community work relationships.

Anti-racist social work is not a case of simply adding 'race' to a basically benign profession. The transformation of social work practice through the creation of social relations fostering equality and justice is critical to moving in this direction, as is adopting a political stance against racism on the personal, institutional and cultural levels within policies, practice, education and social work organisations. Professional neutrality masks support for the status quo. Deconstructing power relations and privileging within professional relationships can begin the processes of changing professional and organisational structures in the workplace and tackling racism perpetrated and legitimated by social workers and welfare bodies.

Social workers wishing to eradicate racism from practice could redefine racism as a social and personal issue to ally individually and as a group with progressive, anti-racist forces within social work and wider society. They can organise for this end in political organisations, trade unions, professional associations, employing authorities and training bodies. Consciousness-raising, as a form of probing beneath the surface of social relations to expose taken-for-granted assumptions and power dynamics, became a tool for social workers to counter racist practices and highlight black people's resilience in resisting oppression.

practice tips   conscientisation processes

Conscientisation processes (Freire, 1970) can facilitate anti-racist social work by involving practitioners working with others to unmask power relations, link personal experiences to structural phenomena and ask questions like:

- What personal and structural attributes are relevant in *this* situation?
- Are these configured to promote racist or anti-racist social relations?
- How do contexts impact upon the positions of service users and workers?
- Does the experience of being white help understand that of a black person? Include differences and similarities in positionality; access to power and resources; and sense of belonging/being accepted by others. How about the reverse?
- Which situations are empowering? Which are disempowering? Why?
- If white, has whiteness conferred taken-for granted privileges? If black, has this been accompanied by disadvantage or discrimination?
- Can inequalities be tackled at the personal and collective levels? How? By whom?

Alliances between black and white working-class organisations can be problematic as white working-class people benefit from racism by being defined as worthy recipients. Group privileging overrides individual merit in these circumstances. Social workers can encourage deeper understandings between both groups to reduce competition over scarce resources and find common cause without disregarding different starting points. Anti-racist social work, a contested and risky business, requires social workers to assess how risks impact upon them, service users or others; resolve ethical dilemmas by helping social workers contextualise and address risks appropriately; and use values like worth, dignity of person and social justice to guide their judgments. A social worker may advocate strongly for resources for one black person. However, individual advocacy does not create precedents for others because each has to press their claim. Collective advocacy, campaigns and 'class' actions that set precedents for others in similar situations are better for promoting group interests. Social workers who support social justice claims may irritate employers, risk dismissal or incur other sanctions. Not acting also has consequences like endangering others' lives.

Attacking anti-racist social work initiatives

Practitioners' ambitions to establish social work as a valued profession may affect the capacity to respond to anti-racist agendas if professional imperatives and social justice issues collide. Claims for equal justice challenge professional aspirations to neutrality and critiques of social and political structures are viewed as political involvement that is eschewed by traditional professionals. Those who attacked anti-racist social work in England in 1993 alleged that social work educators and practitioners were jumping on a trendy bandwagon, not dealing with real practice issues. To make this charge, journalists fabricated a powerful narrative based on an erroneous story alleging that an application for status as adoptive parents by a young couple comprised of an Asian woman and white man had been rejected because the woman had not experienced racism. Norfolk, the local authority in question, denied the allegation, but it acquired potency by being repeated in local and national newspapers and other media across the country. Newspaper columnists like Melanie Phillips (1993) asserted that in being anti-racist, practitioners oppressed clients. The robust defence of anti-racist initiatives surprised its attackers because it encompassed social work employers, practitioners and academics, many not noted for taking overtly political stances on issues.

The attack achieved its purpose, undermining the credibility of anti-racist approaches to the present. CCETSW removed a paragraph in Annex 5 of Paper 30 that referred to anti-racist and anti-oppressive approaches in social work and disbanded the Black Perspectives Committee developing anti-racist teaching materials. The DipSW was phased out and replaced by a three-year degree; CCETSW's functions were assumed by the GSCC. The term 'social work' became disparaged; government literature scarcely mentioned the discipline following this debacle. Social care with a narrower remit than social work as acknowledged internationally is in vogue in England (see IASSW-IFSW definition of social work on www.iassw-aiets.org).

A critique of activities initiated under the anti-racist umbrella was necessary. Examples of poor practice existed in this field as in any other. CCETSW demanded that educators assess anti-racist practice and ensure good practice across racial divides without providing resources or training to reach this goal. Many courses had limited links with black communities and partnerships that could have been developed to facilitate their creation locally failed to materialise; national resources were scarce and overstretched. Social work educators lacked the expertise for cutting the Gordian knot of social work as a complex and contradictory form of social control to develop its anti-racist potential. In the vacuum that existed, people did their best in difficult circumstances, but could not achieve the results sought.

---

practice tips   guidelines for anti-racist social work education and practice

Partnerships involving policymakers, educators, practitioners and service users from diverse ethnic groups working together in a social justice framework to promote egalitarian relations in service delivery, workplaces and broader society can transform social work education and promote anti-racist practice. Deconstructing racist dynamics are crucial to this. The principles below can assist in developing such partnerships:

- Encouraging inclusive social relations.
- Developing anti-racist social work curricula.
- Replacing Anglo/Eurocentric concepts in social work theory, practice, law and policies with anti-racist ones.
- Transforming current definitions of what constitutes social work practice.
- Changing course selection and recruitment procedures so that only applicants committed to promoting equality for all are admitted.
- Developing recruitment and publicity materials that encourage black people to apply for courses.
- Including black people on selection panels to evaluate black and white applicants' willingness to learn how to practice in anti-racist ways.
- Employing substantial numbers of black academics, administrative staff and practitioners.
- Developing links with black communities to provide a substantial pool of placements through which black and white practitioners can evaluate the competence of black and white students to work with black and white clients.
- Providing black students with the space and resources to develop fully.
- Supporting white students in working across social divides including ethnicity.

- Developing mentorship networks for black students and supporting mentors adequately in carrying out their work.
- Lobbying the GSCC to include adequately resourced and enforceable anti-racist and anti-oppressive criteria for assessment.
- Demanding that central government releases resources to employ black people throughout social work education and retrain white staff already within it in anti-racist and anti-oppressive directions.
- Challenging institutionalised racism, making explicit the gains accruing to white people by virtue of its existence, and discussing these on courses.
- Encouraging white social work educators and practitioners not to accept roles as 'race experts' who can teach black and white students the skills that emanate from being a black person living with and tackling racism.
- Making the commitment to working and teaching in egalitarian, anti-racist, and anti-oppressive ways a criterion of employment in social work.
- Supporting and facilitating staff development in anti-racist social work.

(Re)engaging in anti-racist social work

White social workers feel fearful, vulnerable and pathologised by anti-racist writings that hold them accountable for racist practices in the profession. Feeling powerless in initiating change, they focus on the personal and absolve themselves of responsibility for introducing structural initiatives that would improve conditions for black workers, and service users themselves. The fear, linked to difficulty in seeing themselves as privileged or oppressive, inhibits the desire to be anti-oppressive. Receiving personal approbation and recognising self-worth are key factors in overcoming feelings of powerlessness and guilt in initiating change. Becoming conscious of, and reflecting on, the dynamics of racism and their role in perpetuating racism at personal, institutional and cultural levels is crucial for practitioners to fulfil their ambition of practising anti-racist social work. Retaining self-respect, learning from errors made in a process of self-discovery and finding the limits to one's liberality help to become knowledgeable about oneself and facilitate learning and change. This task will not be easy. Working on emotions is central to change processes but difficult when wanting to maintain a 'stiff upper-lip'.

> **practice tips**   working reflectively
>
> White social workers are criticised for their insularity and not understanding
> or knowing other cultures (Winkelman, 2005). Culturally competent,
> intercultural and cross-cultural approaches suggest that social workers
> familiarise themselves with the specifics of each culture (Lum, 2000;
> Winkelman, 2005; Robinson, 2007). Difference is an issue in practitioners'
> relationships with service users, regardless of ethnicity, culture or 'racial' traits.
> Being familiar with diversity does not mean knowing chapter and verse of
> any one culture. More important is practitioners' capacity to ask pertinent
> questions about how diversity and identity impact upon specific lives. Asking
> a person, group or community about the specifics that apply to them,
> focusing on the particularities of an intervention to find out what diversity
> means for a given person, group or community at a point in time enables
> white social workers to respond more effectively. Working in a reflective,
> questioning mode, social workers can do without a 'toolkit' on each and every
> ethnicity that they might encounter.

Gitterman and Schaeffer (1972:282) argue that a 'white professional has the upper hand – in both larger society and in encounters with clients', a view challenged by autonomous black
organisations that provide spaces for black people to create safe
environments; formulate agendas for action; respond to specific
needs; develop skills and knowledge for playing a full role in
society; and create services to meet their needs (Patel et al., 2004).
These reverse power flows that traditionally favour white professionals; empower black people; critique traditional models of
professionalism; and prove black people can run organisations and
activities associated with them.

Some white practitioners worry about their lack of control over
black autonomous organisations, feeling uncomfortable and threatened when in the unfamiliar position of listening to black people
and taking directions from them. Employers should treat practitioners with respect and dignity, positively encourage them to
improve their practice, define and challenge unacceptable behaviour, support and supervise them in developing non-oppressive
egalitarian relationships with black workers and clients. Paying
attention to due process facilitates change as part of a personal

agenda. Group supervision and consciousness-raising techniques can help white social workers to explore their anxieties. Change strategies raise awareness amongst individuals and collective groupings and encourage examination of power differentials at the personal, institutional and cultural levels. Carefully considered interventions enable white people to introduce change that does not undermine black people's strengths or anti-racist actions. Competing with each other to see who is the least racist or most oppressed sows discord and saps energy that could promote anti-racist struggles.

---

practice tips   *personal action in becoming an anti-racist practitioner*

Practising in anti-racist ways makes each social worker personally responsible for:

- Becoming racially aware and conscious of the dynamics of racism and their perpetuation in and through social work practice.
- Exploring their expectations about white people. To what extent are these different for black people? What assumptions underpin these expectations?
- Valuing black people's knowledge and skills. Are black people excluded from positions of power and authority because they are black? Do white people assume that they are not up to the job?
- Eliminating institutional and cultural racism in agencies, workplaces and practice.
- Taking up the general anti-racist struggle, including supportive political action.
- Tackling structural oppression by supporting social justice claims.

Focusing on individual or interpersonal dynamics to eradicate racist behaviour through education and awareness of lifestyles ignores structural elements that embed and legitimate legal, political, social and cultural institutions in marginalisation and exclusion. For example, redefining black people's decision to leave dependants in the country of origin as a rational response to the lack of housing, child care and uncertain job prospects on arrival in the United Kingdom facilitates better practice than seeing it as a cultural trait that creates problems when black families are reunited (Williams et al., 2006).

A social worker who decontextualises working relationships with service users is unable to challenge structural disenfranchisement. Doing that requires an understanding of how structural changes like cutting public welfare expenditures exclude poor people from market-based provisions. Increased public monies spent on 'law and order', defence and subsidies to the private sector through infra-structural developments like roads, communications systems, grants, subsidies and tax relief to corporations divert public resources from improving people's well-being. Social work educa-tors should explore these areas in the curriculum to empower prac-titioners in understanding situations and acting effectively in them. This does not make social workers revolutionaries in a cause, but professionals charged with ensuring social justice for those experi-encing injustice, however caused. They cannot do this without knowing how injustice is perpetuated, whether intentionally or not, or taking actions that initiate structural transformations.

New directions for the social work curriculum

Policymakers can enact legislation that facilitates the development of anti-racist social work curricula. The voices of black educators, practitioners and service users are central to discussions about content. These can be incorporated into learning programmes to understand the links between personal circumstances, contexts, social positioning and locationality; promote individual, group and community well-being; and secure social justice. The curriculum can go beyond casework and engage students in becoming practi-tioners capable of facilitating structural change at organisational, institutional and cultural levels through holistic forms of practice that affirm the realisation of human rights, dignity and social justice. The GSCC has moved in this direction by insisting that service users are involved in all aspects of social work education.

Courses could do more to make staffing, the composition of the student body and curriculum more representative. Creating anti-racist environments involves agencies in employing black staff in significant numbers, catering to the needs of black users, and train-ing practice teachers in supporting students on placements in anti-racist ways of working. Anti-racist placements are central in delivering anti-racist social work curricula; tokenistic responses will disadvantage black students.

Black students are disproportionately represented amongst those who fail academic coursework and placements (Gore, 1998; Curtis, 2006). CCETSW and the GSCC have held conferences to document reasons for the lack of achievement and identified: inadequate support in countering racism on both courses and placements; using black students as 'race' experts to provide learning experiences for white students; and lacking resources that meet their specific needs. Most black students worked with white clients and white supervisors and lacked black practice teachers as role models (NISW, 1994). Some courses offered black mentorship schemes to support black students in white agencies with white supervisors. These are not widespread and can be hit-and-miss affairs conducted on a shoe-string. External consultants engaged on mentorship schemes may be isolated from what is going on in an agency and not well-placed to support students. The outcomes of these efforts need careful research.

---

putting it into practice   deconstructing ethnicities

- How could you use national and international human rights legislation when attempting to provide services to a disabled British Sikh child in a Sikh family originally from India?
- What support would help white social work students practice in anti-racist ways with black service users?
- What support would help black social work students practice in anti-racist ways with white service users?
- Consider what strategies a white social work manager might use to increase ethnic diversity and representation in a pool of practice teachers that is made up primarily of white ethnic groups.

Further reading

Gorman, K., Gregory, M., Hayles, M. and Parton, N. (eds) (2006) *Constructive Work with Offenders*. London: Jessica Kingsley.

Lyons, K. and Lawrence, S. (eds) (2006) *Social Work in Europe: Challenges for Social Work Educators*. Birmingham: BASW/ Venture Press.

4 | Anti-racist social work with children and families

Introduction

Black people have settled in Britain for over 500 years (Fryer, 1984). Families are part of the settlement process, with children representing the link between past, present and future. The majority of black people living in Britain are settlers born in the United Kingdom, but are treated as recent arrivals or immigrants. This configuration of their place in British society has implications for white practitioners' interventions amongst black children and their families. Immigration legislation complicates interventions in black families, actively curtailing black peoples' family life and restricting family reunifications. Reconstructing families in their traditional totality within the United Kingdom is impossible (Cohen, Humphries and Mynott, 2001). Other countries have similar immigration restrictions and encourage transnational movements of people; for example, the United States (Small, 2007).

Children are crucial to the continuation of a people. Considered society's future, they provide continuity between generations. Intergenerational continuities maintain identities over time. Child-rearing practices have become politicised and contested over differences in what constitutes 'good' or acceptable behaviour. These are played out in and through social work practice. Social workers have the power to define what is good child-rearing in a given situation, so their views structure outcomes in client–worker interactions with parents who challenge their opinions of children's welfare. Ensuing tensions can create opposition in relationships between children and parents; children and social workers; social workers and parents; social workers and the state; and the family and the state. Legislation gives social workers authority to make decisions about children's well-being that take precedence over those of parents, creating conflict between them. The potential of social workers to remove children from their families is a contested terrain that casts social workers as 'child snatchers' rather than help-givers. In black communities, the over-representation of black children in the care system is the source of anger and frustration and intensifies black parents' feelings of powerlessness and shame (Barn, Ladino and Rogers, 2006).

In this chapter, I examine persistent over-representation of black children and young people in care and custodial settings (DfES, 2005) to explore how social workers have attempted to improve practice in this area, albeit with patchy outcomes. I consider family diversity, mixed parentage, transracial fostering and adoptions, transnational adoptions, child abuse and neglect, domestic violence and sexual violence within the context of racialised identities with case examples like the well-publicised murder of Victoria Climbié by her carers. I investigate the impact of social divisions like gender, disability, age and mental health on children's lives.

Configuring the black family

In the United Kingdom, direct links with extended family members are more evident amongst some ethnic groups than others: one in six Indian households compared to one in 40 white households lives in a three-generation unit. One-third of families of African-Caribbean origins lives in a single-parent household compared to one in 12 white ones. Black families are poorer, with Pakistani and Bangladeshi ones amongst the poorest (ONS, 2002a). Struggles for survival and basic care consume poor peoples' time and energy.

Global poverty wears a black child's face, assumes various forms and is unevenly distributed on gendered, class, 'race' and ethnic bases. Pakistani children are amongst the poorest. Food poverty leads 5.6 million children to die from malnutrition and 146 million children suffer malnourishment across the world (UNICEF, 2006). Of these, 50 per cent live in India, Bangladesh and Pakistan. Individual country figures include: 8 million in Bangladesh; 8 million in Pakistan; 7 million in China (a figure that has halved since 1990); 6 million in Nigeria; 6 million in Ethiopia; and 6 million in Indonesia. These figures suggest the 1990 target to halve the number of underweight children globally by 2015 will not be met. India and China are doing well as emergent economies, but their wealth is disproportionately distributed. A World Bank report claims India is losing 5 per cent of GDP by not solving child malnutrition. Foster (2006:A9) argues that the Indian middle class benefited most from India's modernisation and is 'insulated from the poverty in which the great majority of Indians still live'. In Canada, children living in poverty are most likely to be aboriginal, recent immigrants, members of visible minorities and those with disabilities. In Britain, 3.4 million children continue to live in poverty despite New Labour's pledge to eradicate it by 2020, a target unattainable at current rates of progress. Children of Pakistani and Bangladeshi origins in the United Kingdom constitute 57 per cent of poor children living on less than £210 per week for a family of four when the End Child Poverty Campaign calculates that £295 are needed.

Creating the mythical black family

Social workers, as part of society, are aware of popular stereotypes about black families. Daniel Moynihan's (1965) work, *The Negro Family: The Case for National Action*, popularised the idea of the black family as pathological and matriarchal, with an 'absent' or submissive father and lacking white middle-class values. Cast as breaking down and in crisis, its divergence from white middle-class family norms was deemed 'deviant' and dangerous for black children. Black families' skills and contributions to children's growth were devalued or labelled 'inadequate' by those who created and reproduced the myth of 'the black family'. Moynihan focused on African Americans, but his views spread throughout the Western world and influenced professional thinking about black families, reinforcing strong misconceptions about their defining characteristics.

Myths about black families are predicated on the notion that there is only one type of black family for each black ethnic group. They rest on the myth of the 'good' white family configured in contrast to the 'bad' black family (Levy, 2004). Myths about families of African or Afro-Caribbean descent portray these in negative terms and as antithetical to raising children. Characteristics ascribed to them cover uncontrolled sexual prowess amongst men; lack of sexual morality amongst women who compose a high percentage of single parent mothers; absence of a stable family tradition; lack of family bonds between members; and strong, domineering matriarchs complemented by weak, powerless men, incapable of forming stable relationships (Staples, 1988). These myths are reversed for families of Asian origins. They are defined as more controlling; under male control; and having passive and sexually repressed women (Berthoud, 2005). Aboriginal or First Nations families are seen as culturally backward and in need of rescuing from their culture (Haig-Brown, 1988).

Black communities challenge these myths by defining families as sources of strength, solidarity, social capital and racial uplift (Hill-Collins, 2000). Robinson (2002:82) argues that individual black children and adults seek to affirm black identities while facing racism throughout the life-course. She critiques attachment theory à la Bowlby for not recognising strength in black families and their significance in children's lives (Robinson, 2002). These strengths offer resiliency, contribute dynamism to everyday life practices in black families and help them survive racism (Hill-Collins, 2000).

Women become signifiers of an ethnic group, responsible for maintaining culture and traditions across time and space and defending the nation. Discourses about women rest on notions of motherhood and sexual abstinence outside marriage. Gilroy (2000:127) associates the integrity of the nation with that of its masculinity: 'it can be a nation only if the correct version of gender hierarchy is established and reproduced' in the family. Ideas about what constitutes appropriate beauty, body shape, youth and age for child-bearing are tied into this. Women's agency becomes circumscribed by the needs of the larger group in which they are ensconced. Not all women accept these inscriptions of their bodies. Concepts of sameness are critiqued by women's everyday life practices. Diversity in women's lifestyles challenges the idea that one family form or woman's body suits all women. Black feminists question their exclusion from black political life, theorise diversity amongst black people regardless of class, gender, age, disability or sexuality and demand inclusivity in facilitating racial uplift across the generations (Hill-Collins, 2000).

The myth of the singular black family flies in the face of black people's everyday realities. While having much in common, black families vary across a range of attributes including ethnicity, religion, language, cultural traditions and sexual orientation. For example, a black British family of Nigerian African origins that is

Baptist will have different family arrangements from one that follows Islam. White people construct myths of black families by combining racism, sexism, classism and other forms of personal and structural oppression to condemn black people whatever they do (Wilson, 1978:24). Black people are castigated for being 'over-ambitious' and wanting their children to succeed while their rejection of racist stereotypes of their capabilities is condemned as 'reaching too far' (Ahmed, 1984). Their skills, strengths and resilience have been problematised as deficiencies rather than resources for social workers to utilise in resolving difficulties within black families. Labelling black parents as incompetent undermines confidence in parenting abilities (Maxime, 1986). Regardless of the type of black family, anticipated outcomes are the same: dysfunctionality in raising children, especially in interethnic relationships; over-representation of black children within the child care and custodial systems (Barn, Ladino and Rogers, 2006). Challenging how white people perceive black families exposes the gap white social workers must bridge to achieve good practice within these relationships.

Lack of acceptable terminology for black settlers is a problem. Describing those born in the United Kingdom as 'second generation' reinforces the view that they are 'immigrants' who do not belong here. This label is routinely used, for example, in discussing Chinese Britons. Dominic Casciani (BBC News Online, 2002:1) reports that 'second-generation' Chinese people organised to speak out against racism linked to Chinese restaurants alleged to having started the outbreak of foot and mouth; and the death of 58 Chinese from Fujan province in China in a lorry in June 2000. They demonstrated in April 2001 and founded the Dimsum website (www.dimsum.co.uk) to ensure that the voices of Chinese Britons are heard and to take Chinese identity and presence beyond the local takeaway. 'We have been silent for too long', claimed Sarah Yeh, founder of Dimsum. Chinese Britons lack a voice in the media, have no sense of citizenship or belonging in the United Kingdom and have different narratives to tell:

> Our needs are different to those of our parents. We have different aspirations. We're debating everything from relationships to how you explain to your parents you don't want to stay in the family catering business all your life.
>
> (BBC News Online, 2002:1)

Chinese have settled in Britain for over 200 years, the largest influx arriving during the 1970s from Hong Kong and Vietnam. Their community is widely dispersed, 176,000 were born overseas (ONS, 2002a). They are more likely to be subjected to racist attacks, but less likely to complain publicly (Patel and Lim, 2004). Few did when Greenock's Sheriff, Margaret Gimblett, claimed that 'Chinese people all look the same' without seeing it as either derogatory or feeding into racist stereotypes.

Nomadic settlers: Gypsies and Irish Travellers

Various minority ethnic groups in the United Kingdom are discriminated against. This general picture of oppression is differentiated according to age, gender and other social divisions. As these stories are different, social workers ought to investigate each for its particularity and not work on stereotypical assumptions. Gypsies and Irish Travellers are amongst groups whose claims to being settlers have been rejected for lengthy periods. Despite living in the United Kingdom for centuries, they are discriminated against extensively. Their traditional lifestyles are rejected as undesirable and accompanied by demands for assimilation. Gypsies and Irish Travellers underachieve in education. Their children have the poorest life chances and die young within an overall life expectancy below the national average (CRE, 2006a). Hostility in the media is rife, especially where encampments arise even if local authorities do not supply sites as the law demands. This picture might alter from 2006, as courts defined Gypsies and Irish Travellers an ethnic group under the Race Relations (Amendment) Act 2000.

Gypsies and Irish Travellers form the largest ethnic minority groups in 13 local authorities. The lack of permanent sites originally identified in the Caravan Sites and Control of Development Act 1960 was reaffirmed in legislation in 1968, 1983 and 2004. Local councillors do not understand statutory obligations to provide for their cultural needs, do so inadequately and without actively promoting good race relations between communities. They have failed to comply with new national requirements for Gypsy sites; promote race equality and good relations with Gypsies and Irish Travellers; ensure that mainstream services meet their needs; monitor the effects of their policies; identify disparities between different ethnic groups; and encourage communication with other community members (CRE, 2006a). Public resistance to creating appropriate sites was evident in 67 per cent of local authorities and unauthorised encampments cause tense relations with locals. The requirement for local authorities to produce race equality schemes that included Gypsies and Irish Travellers came into effect in May 2002, but only 9 per cent have changed policies on unauthorised encampment, and 6 per cent have monitored their effect since then. Consultation with Gypsy and Traveller communities is limited to national organisations, not those on the doorstep. Reasons for this failure include: not perceiving them as a minority ethnic group subjected to racism; focusing anti-racist initiatives on non-white ethnic minorities; and living in rural areas (CRE, 2006a).

By limiting responsibilities to Gypsies and Irish Travellers to site provision, local authorities ignore other basic services like social housing or family survival. Most of Britain's estimated 300,000 Gypsies and Travellers live in conventional housing; 90,000–120,000 travel in caravans reflecting their nomadic cultural heritage, not a 'lifestyle choice' (CRE, 2006a). Officially designated sites are in short supply and in areas inappropriate for raising families. In 2004, 5901 caravans were on authorised public sites; 4890 on private ones; 1594 on land not owned by Gypsies and Irish Travellers; and 1977 on land owned by them but lacking planning permission. The 4000 pitches needed by 2007 are not coming on-stream quickly enough (CRE, 2006a).

Local authorities and the media exacerbate situations by amplifying deviance and treating individuals who behave in anti-social ways as standing for a whole community. Everyone becomes negatively labelled; Gypsy and Traveller requests for the police to deal with specific offenders are ignored; for example, those dumping commercial waste. Blanket approaches to policing and managing unauthorised encampments exacerbate poor relationships between community groups. Police tactics include mass raids and evictions of entire camps, even when seeking to remove only those who cause specific problems. Collective labelling encourages troublesome individuals to avoid responsibility for their anti-social behaviour; punishes the group as a whole for the few; intensifies mistrust; and increases lack of confidence in the police and the broader society that ignore their claims (CRE, 2006a). Blanket surveillance and policing deepen divisions between law-abiding members of a given community and its lawbreakers. Punishing the innocent along with the guilty becomes a miscarriage of justice, intensifies alienation; reinforces racist dynamics that 'treat everyone the same'; and perpetuates problematic stereotypes of communities as outside the law.

More than half of local authorities use private bailiffs to remove Gypsies and Irish Travellers from unauthorised campsites. Evictions are conducted without consulting social workers and specialist workers providing services. Welfare checks are not carried out and the services that these workers provide are not reported to the enforcement officers carrying out the evictions. Social workers intervene as Gypsy and Traveller Liaison Officers (GTLOs). GTLOs aim to support them but lack resources and backing from local authorities. Working in constrained circumstances limits GTLOs achievements with schoolchildren, older people and homeless families. Another structural difficulty is that GTLOs are employed by county councils while district councils supply services and policy frameworks. Poor communications between these bodies fragment service delivery and undermine community cohesion (CRE, 2006a).

---

practice tips   building community cohesion

The principles outlined below enable social workers to engage with cultural diversity, promote community cohesion and facilitate egalitarian relationships between Gypsies, Irish Travellers and local communities. These include:

- Countering the social exclusion of Gypsies and Irish Travellers.
- Encouraging cross-community communication and participation.
- Involving Gypsies and Irish Travellers in local decision-making.
- Advocating for adequate services in housing, education, health, the personal social services and employment.
- Promoting local leadership amongst Gypsies and Irish Travellers while including women and young people.
- Demanding the enforcement of legislation aimed at assisting these groups.
- Liaising with police departments to eliminate blanket policing of these groups.
- Helping Gypsies and Irish Travellers present action plans to local authorities.
- Monitoring the effects of policies on the lives of Gypsies and Irish Travellers.   ➡

- Working with other agencies to coordinate and deliver needed services.
- Building bridges between Gypsies, Irish Travellers and other local residents.
- Following-up instances of racial harassment and, with those affected, monitor action taken by police and local authorities; respond to the needs of victim-survivors and ensure that perpetrators receive treatment and support.

White social workers' intervention with black children

Black children constitute 3 per cent of all British children, but 8 per cent of those in care as 'looked after' children (DfES, 2005). During the 1980s, 71 per cent of black children in care were placed in white families, a position that has altered little (Norford, Rashid and Thoburn, 2000). Currently there are disproportionate numbers of white foster carers; shortage of black foster carers and adoptees; lack of institutional provisions that respect black children's cultural traditions; predominance of white staff in care agencies; and lack of institutional milieus that nurture black children's identities and cultural needs. These black children have to ignore or suppress different cultural identities or do without services responding to their needs as is their right under the 2004 Children Act and United Nation's Convention on the Rights of the Child.

White social workers have difficulty accepting black foster carers as *bona fide* carers or substantially changing institutional environments to support black children's identity needs or foster white children with black families. An explanation is that they operate within general cultural discourses that pathologise black families and child-rearing practices; relationships between black parents and children; and women's roles in families. This makes white social workers anxious about 'risks' they might take if they do not act with caution when they intervene. And, it affects their professional judgment, causing them to play safe by minimising anticipated risks and excluding black families as appropriate carers for their children.

'Risk' is a key feature of modern life. Living in the 'risk society' intensifies concerns to reduce risks (Beck, 1992). Foucault (1988) defined risks as 'practices of the self'. Contemporary configurations of risk refer to professionals calculating the potential of specific individuals to harm others or themselves. Beck (1999) suggested that greater knowledge increases uncertainty and the inability to deal adequately with risk. Child welfare workers constantly assess risk, using bureaucratic tools known as risk assessments to assist their calculations. They are enjoined to be 'culturally sensitive', but overriding fears about protecting children from dangerous individuals means that current constructions of black families predispose practitioners towards configuring relationships between black children and parents as risky and utilising harm reduction strategies rooted in services provided by white rather than caregivers.

Case study   Black practitioner activism

Black practitioners have criticised white social workers' poor responses to black children's needs and for not seeing black families as appropriate carers. Traffic in children was one-way: black children going to white families without white children being placed in black ones. They defined such practices cultural imperialism with black children as commodities of exchange and began initiatives to change these. Under pressure from the New Black Families Unit created in 1980, the Soul Kids Campaign and Black and in Care, Lambeth Social Services Department altered its procedures and criteria for selecting foster parents so that they became more inclusive and selected sufficient black foster parents (Small, 1987). Their criteria included: the ability to love and relate to a black child *as a black child*; skills in handling racist onslaughts; knowledge of black culture, language, religion and ethnicities appropriate for a specific child; a positive sense of black identities to assist the development of black children as whole human beings; and positive ongoing links with black communities including extended families located overseas. Black practitioners formed the Association for Black Social Workers and Allied Professions (ABSWAP) in 1983 to add collective voice to these critiques; give evidence to the House of Commons Select Committee revising child welfare legislation; and have racial, linguistic, religious and cultural factors included in the 1989 Children Act including Section 22(5)(c). Norford and colleagues (2000) reviewed the outcomes of these changes and confirmed that holistic approaches that go beyond 'race' meet black children's needs. This section of the Act is poorly enforced and resourced, whether training social workers or observing requirements in practice. Its provisions are affirmed by the Children (Leaving Care) Act 2000, *National Service Framework for Children*, Children Act 2004 and *Every Child Matters* (DfES, 2004).

Similar pressure from Maori peoples led to the 1989 Children, Young Persons and Their Families Act in New Zealand/Aotearoa, entitling Maori children to culturally sensitive intervention in Family Group Conferences (FGCs), later adopted for working with children and young people elsewhere, e.g., youths in custody in the United Kingdom (Jackson and Nixon, 1999). First Nations peoples in Canada created their own child welfare system to boost communal growth and spirituality (Thomas and Green, 2007).

Black professionals saw that the poor treatment of black children in residential care applied to those undergoing adoption and argued for a 'same race' policy in adoption and fostering so that they could be matched for ethnicity and culture, thereby supporting black identity formation and links to black families and communities. This policy has been and continues to be contested, although research has highlighted the importance of knowing about one's cultural heritage and community (Banks, 1999; Moffat and Thoburn, 2001). Attacks on the integrity of 'same race' policies and anti-racist social work include spurious allegations of bad practice as occurred in the United Kingdom during the summer of 1993 (Dunant, 1994). Such attacks undermine black people's right to self-determination because their struggles against colour-blind practices led to more culturally aware policies being enshrined in law. 'Same race' policies do not obviate a full assessment of an individual or family in reaching a judgment about their specific capacity to care for a black child. Nor does it cancel the need for supportive resources for black carers to maintain children's welfare or permit white social workers to use black families only for 'hard to place' children.

Transracial/transethnic adoptions

Rescuing black children

Transracial/transethnic adoptions occur when parents adopt a child from a different racial or ethnic grouping. Whether this should happen has been/is hotly contested. Multi-heritage children (those with one white and one black parent) come to the attention of social workers in the absence of support from an extended family that is often not there according to Jill Olimude, a white woman married to a Nigerian (BBC News, 2002:4). Children are treated as black when they should not be (Alibhai Brown, 2001a). Discourses on familial-ist ideology and 'otherness' intersect to construct a black child as needing rescuing by white parents. 'Rescuing' multi-heritage children born in Britain occurs alongside 'rescuing' children from overseas. Multi-heritage children are over-represented in the care system and custody. A PSI study found that 50 per cent of black men, 34 per cent of black women, 20 per cent of Asian men and 10 per cent of Asian women had a white partner (Berthoud and Modood, 1997). The 2001 Census revealed that 10 per cent of the minority ethnic population in the United Kingdom or 415,000 people, were 'hybrids' or 'mixed race' (ONS, 2002a). And, 40 per cent of black children living with both parents had one black and one white parent. 'Hybridity' has become a national characteristic and produced fused and separated identities. Often excluded by both communities, these families' experiences differ according to whether the mother or father is white. The terms 'hybrid' identity or mixed 'race' identity do not address the specifics of the people concerned. Hybrid discourses have their roots in biology and risk essentialising social relationships and blur distinctions between cultural heritages, ethnicities and nationalities. Multi-heritage or multi-ethnic better describe children with parents of different ethnic groups; multinational if another nationality, but the same ethnic group.

In the 1960s and 1970s, transracial/transethnic adoptions impacted primarily on black children as part of a 'rescuing' mission undertaken by white parents who focused on 'loving' a child and providing a broader range of opportunities than would otherwise be available. The fall of the Berlin Wall in Eastern Europe expanded the ideological reach of this practice during the 1990s to children 'abandoned in squalid orphanages' in the former communist regimes. This rescuing mission is evident today when children of non-majority ethnic groups are taken into care. Brinkworth (2005) paints a loving portrait of four young women saved from Romanian orphanages by the British charity, Children on the Edge (COTE) to avoid the path to prostitution and life on the streets followed by others. 'Celebrity' adoptions in the lowest income countries in the world revive Western rescuing discourses and affirm that African children need rescuing from poverty and parents unable to care for them; for example, Angelina Jolie adopting an Ethiopian child in 2005, Madonna a Malawian child in 2006.

International adoptions are problematic. Racialised class inequalities abound as poor black children are adopted by rich white people (Nolan, 2006:A3). Difficulties are compounded in cultures that foster children in extended families if children lose links with their communities of origins. Rich people can bypass local safe-guards that ask prospective parents to live in the country for a period prior to adoption, as Madonna did in Malawi. Unscrupulous agents can extort children from reluctant village women that they pressurise into giving their children to wealthier foreigners who promise them better material opportunities. These transactions can impact on home adoptions. For example, in-country adoptions in Canada might take 10 to 12 years to process compared to 18 months for an Ethiopian child. This huge time differential encourages prospective parents to go for the latter option. The adoptive process also costs from $Cdn15,000 to $Cdn20,000, so mainly high income people can access it. Adopting children who have been trafficked or stolen from their families of origin also reduces waiting times and draws people desperate to become parents into the ambit of unauthorised adoption agencies and criminal traders in children. Knowledge of the illegal basis of their involvement may be absent. Concerns over the legality of adoption processes in Guatemala led the United States to introduce further DNA tests to link children to birth parents in the visa-granting process in 2007. Europeans connected to the charity, Zoe's Ark, were detained in Chad for allegedly attempting to abduct 103 children from Darfur for fostering by families in Europe (Chrisafis, 2007).

Discourses of 'rescuing' children from other lands go beyond individual celebrities and become part of the global exchange in children. These are incorporated into policy discussions about transracial adoptions of children even when attempts are made to grant equality to all. For example, the Conservative government in Canada announced it would equalise treatment by ending an anomaly that allows children born to Canadians overseas automatic citizenship (provided parents complete the required paperwork in time), but not adopted children. All children in 'Canadian families deserved to be treated the same way', Prime Minister Harper announced when streamlining the 'foreign adoption process to allow parents to submit citizenship applications for foreign-born adoptees at the same time as they begin the adoption process' (Graham, 2006:A3). Harper's terminology of 'foreignness' 'others' these children and legitimates the rescuing of black children:

Those parents . . . go to great effort and expense to bring those children into their families . . . They open their hearts and their homes and they provide opportunities to children who often come from impoverished or war-ravaged countries.

(Harper quoted in Graham, 2006:A3)

A delighted prospective adoptive parent awaiting clearance for a second adoption from China expressed her appreciation of this change by locating her response within familialist discourses: 'This is a great Mother's Day present' (Graham, 2006). The Adoptive Families Association of British Columbia (BC) shows that half of the 600 children adopted in the province yearly are overseas adoptions, mainly from China, the United States, Russia, Haiti, Thailand and Korea (www.bcadoption.com). The United Kingdom, less committed to such equality, refuses to grant British citizenship to adopted children of British parents living overseas or those born in the United Kingdom without a British parent unless they meet other stipulated conditions.

---

practice tips assessments to support black children's identity development and community connections

The problem with rescuing discourses from an anti-racist perspective is not that parents aim to give children better opportunities, but that doing so within rescuing discourses affirms the superiority of white Western culture and can negate a child's heritage and the significance of retaining a sense of self that reflects the complexities of their situation. In practice, white parents should not automatically be ruled out as inappropriate. Each applicant has to be fully assessed against criteria about providing adequate care for a black child *as a black child*, who can explore identity issues and feel at ease within both black and white communities. Alongside this, practitioners should explore peoples' motivations for adopting a black child and the social networks they access. White people may be overtly racist and lack connections with black communities, but some black people have internalised racist values and need support in establishing connections to their heritages. Social workers can use these insights to undertake sensitive assessments that do not collude with or sustain racism.

A 'one size fits all' response is unlikely to meet the specific needs of a given black individual or family. Expecting services developed for white women automatically to meet the needs of black women assumes that different needs can be neglected and white social workers 'know best'. Such attitudes ignore black women's struggles for gender equality in their communities and portray white people as experts on how to organise relationships between black men and women. It also suggests an absence of sexism in white communities, a reality exposed as false by white feminists who have identified a continuing 'glass ceiling', a pay gap between women and men and lack of political representation (Brook, 2004). Homogenising identities also neglects the needs of white children with multiple white heritages; for example, a white working-class Welsh-speaking child growing up in England. Systems that account for diversity in assessing, processing and evaluating referrals enable social workers to intervene appropriately in complex identity relationships.

Fear of 'race' issues leads to inappropriate interventions for black children

Around 80 children a year die at the hands of their carers, a figure that has persisted for many years. A number of high-profile ones involve black children. The most horrendous of these are subjected to a public inquiry (Berridge and Brodie, 1996). There are many reasons why the state's safeguarding of children's welfare fails both black and white children (Dominelli et al., 2005). One of these, fear of being labelled racist, impacts primarily upon black families. White social workers', anxious about their inability to address problems that affect black families, undermine their interventions and endanger black children's lives so that some have been murdered by carers whilst under their scrutiny. Jasmine Beckford (Blom-Cooper, 1986), Tyra Henry (Lambeth, 1987), and Victoria Climbié (Laming, 2003) provide classic examples of the deadening effect of such fears, albeit in the last case it was white social work managers at the higher levels who failed to adequately support black frontline workers or challenge the assumption that 'all black cultures were the same'.

Case study Failing 'looked after' black children

Jasmine Beckford died in 1984. The white social worker working on the case did not challenge the black parents' refusal to let her see the child and accepted their excuses until it was too late. Tyra Henry died that year in similar circumstances. Her white social worker, unable to overcome fears of being seen as racist if she challenged the black parents' versions of events, did not meet her obligations to look after the 'best interests of the child'. Tyra ended up being killed.

Agencies have a duty to address white social workers' fears, support them in overcoming these and acquiring the skills for working appropriately with black families. Helping workers to understand black families is part of this. Having the confidence to do assessments without assuming that everything is racism will allay fears of being labelled racist. Learning about racism and how racist dynamics are perpetuated in an agency at personal, institutional and cultural levels requires additional training resources to reach this goal. As Victoria Climbié's death revealed, black practitioners have to be supported differently. Managers should not assume that just because they are black, they know how to tackle issues raised by another culture or racism.

Victoria Climbié's death on 25 February 2000 highlighted systemic failure and the inability of black social worker Lisa Arthurworrey, supervisors Carole Baptiste and Edward Armstrong, manager Angela Mairs, and other white professionals including health professionals and police to intervene and protect Victoria's welfare (Laming, 2003). Lord Laming (2003) summed up professional shortcomings by commenting:

> Never once was an assessment of need made; never once, whether by the hospital, social services or the police service. What happened to this little girl was shocking in the extreme.

No one picked up on the cruelty and abuse Victoria suffered at the hands of great-aunt Marie-Thérèse Kouao and her boyfriend Carl Manning, both subsequently convicted of her murder. Lisa Arthurworrey was dismissed from her post and banned from working with children. She successfully challenged this outcome. In reversing this decision in 2006, the Tribunal agreed she had been unsupported by her employers.

Laming felt Victoria's death occurred through 'systemic failure', not the shortcomings of one individual. His indictment covered all the agencies safeguarding Victoria's welfare – 4 social services departments, 3 housing departments, 2 specialist child protection teams in the Metropolitan Police, 2 different hospitals and the National Society for the Prevention of Cruelty to Children (NSPCC). Victoria was referred to Haringey Social Services as a 'child in need' under the 1989 Children Act instead of as a child both in need and requiring protection. Investigating child protection cases diverts substantial resources away from supporting those defined as 'in need' whereby social workers can address issues of discrimination, disadvantage and deprivation, and leaves inadequate resources to meet the needs of families with children. Rationed resources subvert child welfare to produce 'systemic failure' and place social workers in impossible situations.

Failing to prevent the death of a child and not knowing what to do in such situations increases a social worker's stress levels. McLeod (1987) argues that child protection practitioners who work within community health settings suffer high rates of stress and are more likely to experience higher levels of burnout if inadequately supported by managers and lacking appropriate supervision in difficult and complex cases. Worker neglect seriously compromises professional competence and damages their emotional well-being. These issues are further complicated by high rates of turnover and a shortage of social workers in children's services. Lisa Arthurworrey's tale is instructive here.

Butler and Drakeford (2003:221) deem the inquiry a 'player in the construction of events' that 'manages the scandal' and leaves the system intact. Blaming the social worker is integrated into its narratives, as Victoria's social worker and others have found out. Laming (2003) hoped Victoria's death would be the last and proposed wide-ranging changes to prevent wholesale failure in future. Despite his wishes, children continue to be murdered by their carers as occurred, for example, to Lauren Wright later in 2000, Ainlee Walker in 2002; Leticia Wright in 2006. Shutting the revolving door of systemic failure requires fundamental changes including tackling poverty within families and seeing child-rearing as *both* a private family and a *social* responsibility.

practice tips   key messages from public inquiries

Over 70 major inquiries into cases of child abuse from 1948 up to Victoria's death gave largely the same key messages, namely:

- failure of inter-agency communications;
- inexperienced and inadequately informed workers;
- inadequately trained workers;
- failure to follow established procedures; and
- inadequate resources to support workers and families.

Social workers require resources, emotional stability and creativity to address both convergent needs that cross ethnic divides like food, clothing, shelter or safe environments and divergent needs linked to specific ethnicities, culture, languages or religions. Divergent needs involving culture, language and religion and convergent needs like poverty, isolation, powerlessness or being in abusive relationships intersect with racism but are relatively independent of it. Convergent needs impact on both black and white children and the parenting abilities of mothers and fathers, but racism and other 'isms' make their experiences different. These should not be essentialised or presumed to be the same for all people in a specific ethnic group but established in their particularity with service users. Below, Figure 4.1 on Convergent and Divergent Needs indicates that there are needs common to both groups while others differ. These considerations are relevant to social workers who support black families through family centres, outreach services and home-based family support services.

Figure 4.1   Convergent and divergent needs

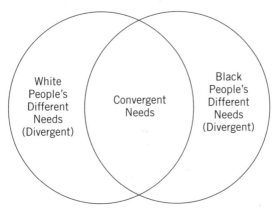

White People's Different Needs (Divergent)

Convergent Needs

Black People's Different Needs (Divergent)

Translation

High quality translation resources are integral to delivering appropriate services to families with limited knowledge of English. Demands for these services are rising, but funding for them is scarce (Turton, De Maio and Lane, 2003). The absence of such supports for social workers constitutes institutional racism. Often disguised as a shortage of resources, it indicates lack of priority for their provision. Translation involves interpretation and transmitting meaning and significance across language barriers. Translators require training to handle diversity and unequal power relations sensitively. Social workers should be familiar with how different values and social divisions like gender, class, age, disability and sexual orientation shape translators' responses and ability to communicate without oppressing black people whose values or attributes they do not share. These issues arise in the case study below:

Case study   Gendering and classing 'race' appropriately

A Muslim Gujerati woman with two children had been left in poor housing and without money by her husband of five years after an acrimonious divorce. The husband's family, who lived nearby, wanted the children and were willing to raise and support them. They refused to support the wife whom they blamed for the failure of the marriage with unreasonable demands about the lifestyle she wanted to lead. The woman was determined to keep her children and asked social services for help. She spoke little English and wanted a translator. Social services employed a woman, originally from the Gujerat, to assist the white social worker assigned to the case. The translator was a middle-class Brahmin woman; the client a working-class Muslim. The practitioner sensed 'discomfort' between the two women when she entered the client's house, but continued the interview as she was worried about the children. When she asked the translator what the client said, she replied, 'Don't worry about her too much. She is a peasant who doesn't know what she wants or what is good for her children.'

Fortunately, the social worker discontinued the interview to resume it later and learnt how complex 'matching' translators and clients could be. This translator had been on social services' list for several years before arrogance about those with different religious, class and cultural needs surfaced. The repercussions of not having paid translators can be disastrous in some situations; for example, where children act as translators. How can a black child being abused by family members translate dialogue for them without further trauma and abuse occurring through and from the telling? Lack of skilled translators could result in social workers relying on translations given by children they are required to protect, with the ensuing silences and conflicts of interest between parents and children. Children may be unable to grasp and convey complexity or it may be outside their knowledge and experiences as occurs below:

Case study   Poor translation practice

Catherine, an 8-year-old girl of Chinese descent, accompanied her mother who spoke no English to a white English gynaecologist. As there were no Chinese-speaking interpreters available, the gynaecologist asked her to translate. Some questions were of a highly explicit intimate sexual nature and Catherine did not understand what was being asked. She felt confused and unhappy about being in this position. When the mother asked her what the 'doctor' had said, the child replied, 'Everything. He says you need a hysterectomy', but could not explain what this was.

This case exposes the fallacy of assuming that anyone who 'knows the language' can provide translation. Translation agencies that aim to root out bad practices and insist on appropriate qualifications can be found on the Internet. Professionals may not know of these facilities and not use them. Social workers were not there for Catherine, yet the GP's surgery that made the referral had social workers attached. If one had been, Catherine's 'best interests' in *not* translating could have been safeguarded.

Clientising black women through interactive processes: sexism and racism

White sexism intersects with white racism to provide different experiences of gender oppression between black and white women and different forms of racial oppression between black women and black men. Myths of the sexually active Afro-Caribbean woman and sexually repressed Asian woman configure their experiences of oppression differently. Asian women are subjected to stereotypes like 'arranged marriages', are 'forced' or 'bogus', and preferring boys to girls (Hocking, 2006). These narratives inscribe relationships, structure interpretation and invest meaning with stereotypes of diverse cultural practices as lacking value. Social workers require skills to distinguish between these practices and the stereotypes associated with each.

---

practice tips   changing narratives, developing new possibilities

Changing the narratives that white social workers associate with black families will yield opportunities to create and orchestrate new knowledges that can reconfigure practice in more egalitarian, life-affirming directions, e.g., arranged marriages are generally successful. Reworking narratives within egalitarian anti-racist and social justice perspectives would help white social workers retain a critical reflective perspective that deconstructs oppressive practices and enables them to make judgments based on the particulars of a situation and the specific actors involved.

Black women who challenge a cultural norm should not be presumed to question its entirety, let alone a whole culture. Not thinking of the repercussions of intervening in black women's lives can be counter-productive, complicate their position or endanger them. These concerns become important when Asian women ask for social work support to avoid 'honour' killings or *forced* marriages or when a community rejects a woman to enable a family to maintain *izzat* (honour) and she becomes isolated (Hocking, 2006). The complex interplay between sexism and racism requires white social workers to be extremely sensitive about their interventions and conduct. Action has to occur within specific contexts explicitly explored for their implications in particular circumstances.

How white social workers challenge what they are told by black people matters and should be handled with sensitivity, tact and awareness of their own impact on others. White social workers engaging and working effectively with a black woman would listen and learn from her. If intervening appropriately is beyond their capacity, they can refer her to a black woman worker. To do this, they should know about specific resources in black communities, and understand both how they operate and their appropriateness for any one woman. For example, Southall Black Sisters help black women experiencing domestic violence obtain needed resources. Working with other black women is crucial if a black woman has been ostracised or isolated from a community for challenging its traditions. If this occurs, black women may become more vulnerable if exposed to white racism without appropriate support.

White social workers should not assume that a black culture is either monolithic or not being challenged internally. Black family lives should not be considered static and unchanging any more than white ones. Definitions about what is appropriate in black families' arrangements are being contested, as are those in white families. For example, in Britain, Women's Aid aims to help women fleeing domestic violence. Mama (1989) highlighted different experiences of domestic violence for black women and revealed how state responses and immigration legislation institutionalise sexism and racism by labelling black men as wife abusers and threatening deportation. Indo-Canadian women in Vancouver formed alliances with Indo-Canadian men to protest honour killings and demand cultural change. Families and cultures constantly undergo changes that members either contest or support. Gilroy (2000:213) claims that the repositioning of black conservative thought amongst black middle-class elites in the United States has reaffirmed masculinist versions of racial identity and undermined the ethics of care between black people living in affluent areas and those in ghetto communities.

For Gilroy (2000), transformational change cannot occur solely in the interstices of interpersonal relations. He lays the blame for the vacuum at the heart of black community life not on a conservative personal sphere dominated by family life, but on the absence of an inclusive black political leadership interested in social change. He claims that his vision of a 'planetary humanity' that rejects racialisation and reconnects 'with democratic and cosmopolitan traditions that have been all but expunged from today's black political imagery' can replace the emptiness of corporate spaces that benefit few people, black or white, (Gilroy, 2000:356). Encouraging black and white people to find common cause in realising this 'planetary humanity' allows the best in specific societies to be preserved. Gilroy's cross-ethnic alliances that go beyond the 'colour line' in interpersonal and public life can help to achieve this goal. Finally, skills that social workers learn working with black people make them better practitioners with white people. They, too, require contextualised interventions that engage with their specificities and promote strengths and resilience. Racism makes these different from those of black people. Anti-racist practice contributes to the development of good practice for all, regardless of 'race' and supplies transferable values and skills for dealing with 'isms' like classism, sexism, disablism.

Social workers' legacies of oppression

Social workers have been implicated in the obliteration of peoples and their cultures, as exemplified by people of Jewish origins in Nazi Germany (Lorenz, 1994) and aboriginal peoples in North and South America, Australia and New Zealand (Haig-Brown, 1988; Briskman, 2005). In these, cultural intolerance and assimilationist arguments about sameness and cultural purity resulted in physical genocide. For indigenous peoples, the psychological damage these processes inflicted on survivors was severe and impacted negatively on child-rearing practices as they became parents (Dominelli et al., 2005). First Nations families have lengthy histories of institutional abuse that caused individuals to misuse alcohol and drugs to the detriment of their parenting (Thomas and Green, 2007). In Canada, campaigns initiated demands for legislative reform to change the Indian Act that denied women their rights and status as Indians. Achieving this success under Bill C-31 was a long, difficult journey. At one stage the issue was internationalised by coming before the United Nations. Equality of treatment evades First Nations peoples today and the transfer of resources by the few to the majority continues. For instance, Hume (2006:A19) exposes inequalities in the agreement with the Nuchatlaht. Each person in this small band of 130 members on 11 reserves in Vancouver Island receives $1.36 per day while the provincial government gets $55 a minute. Compare these earnings from one project to $8 billion in aid yearly for Indian bands across all national government programmes in Canada.

Briskman (2006) highlights the appalling treatment of aboriginal children and asylum-seekers in Australia. She complains that dominant white ethnic groups promote cultural assimilation, especially for 'dual heritage' children with a white and an aboriginal parent. The Stolen Generations describes the genocide perpetuated on them (HREOC, 1997). The abuse of Australian aboriginal children was a crime of white colonisation (Briskman, 2006:214). The film, *Rabbit-Proof Fence*, exposed the privations including death that small children encountered in resisting subjugation by running away. Enduring hardship, they broke the secrecy that hid their suffering; loss of families, names and culture; and oppression as indigenous children.

Social work intervention with young black people

Young people, black and white, have limited opportunities for contributing to society and acquiring a sense of belonging to it. Young black people are more frequently unemployed, thrown out of school and represented in crime statistics than white ones (Young, 1999). Young people are cast as constantly out of control, threatening social order, and are demonised as a result. Young black people are more likely to be stigmatised and defined as dangerous, although this varies by gender, class, ethnicity and religion. Society's control of rebellious young people who threaten its fragile stability encompasses their lifestyles or relationships with one another and authority. Social workers in inner city areas collude with these definitions, pathologising black youth's resistance to racism and instances where they identify as positive black people. As a result, their rights in encounters with the law become precarious (Home Office, 2002a). Young Rastafarian men are perceived as particularly dangerous and difficult for smoking ganja in religious rituals. Those with dreadlocks are more likely to be stopped and searched by the police under the guise of ensuring public safety. There have been several campaigns against what were called 'sus' (stop and search) laws in the 1980s, despite their amendment after the Brixton Riots in 1981 (Scarman, 1981) because the police, especially in London, stop disproportionately more young black men than other groups and then find no evidence to charge them. The Crime and Disorder Act, 1998, initiated new versions of this practice. In 2005–6, the police stopped 878,153 people on 'reasonable suspicion' of committing offences, especially those associated with drugs. They were disproportionately black (Dodd, 2007). The issue is controversial, for example, Keith Jarrett, President of the National Black Police Association calls for more action to curb gun and knife crime while Milena Buyum, Coordinator of the National Assembly Against Racism demands the opposite.

Although concerns about terrorism have exacerbated the labelling of black youths as deviant, only 1 in 400 anti-terror stop and searches result in charges. These have increased 44 per cent to reach 44,543 during 2005-6. Asians were more likely to be stopped under these provisions, then black and then other ethnic groups, and last were white people (Dodd, 2007). The Prevention of Terrorism Act 2005 has exacerbated stereotypes of dangerous young black men, especially those of Islamic faith, as threats to society. The killing of Brazilian, Jean Charles de Menezes, by the Metropolitan Police in London who thought he was a terrorist (BBC, 2006) provides a high-profile recent example of this development. No charges will be laid against individual officers concluded the inquiry conducted by the independent Police Complaints Commission. This is disputed by the young man's family, who wants a public inquiry and might lay civil charges. Netter and colleagues (2001) term this 'xeno-racism' and argue that it is a strategy for managing migration.

Expectations that black communities exercise internal control, display docility and 'look after their own' mean that activities that white social workers would tolerate in white clients become alarming in black ones. Juvenile crime and adolescent struggles for individual autonomy are seen as especially threatening. Black people's alleged deviance is amplified, raising white people's fears about them (Young, 1999). White social workers encase black people in a web of stricter surveillance and control, rapidly clientising them as a host of welfare agencies descends upon them. Collective action may be necessary to safeguard the rights of young black people and affirm ties of solidarity. Social workers have a role to play by ensuring fair treatment in legal processes as Hutchinson-Reis (1986) describes for the young black people arrested in the aftermath of the riots on the Broadwater Farm Estate in the mid-1980s (see p. 218).

Organisational change

Changing organisational structures involves altering an organisation's culture, practices, policies, perceptions, priorities, commitments and the behaviour of clients, colleagues and managers. Orienting these in anti-racist directions entails long and protracted processes and may strain relationships amongst those involved. Smooth progress cannot be assumed and even if worked for, there is no guarantee of success. For example, tackling racist attitudes and behaviour amongst white clients will be difficult and challenging. Undoing the damage of internalised racism amongst black clients will not be easy. Both will require resources, support, commitment and time if the people concerned are to be helped to grow, and to believe in their dignity, worth and entitlement to services that meet their needs. Matters can be complicated by client and worker resistance to such a journey and contested in various ways. Agency priorities may conflict with personal ones and create tensions between employees and employers. Gaining the support of the wider public can be problematic. Changing the perceptions of those who argue that black people are privileged by anti-racist initiatives will take a lot of convincing that this is rarely the case. Forming alliances around agreed goals with several different groups and preparing for their fragmentary and transient nature is essential. Complementarity between different groups might help this process. Organisations can seek research and training to secure these goals.

Developing transnational links is crucial to protecting children who cross borders with adults who end up abusing, exploiting or killing them. The internationalisation of social problems, like people smuggling, prostitution, the sex trade, arms trade and drugs, involve children and illustrate this need. Victoria Climbié's case highlights the internationalisation of social problems alongside the system's failure to deal with this, an aspect ignored in Laming's Report. Laming (2003) paid insufficient attention to: 'race'; racism; agency failure under conditions of globalisation; and working out how to deal with children privately fostered out to relatives for the chance of a better life, as is traditional in several African countries (Palmer-Hunt, 2003).

Victoria was born near Abidjan in Ivory Coast, a former French colony with French as a main language. Was this the one Victoria spoke? How much English did she know? Could Lisa Arthurworrey speak French? Were French–English translation services available? Victoria travelled to France on her great-aunt's passport as her daughter, Anna. She was not properly documented, but immigration officers noticed this neither in France nor Britain. How do they engage with safeguarding the interests of children? The school in Villepinte, France, had issued a 'Child at Risk Emergency Notification' in February 1999 over concerns about Victoria's health. School officials accepted Kouao's word that she was taking the child to London for treatment without further follow-up. There are no established procedures for passing such information between jurisdictions. They need to be devised. On arrival in London in April 1999, Victoria was responded to as a child 'in need' of housing, not one already 'at risk'. This exposes the convergence of transnational institutional failures alongside individual and national ones. All have to be addressed to safeguard children's lives, adding weight to calls that define the raising of children as a social, not private responsibility.

---

practice tips   sustaining change

Social workers can sustain change by:

- Becoming culturally aware from an anti-racist perspective that does not ossify culture or lay responsibility for all that goes wrong on cultural differences.
- Not using value judgments that presuppose white superiority.
- Becoming conscious of how institutional and cultural racism link to personal racism and impact upon their work.
- Working to overcome racism within the profession and broader society.
- Exploring the privileging of white power in relationships with black people.
- Drawing connections between racism and social control in social work.
- Connecting eliminating racism to getting rid of other forms of oppression.
- Promoting institutional and organisational change alongside personal change.
- Receiving supportive supervision.

Conclusions

White social workers' assumptions permeate their work. If negative, interventions devalue black peoples' knowledge, skills and contributions to the wider society. Whether with black children, young people or elders, these will be detrimental, decontextualise their activities and 'dump' responsibility for eradicating racism on them. Not facilitating black social workers' capacities to practise with other ethnic groups and develop a broad range of competencies could segregate the workforce to the detriment of black workers and ghettoise services for black communities. White social workers could enhance their skills in working with diverse ethnic groups, including white ones, who differ from them to provide clients with real choices about available services. Anti-racist workplaces can support both black and white social workers in acquiring the relevant skills, knowledge and values. Progress in developing anti-racist workplaces and practices can be monitored alongside agency and managerial support for staff development. Black and white practitioners can work together and separately to eradicate racist practices from the profession and legitimate struggles for egalitarian social relations in the wider society. This goal is attainable if supported by structural and organisational changes.

---

putting it into practice

- Consider your assumptions about black families' positions in society. How do these take account of racism?
- How would you deal with differences over cultural practices in child care?
- How would you work with parents who reject invasive medical treatment when a child's life is at risk?

Further reading

Barn, R. (ed.) (1999) *Working with Black Children and Adolescents in Need*. London: British Association for Adoption and Fostering.

National Children's Bureau (NCB) (2004) *The Care Experience: Through Black Eyes*. London: NCB.

5 | Anti-racist social work with adults and older people

Introduction

The Western population is ageing or getting proportionately older with views of old people as burdens gaining ascendancy. Demographers expect older Europeans post-retirement age to rise from 34 million in 1960 to 69 million by 2010 (EC, 2003). Constituting a small part of the larger whole, black elders fit into this ageing pattern, having come to the continent in their earlier years as labour power for European economies or to be reunited with family members, a picture also found in Britain (Patel et al., 2004). Black elders are oppressed on ethnic grounds alongside those of age and 'race'. Black women elders also endure gender discrimination.

Elders experience ageism or oppression on the basis of old age. Ageism undervalues older peoples' contributions to society and portrays them as incapable, vulnerable and dependent. It involves an abuse of power over a person on the basis of age and consequent loss of personal dignity and status. Ageism, a defining feature of old age in the West, is reinforced by cultural practices that treat age as an essentialised, unitary, unchanging entity. It contrasts to youthism that celebrates young, vigorous bodies and links to consumerism's players in the marketplace. Marketable bodies are manufactured by a host of entrepreneurs that advocate agency and glamour by having the 'correct' body. Ageism is expressed in personal, institutional and cultural forms structured into everyday life practices and professional routines. Government policies that fail elders, evident in low incomes, poor health services and inadequate provisions for an active, healthy old age are institutional expressions of ageism.

Ageism curtails agency in older people, subjecting them to regimes of control under professionals or carers. Older people have challenged their depiction as dependent subjects. The Centre for

Policy on Ageing, established by the Nuffield Foundation in 1947 has promoted positive views of older people through research and dissemination activities. The same can be said for PRIAE (The Policy Research Institute on Ageing and Ethnicity), which focuses on evidence-based studies to lobby for policies that benefit ethnic elders. Better Government for Older People (BGOP) is a partnership that includes older people in decision-making at many levels. Active Ageing Units and Advocacy Schemes for Older People seek to empower older people. These groups' commitment to demonstrate active ageing contrasts with those in the Debate of the Age who define older people as burdens and ignore unpaid carers.

White older people have rejected their image as vulnerable and incapable adults and organised to press their cause with direct action in relation to pensions, council tax and mandatory retirement. They also worry about relationship loss and the death of close ones, including ultimately their own. These concerns are shared by black elders and belie their caricature as passive and powerless victims. Black elders with cultural traditions that venerate old age hold continuing roles in their communities as sources of wisdom, advice and care for others especially children; and argue for interdependency between generations (Thomas and Green, 2007). Intergenerational relations differ between ethnic groups and have significant implications for service provision. Janet Boateng (1999:5) suggests that 'age is a resource' useful in creating services for black elders and 'trust, credibility, equity, inclusiveness and effectiveness in all our services should be seen as the status quo', a goal that befits all elders.

Adults seldom receive social services in their own right unless they have problems requiring external intervention. These are usually linked to disability, learning difficulties or mental ill health. Service provision for older people is premised on notions of vulnerability, dependency and medicalisation (Scruton, 1989), making older generations key users of adult social care services. Black elders are under-represented amongst these users and, if included, mainstream ones usually do not meet their specific needs. Examining patterns of provision can expose failure in a service's capacity to meet a wide variety of black elders' needs. Ironically, neo-liberal forces that caused the demise of public provisions in residential care opened up competition and created spaces for new providers. These enabled black voluntary organisations to offer black elders an array of resources under their control. This reinforces their role as primary providers so that ultimately, 'They really have been looking after their own' (Patel, 1999a:19), giving this worn phrase a new twist.

Patel (1999b) highlights a further problem: once autonomous black organisations identify or begin to meet needs, larger white organisations move into this space, creating rivalries that intensify pressures on smaller black agencies, as has occurred around dementia (Patel and Mirza, 1998). Recognition of the contribution made by these bodies and supporting them to extend their work would enable larger numbers of black elders to be served by black autonomous organisations. Mainstream service providers' neglect of black elders affirms racist social relations.

In this chapter, I use case studies to consider the impact of racism and ageism in delivering services to adults with complex needs and argue for an active old age. I highlight how professional discourses about dependency undermine adults' right to make their own decisions. People accessing services challenge these dynamics to: create less oppressive ones; replace vulnerability and dependency with interdependency; and argue for strong links across age divides to bridge generations.

Vulnerability and dependency

Dependency and vulnerability underpin ageism. In contemporary white Western societies, ageism formulates old people as burdens or the flip side of 'youthism', a culture that extols young people as able-bodied consumers (Dominelli, 2004b:136) and constructs old age as vulnerable and dependent. Vulnerability is the likelihood of a person being subjected to some risk, foreseen or unforeseen and lacking the capacity to tackle it effectively. Vulnerability is structural and beyond the direct control of the individual. Dependency is the state of relying on others to meet daily needs. It lacks reciprocity and is pitched against independence (Memmi, 1959). Frailty, coupled to disability, configures a 'deserving' older person. Practitioners use this configuration to target resources on very frail elders. Responsibility to care for an older person in the most appropriate manner goes hand in glove with vulnerability and dependency and is enshrined in the United Kingdom's legislation on community care, the basis of social care.

Notions of dependency in black elders build on ageist stereotypes and are complicated by racist views that black people abuse and overuse welfare systems (Murray, 1994). Research by Patel et al. (1999a, 2004) undermines this myth and indicates that black elders seldom use mainstream services, relying instead on family and black voluntary organisations to meet their needs in old age. This has been possible for an under-resourced sector whilst their overall numbers were small – 3871 in the 85-plus age group during the 1990s (Patel, 1999a). In time, those who arrived during the 1950s and 1960s will increase numbers tenfold, stretching these limited resources beyond capacity (Patel, 1999a). It is crucial that black organisations receive adequate funding and mainstream providers take seriously the duty to provide culturally appropriate services for all peoples under the Race Relations (Amendment) Act, 2000 (RRA). This Act can contribute to social cohesion, social inclusion and civic participation.

Ethnic elders challenge dependency myths in favour of active ageing (Patel, 1999a:15):

> Policymakers, planners and professions should not regard Black and minority ethnic elders seeking support as increasing dependency. They . . . require forms of support which help as well as provide autonomy for better living.

Black elders have emphasised the centrality of preparing for a fulfilling retirement. By promoting an 'active, healthy old age' they challenged Murray's (1994) stereotype of a 'dependency culture' and fashioned discourses around the idea that receiving state aid enables people to deal more effectively with life circumstances. This includes capacity-building endeavours that help black elders create social networks that reduce isolation and foster egalitarian forms of interaction with majority communities. An active and healthy retirement is an objective for white older people. Assisting all older people to retain physical strength and valued social roles will cost society less in the long run and be personally rewarding for individuals. The state can play a key role in creating an enabling culture to promote active well-being and interdependency amongst citizens. Interdependency facilitates active interaction across social divides because it involves recognising that each person relies upon others for help, but also contributes to their well-being.

Peter Robb scathingly subverts discourses about baby boomer elders as burdens who cause intergenerational strife by consuming social goods:

> We are ... self-centred greed heads who ... pile on the debt and rip off their future ... we occupy all the good jobs and show no signs of giving those up.
>
> (Robb, 2006:A19)

Using irony, he rubs in the point:

> We boomers have been avoiding this confession for too long by ... living our lives, raising our kids, working, stuff like that ... Younger generations, smaller in numbers, seem to believe that they are going to have to shoulder a burden of debt that is not of their making but will be exacerbated when the great blob that is the baby boom enters a dissolute retirement.
>
> (Robb, 2006:A19)

Ageism in the West has contributed to decline in the status of older people for over a century (Cowgill and Holmes, 1972). Old age has been medicalised and associated with declining mental and physical prowess, despite evidence indicating that older people today have better health than previous generations. Other cultures continue to venerate elders; for example, Chinese society. Older people, black and white, have resisted ageist characterisations of disability, dependency and vulnerability with social movements like the Gray Panthers in the United States and Association of British Pensioners in the United Kingdom. They portray themselves as agents of their own destiny, capable of creating the social resources they need to enjoy life as they see fit. Black elders have also high-lighted their position as positive contributors to family life. In extended families of African and Asian descent, they maintain child care services and strong intergenerational relations (Patel et al., 2004). Recent studies in the United Kingdom (Patel et al., 2004) and Grandmothers Project in Canada (Brown et al., 2002) show grandparents as major providers of child care services to grand-children regardless of ethnic group. Despite these activities, ageist discourses remain articulated in the popular media. In poking fun at their caricature, as does the TV comedy, *One Foot in the Grave*, stereotypes of incapacity, vulnerability and dependency are reaffirmed.

Black elders are part of mainstream society

The 2001 British Census showed 19.6 million people aged over 50 compared to 16.0 million in 1961. This is set to increase to 27 million by 2031. Those over 60 rose from 16 per cent of the population in 1951 to 21 per cent in 2001, but the percentage of under-16s fell from 24 per cent to 20 per cent during this period. Those in the 85-plus age cohort numbered 1.1 million, up fivefold from 1951. Black elders over-65 made up 6 per cent and white elders 16 per cent of the population (ONS, 2002). Black people over age 50 numbered 672,000 in 2001; Afro-Caribbeans held the oldest profile (ONS, 2002). The ONS estimated that the United Kingdom will have 1.7 million black elders by 2030 (ONS quoted in Patel, 1999b:25). Like all older people, they are part of society and located within diverse ethnic groups (Askham, 1995). Only 5 per cent of all elders receive mainstream social care services (Higgins, 1989), few are black.

---

practice tips   mainstreaming services for black elders

Relatively low numbers have delayed the development of appropriate mainstream services for black elders and shifted the load to family and black voluntary agencies (Patel et al., 2004). The growing black elder population will require more services in the next decade and beyond; service providers are poorly prepared to respond. Mainstream, voluntary and commercial providers have to expand services to meet the needs of black elders who have been contributing to the country's economic and social well-being for some time (Patel, 1999a,b). Current ad hoc provisions are patchy and inadequate.

Mainstream providers can offer 'culturally appropriate' services to all ethnic groups and assist autonomous black organisations in becoming fully funded primary providers rather than stop-gap ones because they outstripped this role long ago. By engaging in long-term strategic thinking, local authorities and primary health trusts can provide well-developed, accessible and suitable services for black elders; promote an active old age; enable elders to contribute to their communities; and be sensitive to how 'race', ethnicity, gender, class, disability, sexual orientation, religion, language expertise and other social divisions impact upon services. An Office of the Deputy Prime

Minister (ODPM) report indicates that such thinking is providing 'wider choice, greater independence and control for older people' (ODPM, 2003:7). Yet, the document lacks joined-up thinking on how 'race' intersects with other social divisions to shape the experiences of old age differently.

Tailor-made resources would not be a problem if all elders, black and white, could access services that meet their needs as is required under the Health and Community Care Act (CCA) 1990 because all providers would cater for the specific needs of each individual. A range of high-quality services to meet diverse needs, simple to access and easily monitored, would fit the bill. User-fees or charges for services for older people can entrench inadequate services for black and white elders along a range of social divisions including gender, class, disability, ethnicity and culture. Services should be publicly funded and free at the point of need. Older people's earlier waged and unwaged labour justifies eliminating user-fees as they have already contributed to the social pool of resources required to make specific services available free (Patel, 1999a). Charges divide users into those who can pay and those who cannot and create narratives that promote a lesser sense of entitlement amongst poor older people and neglect demands for eradicating racism. User-fees link ageism and racism by pitting minority ethnic group interests against those of the majority and reinforce class divisions. Class is a strong indicator of the ease individuals have in purchasing care. Residualised public services enforce class-based discrimination and should be declared illegal. British legislation against age discrimination in employment was enacted in October 2006.

Securing state support for elders is a social responsibility. Assistance from family members is increasingly difficult to count on as a substitute for public care because women increasingly engage in waged work leaving little time for unpaid care and family demographic structures are changing. Pittaway's (1995) Canadian study found that only 11.3 per cent of all elders had reliable family assistance while 19 per cent had none, making state-funded care crucial for some older people. Research by Patel and colleagues' (2004) shows that family support for black elders was somewhat higher than this in the United Kingdom.

Ensuring that these resources provide the most effective person-centred care possible is a core professional responsibility, as is getting sufficient resources to meet cultural needs. In its absence, carers bridge the gap through goodwill gestures or extra contractual care that presupposes the existence of a good relationship between the person providing care and the one receiving it (Dominelli, 1997:216). In relational care, social workers will go the extra mile to give service users the care they need rather than stick strictly to a regime of entitlements. The extra-contractual element in relational care is significant in allowing service users and carers to transgress the boundaries and limitations imposed on their interactions by those purchasing services on their behalf and subvert the bureaucratic tools managers use to control workers. Caring founded on good relations between participants in a care relationship without external scrutiny can be exploited in a resource-scarce context and is to be guarded against. The National Service Framework (NSF), introduced in 2001 to improve services for older people, established outputs for measuring progress in health service delivery.

Social work interventions with older black people

Black and white elders are subject to ageism and share aspects of it. Age as a social division interacts with racism to vary black elders' experience of it (Patel, 1999a,b). Social workers' lack of awareness of these matters has been highlighted in a raft of studies (Patel, 1990; Murray and Brown, 1998). Patel and colleagues (2004) reveal a dismal portrait of inadequate or missing provisions throughout Europe. Professionals in the United Kingdom and Germany were credited with higher levels of awareness and better links to black voluntary organisations offering black elder services than in other nations.

---

practice tips   tackling ageism

Social workers tackling age-based oppression for black elders can advocate for:

- Increased pensions to overcome a historical legacy of discrimination caused by low waged employment.
- Immigration controls that allow entry for significant family members living overseas to reduce isolation and sustain black family care structures in old age.

➡

- Facilities that meet black elders' specific needs.
- Higher take-up of services available.
- Useful information about services black elders can access.
- Delivering culturally appropriate services to older people.
- Culturally sensitive routines in residential care.
- Research for policies and practice that promote black elders' well-being.

Culturally insensitive responses discourage black elders from using existing facilities. Social workers could alter this record by accepting black elders as part of the settled population; taking their views into account in designing, developing and delivering services; and addressing issues of poor communication and isolation. Practitioners can provide information about services in other languages without limiting these to written forms. Videos, personal contact and translation can be highly effective means of communication, especially for those with literacy problems. Religious and cultural traditions could be respected in dietary requirements, religious observance and personal care.

Black workers from diverse ethnicities can be employed in higher numbers, promoted fairly and treated as valued colleagues. Forums and committees discussing services for elders should include black elders. Health care professionals facing similar problems have sought culturally and linguistically relevant standards as routine in service provision (Goldsmith, 2000). Being flexible and thinking creatively are assets in working effectively across racial divides as Agnes's story below indicates.

Case study   Sexism, racism and disablism converge

Agnes, an 83-year-old black elder had been in the United Kingdom for 50 years. She and her husband raised children without claiming income support or state help. Agnes had been diagnosed with glaucoma for which she received treatment. Her consultant aged over the years and the practice was taken over by a younger man. Meanwhile, her husband died and having been depressed over his loss, Agnes had missed several check-up appointments. She finally attended for one, only to be 'told off' for skipping the others, although she explained why. When her eyesight was checked, she was asked to read letters flashed onto a machine on the wall. Agnes explained that she

➡

was unable to read letters, having had no schooling and asked for numbers to be used as she recognised these. She was told that 'the office does not have such options' and as there were 'no alternative services' for her, she should just 'accept what was given'. The previous consultant had asked Agnes to thread a needle with different lenses, deducing that the correct lens had been found when Agnes could thread it. The new doctor used advanced technologies and powerful machines. He asked her, 'Is this better than this? Tell me which one, a, b, c or d?' When she answered, 'd', he kept switching lenses around saying, 'Which is better, d or c, d or f, d or g?' confusing the poor woman completely. Although the doctor proceeded with the examination, Agnes left the office feeling 'humiliated and ashamed'. She had her prescriptions filled out, but she 'could not see' with her new glasses and the medication she received made her 'eyesight worse'. Agnes refuses to go back or complain about her treatment.

Today's older people are yesterday's young people; today's children will become the elders of tomorrow. There is connectedness between different parts of the life-cycle. The seamless slippage from youth to old age as part of a life process is an integral, albeit socially constructed, part of existence that calls for a holistic approach to old age. Black elders' needs are not 'special needs' because defining them so draws on a deficit model of intervention and facilitates the marginalisation of services for them, as occurred for Agnes. Contrasting approaches between the two doctors made matters worse for her. Agnes explained the difference in intergenerational terms by saying, 'He's a young doctor and doesn't understand old people'. To me, the second doctor's practice reveals institutional ageism, sexism and racism. The doctor's youth, arrogance and insensitivity exacerbate the situation and deny her right to be treated with dignity and respect. Agnes had not been educated in her country of origins because she was a 'girl' – a position she shares with millions of women on the planet, young and old (Rose, 2002). Ignoring its impact reaffirms a past sexist practice and is sexist. Her treatment is racist because she was expected to conform to the dominant health service norm – the assumption that all people in white society are literate. Agnes is old so no notice is taken of her wishes to 'use numbers', an ageist practice. A social worker could advocate for Agnes to be treated with dignity and respect; have a proper diagnosis; and receive appropriate treatment.

As it was, Agnes was a dissatisfied and scared customer and scarce medical resources had been wasted.

There are models provided by the black voluntary sector that offer positive models of service delivery to black elders. The Asian Sheltered Residential Accommodation Association (ASRA) provides black elders with housing that is sensitive to their needs and includes strong intergenerational interactions as routine. Other success stories come from: Ujama, Ashiana, Sadeh Lok, Pine Court, Eastwards Trust, Unity. Some organisations provide for a mix of elders, for example, Milton House and the Minority Ethnic Carers of People Project. These provide alternative models to mainstream care. They show that social workers and health professionals can create apt services for black elders. By following their lead, existing mainstream specialist units, sheltered housing and domiciliary services could include black elders' needs more fully. Black elders resent the use of black voluntary organisations to absolve statutory services of providing suitable mainstream services. Their role as *primary* providers suggests this is already occurring, making funding them properly crucial (Patel, 1999a).

Capped budgets reduce autonomous black organisations' capacity to expand and respond to changing needs amongst black elders as more reach retirement age. This can be problematic in future. Patel (1999a) claims that black elders are entitled to services because their contribution to society has already been made: 'Yesterday's work paid for today's care'. As their entitlements are not guaranteed by the state, budget restraints collide with personal needs, leaving huge gaps in provisions. A publicly funded, flexible care system would enable black and white elders to choose from a range of services including: being supported in their homes and communities; paying for a carer of their choice; staying in residential accommodation that would cater for spiritual, religious and cultural needs; and maintaining links with family members and friends living in communities of residence and origins (Goldsmith, 2002).

Patel (1999a) suggests that seeing black elders' needs in the round enables access to low-cost or free transportation to be included as a benefit to avoid discrimination against them. Removing current restrictions to enable elders to travel throughout the day and reasonable fares on both road and rail would promote this objective and help reduce social isolation. Outreach into communities through activities like Age Link Line and road shows could enhance black elders' involvement with others and facilitate intergenerational mixing for both black and white elder communities. Social workers could facilitate their implementation.

Elders are valuable members of communities despite popular stereotypes to the contrary. They play significant social roles and contribute to the wider society as volunteers. Patel (1999a) portrays the quiet heroism of black elders who lead their lives without complaint, helping whoever they can, looking after children and grandchildren and doing domestic chores for those in waged work. These activities comprise valued caring and are socially useful too. Patel (1999a) argues that black elders, especially women, could do more for their communities if their energies were channelled more effectively and their integration into communities was less hit and miss. The message of valuing black elders holds for white elders too. And so, anti-racism, as part of the democratisation of services to older people, can promote greater user-participation and contribute to making services more elder-friendly for all older people, points that social workers can endorse.

Elder abuse

Elder abuse is the perpetration of violence against older people and can take the form of physical, sexual, emotional or financial ill-treatment. Elder abuse is more easily perpetrated if an older person is isolated or wholly dependent on a given carer without outside scrutiny. Pittaway's (1995) Canadian study had 28.6 per cent of elders suffering physical abuse. Biggs and colleagues (1995) indicate similar levels in the United Kingdom. Elder abuse traditionally refers to violence *individuals* perpetrate against elders. This type involves the misuse of trust and is especially hurtful if carried out by people an elder knows. Every person is entitled to be free from age and 'race' related attacks, or elder abuse. Preventing elder abuse and exploitation is a social responsibility. The state's failure to provide the care needed by older people to live healthy, active lives could be characterised as institutional elder abuse because its lack constitutes a deprivation of people's human rights, particularly Article 25 of the Universal Declaration of Human Rights and the European Human Rights Act (EHRA) (Audit Commission, 2003). Public homes are covered by the EHRA; private homes are not.

Action on Elder Abuse has run campaigns to close this loophole and secure redress for abuse and neglect in such establishments, a failing illustrated by events at the Maypole Nursing Home, Birmingham, in 2003. Social workers have a poor record in preventing elder abuse, despite the duty to safeguard human rights and can do more through individual and collective advocacy; advice centres for elders; and helplines.

Community care

The main institutional provisions for older people, community care, were initiated by the National Health Service and Community Care Act (CCA) 1990. It sought to decrease reliance on residential care by supporting people in their communities and introducing market mechanisms into the care system, increasing the likelihood that providers of services for older people, black and white, would be drawn from the 'independent' – voluntary and commercial – sectors. This development has created new challenges and reasserted old problems. Community care has changed social work practice by intensifying managerial control of social workers' activities; opening up service provision to private and commercial providers; and commodifying services by commissioning rather than providing services.

Market-led opportunities have enabled agencies in the under-funded black voluntary sector to bid in competitive tenders for specified facilities under contract. This has eased black organisations' access to funds, created employment opportunities for black workers and improved links between statutory providers and black agencies. Contracting processes can leave small community-based voluntary organisations behind because expensive expertise is needed to submit tenders. Small organisations cannot afford this prior to being awarded a contract because preparing bids is unfunded. Larger organisations employ fund-raisers to secure funding for their activities and can more easily carry such costs.

Culturally appropriate services are more expensive, disadvantaging black autonomous organisations in bidding processes where tenders are awarded to the lowest bidder. This restricts black organisations' autonomy to develop the services they think best as funding criteria drive provisions paid for by government and other funders. Their contracts enforce high degrees of control over the nature of services provided and to whom, and prioritise budget-led assessments over needs-led ones. Competition between different agencies is rising, making the playing field between them more unequal. Policies impact disproportionately on small autonomous black organisations (Patel et al., 1999), add to burdens the black voluntary sector already carries and allow statutory providers to exclude black service users through poor services leaving gaps for those needing them (Murray and Brown, 1998). Discriminatory assessments are illegal; service providers can 'meet the same needs differently' (Patel, 1999a:278).

Volunteering makes major contributions to services for older people who provide much of it. Black elders suggest that 'volunteering is too important to be left to volunteers' and that a payment system for recovering costs should be put in place (Patel, 1999a). The state occupies an ambiguous position over the use of volunteers for older people: actively promoting schemes to help neighbours while ignoring activities worthwhile enough to invest in. Stigma attached to old age as a non-productive period in the life-cycle persists (Phillipson, 1998) and impacts on volunteers whose work is devalued in consequence. Resources the state expends on services that older people find inadequate could be diverted to create those that older people, black and white, actively seek and involve them in their formation. Social workers and volunteers could participate alongside black elders to develop care centres for them; locate these where people want them; and facilitate interaction and knowledge-sharing across generations and ethnic groups.

Appropriate professional training

Calls for better co-ordination between health and social services have been around for several decades. If holistic, community-based provisions are to become the norm, it is crucial that social workers and health professionals work effectively together and undertake joint training, but its implementation has rarely been well-resourced.

Case study   Multi-professional training

An exception is the University of Southampton's New Generation Project. Begun in 2002, it grew rapidly. In 2005 a cohort of 2000 students in 12 different professions trained together. Health professionals dominate this

➡

Project; social work students are a minority. Social work student tutorial feedback rated the Project useful. Exchanges with other professionals enabled them to appreciate how different professional cultures, traditions and values impacted upon service delivery. However, some social work students felt that their interests were not adequately addressed and that the greater numbers of health professionals resulted in their needs being prioritised. This was especially problematic for those who were the sole social work student challenging oppressive practices in a group undertaking specified projects. Their views suggest that 'mass' interprofessional education is not the best way of teaching professionals how to work effectively together. Small groups with evenly matched numbers from each professional group and better trained interprofessional tutors might be more productive in the long-term. Higher costs could discourage cash-strapped educational institutions from running staff intensive provisions.

Joint Investment Programmes (JIPs) encourage partnerships amongst different stakeholders. JIPs aim to improve services for older people, disabled people and those with mental ill health to enhance their capacity to undertake paid work. The Health Improvement Programme (HImP) is another multi-agency partnership initiative that targets health needs to prevent unnecessary medicalisation and enable people to lead active lives longer. Social workers could play important roles in bringing older people and providers together through these schemes. As locality-based partnerships, these can respond to the demographic make up of populations and promote culturally appropriate services for elders, including those in rural areas where, Chakraborti and Garland (2004), argue racism is largely hidden. Multi-agency partnerships can be sensitive to different needs and utilise resources more effectively in responding to unmet needs.

Meeting the diverse needs of black elders from different ethnic groups

Black elders are a diverse group, made up of different ethnicities, nationalities, cultures and other social divisions. Racism in its various forms perpetrated against elders impedes their enjoyment of the artefacts of everyday life and perpetuates their marginalisation. This occurs if immigration officers refuse visitors' visas to extended family members for crucial family occasions and celebrations. Patel (1999a) describes how an Indian elder's brother was refused a visa for a Golden Wedding Anniversary.

Professionals in health and social care fail to meet ethnic elders' varied needs if they do not explain hospital treatment or carry out social care assessments (Patel, 1999a,b). Social workers should keep an eye on institutional shortcomings and the impact of cultural practices on black elders. Disablist assessments of older black people's skills can affirm racist assumptions about intellectual capacities as occurred below.

Case study Stereotyping black elders as mentally impaired

Social workers who assume they understand a situation when they do not can do untold damage. Patel (1999a:293) tells of a Ghanaian elder labelled 'dumb' for saying nothing when at a day centre. Yet, when a visitor to the centre spoke Kentaku to him, he conversed freely.

Disabled elders favour direct payments as these give them control over who provides their care and how (Hughes, 1995). User charges create institutionally racist practices if assets are shared amongst extended family members and are not accessible to a specific individual. Public funding of provisions for older people is a social issue. Attitudes about how this should be addressed vary amongst different ethnic groups (Clarke, 1998), although most welcome shows of solidarity between rich and poor community members (Patel, 1999a). Heterogeneity of needs amongst elders facilitates the creation of spaces for alliances across ethnic divides to meet diverse needs through the creation of unity amongst diversity and diversity within unity, by locating different ethnic groups 'under one roof' to address their specific needs. Patel (1999a) suggests this could be done by responding to 'person-centred' assessments and promoting better race relations. Below, I consider anti-racist practice with Chinese elders.

Chinese elders

Chinese-origined elders will double from 1991 levels by 2011 (Patel and Lim, 2004). Chinese communities are diverse, widely dispersed, clustered in catering and compete with each other as self-employed workers (Kam Yu, 2000). This has hindered the development of community capacity in providing services for elders, prevented individuals from setting aside income for retirement and kept poverty within families secret. Chinese elders feel ashamed to 'burden' families with their care if unable to work and under-report ill health. Their position is complicated by a reluctance to take up welfare entitlements if they do not speak English, lack knowledge of benefits or have insufficient support networks to help claim these (Kam Yu, 2000).

Resource shortages, poor infrastructures and inadequate funds made service providers unable to meet demand. The Chinese Community Centre in Camden seeks to respond to the needs of all elders and carers with two part-time workers. Shu Pao Lim, founder of the Great Wall Society, worried about the lack of facilities for this group, including those generated by the community, is campaigning for an 'extra care home' for them in London (Patel and Lim, 2004). The London Chinese Community Network and Chinese in Britain Forum are tackling these issues with Somalian, Chilean and Vietnamese elders following suit. Patel and Lim (2004) argue for services for Chinese elders to have simple entry and exit policies; rules that are easy to follow; spaces that create a sense of belonging; and Chinese-specific services for those unable to live independently. Their culture is not static, but constantly evolving.

Case study   Services for Chinese elders

The Hanover Housing Association (Hanover) created extraCare housing in the mid-1990s to meet the needs of frail elders in culturally suitable ways, e.g., space for 'shrines' in Chinese elders' bedrooms. These are joint ventures jointly managed and funded by Hanover, charitable agencies and public grants. Hanover estates encourage active lifestyles with a dedicated Warden/Estate Manager and a team of carers on duty 24 hours a day organised by social services. The Hanover partnership exemplifies good practice, straddles several providers and indicates interagency collaboration. Social workers can research which partnerships and public provisions work best.

Carers: a diverse group

The issue of paying for care is a thorny one. Negotiating bureaucratic hoops can be insensitive, stigmatising and nightmarish for those cared-for and carers. Feminists have demanded the 'right to care' alongside that 'to be cared about' (Knijn and Underson, 1997). Carers are a diverse group and will have different needs as well as some in common. Supporting carers involves providing adequate respite care, domiciliary support and paying carers for services so that they can lead their own lives. Caring provided by unpaid carers should not be considered 'care on the cheap', acquired at the expense of women and other family members. The British government claims 3.5 million *formal* carers are needed by 2037 (DoH, 2001b). This is likely to be an underestimate. The majority are women, but men carers often look after their spouses; young carers after parents or siblings.

Young carers are particularly vulnerable. They may feel ashamed of their role in caring for older or disabled parents, especially if negotiating school at the same time. They can be bullied for doing this important work and may under-perform in their studies (Undergown, 2002). Young black carers face additional hurdles, for example, translating if a parent does not speak English; finding information about ethnically sensitive services. Young carers are often not assessed as being 'in need' themselves as authorised under Section 17 of the 1989 Children Act and the Carers (Recognition and Services) Act 1995. Dearden and Becker's (1998) study revealed that only 11 per cent of interviewees had been assessed.

Black carers are likely to remain outside waged employment. The ensuing lack of pension credits will lower their income in old age and cause poverty which is likely to remain hidden within the household. Patel (1999a) argues that responsibilities for family members overseas further reduces resources and income for paying into pension plans and exacerbates poverty in later years. For black elders, discrimination in employment through slower career progression, work in low-waged declining industries and having poor language skills also decrease incomes in old age. Black carers' position is further complicated by older black people's lesser use of health services in general though some illnesses are linked to ethnicity; for example, sickle cell anaemia in people of Afro-Caribbean descent (Smith et al., 2000; CRE, 2006).

Holistic approaches to meeting the needs of black elders

Holistic approaches to individual need situate individuals in their social contexts and respond to the person-in-the round (Dominelli,

2002b). Defining elders as burdens creates funding shortages that prevent social workers from responding holistically.

Case study Holistic analysis

Aysha requests a downstairs bathroom with shower for her mobility problems. This is denied, but she is given one hour of personal care a week. The response, nonsensical and unacceptable, is permitted under bureaucratic economistic cost-benefit analyses that underpin the new managerialism. It is short-sighted and undermines Aysha's dignity. Climbing stairs to use the bathroom causes her mobility to deteriorate rapidly. Aysha then needs hip and knee replacements. In the long-run, NHS hospital care costs outstrip those of providing a bathroom. Bureaucratic responses fragment care and mock rights-based service provisions. These could have been avoided had a holistic cost-benefit analysis been done.

A fully-costed holistic approach (Figure 5.1) would include a time dimension and the price borne by individuals in unnecessary pain, foregone physical activities and heavier long-term costs to public services. This occurs because people receive health treatment when more sick or become disabled by illness the longer they have to manage without receiving medical attention.

Figure 5.1 Holistic cost–benefit analysis

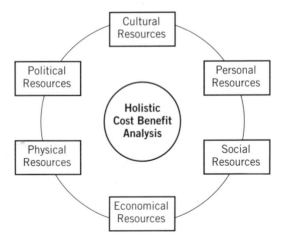

Holistic cost-benefit analyses would calculate the entire costs of delays to necessary operations caused by lengthy waiting lists for NHS treatments and admission to nursing homes, residential care or hospices. It would show better patient outcomes and reduced overall costs if care is provided early. A further benefit is the social one of generating additional services, facilities and employment opportunities for people, black and white, in providing the facilities required.

Home-based care has to become more person-sensitive. Below, a black elder I interviewed graphically terms its absence a 'home invasion' or 'institutional abuse'.

Case study   Home invasion

William, a 92-year-old black elder, had maintained his independence and integrity until five years ago when a heart attack made his respiratory problems and immobility from arthritis worse. His wife, close to him in age, was frail but continued to look after him and the house. As her infirmities increased, she could no longer get him out of bed or assist with personal care. They asked social services to help. After several representations and assessments, they were offered two hours of personal care two days per week. Assistance with cleaning the house was impossible and financial support to adapt it was refused.

The carer providing personal care worked as authorised, politely and efficiently. These weekly visits became an ordeal. They took over William's life which had to fit around their 'calls'. William felt his 'whole life had been taken over'. He could not leave home as he wished because he had to be there for scheduled 'personal care including bath' twice weekly. The timing was often changed at short-notice. He felt that home care workers could 'snoop' into all of his personal things with impunity, but would not complain in case the service was withdrawn. William called this treatment an 'official home invasion'.

William endured institutionally driven agendas at home for five years and then had similar experiences in hospital. Having undergone a major operation, he was unable to get physiotherapy at a pace he could handle as the 'hospital was understaffed and there were too many patients to fit in'. Dietary requests to meet religious needs were ignored, so he ate little. Thus, despite successfully enduring surgery, he died after a two-month stay because his care left him too weak to move out of bed without help.

Assistance was grudgingly given and intermittent. He often waited for lengthy periods to get assistance, e.g., lying in faeces for nearly two hours when having diarrhoea caused by clostridium difficile and no one was available to change him or his bedding.

Although he spoke adequate English, William's ethnic background was used as an excuse to deny his rights and entitlements and ignore those of his extended family. William was usually referred to in a condescending manner that exposed a racist view of this man who was labelled as having lost his 'marbles' rather than only his 'mobility'. His family asked for help in attending to his personal needs and support at home so that he could be discharged and cared for there. His hospital social worker rejected this as 'too expensive'.

William had nowhere else to go. His wife was too old and weak to look after him; his family too far away for the round-the-clock care he needed. He was stuck in hospital. The hospital social worker responsible for his care accepted the medical definitions of his condition and proved unable to advocate for his right to be treated with dignity, get his specific needs met, or see that he went home with appropriate home care support. William became a homogenised consumer of 'one-size fits all' services that became institutionally racist but were enacted through the actions of specific health and social care professionals. The family's anger at their treatment and that of their loved one persists. As one said, 'Fighting the hospital system won't bring Dad back. I just want to forget it all.' Thus, the merry-go-round of churning people in and out of care carries on.

William's treatment affirms Goffman's analysis (1961) of patient discipline and order being dictated by the needs of the institution and staff. The term 'institutional home invasion' is this elder's description of being cared for by the state. 'Home invasions' by burglars traumatise. This elder and his family were traumatised by the caring state. Government institutional abuse is also exemplified by personal asset stripping, or the obligatory sale of people's homes, to pay for elder care. These are homes that old people on modest incomes have saved for all their lives and had hoped to pass on to their children. The original £16,000 disregard has reached a maximum of £21,500 and is strongly disliked by black and white older people. Having paid taxes and national insurance all their lives, they feel they have already paid for their care. And, they claim that having saved to buy their houses in difficult financial situations, their thriftiness is now being penalised (Dominelli, 1997; Moulds and Weale, 2007). Elder care involving nursing care currently costs £2,500 per month. Thus, the cash from the sale of the house will not last long. This personal asset stripping impacts more heavily on black elders as owner-occupiers buying housing to avoid discrimination in the rental market during their younger years, an act often made possible by pooling resources amongst a network of extended family members (Patel et al., 1999a).

The hospital social worker suggested this option to William when he asked for 24-hour home help to discharge him. Yet, his wife still lived there! William's experience is likely to resonate in countries with inadequate funding for health and social care. Staffing shortages in Canadian hospital care hit the headlines in the summer of 2006 when doctors spoke out against unnecessary deaths caused by worker shortages in emergency departments. Initial problems were reduced, but difficulties remain. Preparing health services for private providers skews government responses. Britain's experience of quasi-markets in the NHS suggests that higher user-fees and fewer services provided free of charge are the future, especially in dentistry, optometry and chiropody, making dental care, eye checks or foot care luxuries.

Conclusions

Black and ethnic minority elders have argued for 'choice, voice and control' that enables them to 'live their old age with dignity, respect and independence' (Patel, 1999a:33). Service providers in the state, voluntary or commercial sectors can work together to make this happen. Defining older people as fiscal burdens indicates a lowered status amongst the deserving poor (Estes, 1989; Walker, 1990). Turning elder care into an individual responsibility relegates it to private realms and intensifies intergenerational conflict. It encourages privatisation, decreases pressure on government to adequately fund services for older people, and lessens the social solidarity essential to social cohesion (Dominelli, 2004a). These meta-discourses impact upon black and white elders by focusing on age as a key definer of unlimited need, often disregarding ethnicity or other social division. Older people have challenged this depiction of them by exercising agency and arguing for citizenship-based entitlements and services. Black elders are making these statements to policymakers (Patel et al., 1999a) and the baby boomer generation of white people are making and will increasingly make similar points as they retire in larger numbers during the next two decades.

Older people are becoming more electorally important and using their power in numbers to register claims. Black and white elders can form alliances to improve the position of all elders and get their diverse needs met. This has occurred in the United States where mandatory retirement has been abolished under pressure from the social movements of elders. Holistic strengths-based interventions are essential to realising elders' visions of active ageing. Different paths to service provision for black and white elders should result in the same outcomes: a healthy and active old age in which elders are respected and enabled to play a vital role in their families, communities and nation. Publicly funded investments for universal elder care in recognition of their earlier contributions to society would destigmatise old age and embed interdependency to assure the care of one by all.

---

putting it into practice

- How would you take account of age, ethnicity, class, disability and family roles in responding to a 78-year-old elder of Chinese descent who is a wheel-chair user, has chronic depression, but wishes to live independently in the community where a daughter and son live nearby?
- How should black voluntary organisations that provide care for black and minority ethnic elders be funded?
- How would you support a young black carer who is worried about attending school and passing exams?

Further reading

Daatland, S. O. and Biggs, S. (eds) (2004) *Ageing and Diversity*. Bristol: Policy Press.

Wilson, G. (2001) *Understanding Old Age: Critical and Global Perspectives*. London: Sage.

6 | Anti-racist social work with offenders

Introduction

Matters of justice, crime and punishment are hotly contested, with government and media playing key roles in how discourses about their purpose, operation and worth are conducted. These construct black people as dangerous deviants in need of control. They are over-represented in the criminal justice system, especially in prisons and the police DNA database where four out of ten entries are black men (Randerson, 2006). Precise percentages vary according to ethnic group; those of mixed heritages being over-represented (90 per cent) in comparison to African-origined (85 per cent) or Asian-origined (76 per cent) groups (Calverley et al., 2004:50). Unflattering media images of 'No Go' Britain and 'Yardie Gangs' portray black men as muggers and gun-toting drug runners who make the streets unsafe for other citizens (Muncie, 2004). The dynamics of over-representation are evident across age and gender spectrums (Home Office, 2006). Black women offenders are considered 'dangerous' and in need of harsh punishment (Dominelli, 1983), while white women offenders are deemed 'mad, bad or sad' and in need of help (Worrall, 1990), stereotypes that result in the over-representation of black women in custody (Walklate, 2004).

Black people's under-representation on police cautions speed their entry to the higher tariffs of the criminal justice system (Dominelli, 1983), a depressing finding replicated by Calverley and colleagues (2004) much later. Their research revealed that the police stopped 84 per cent of 'black and Asian' respondents; more often if in cars. The police were more likely to lay charges against black people than white ones. In May 2001, four black members of the Metropolitan Police Independent Police Authority, set up in

July 2000 following the Macpherson Report (1999), resigned claiming it was controlled by the police, lacked independence and credibility, and reduced them to 'nodding dogs' (BBC News Online, 7 May 2001).

Images of black people as deviant and criminal are a recurrent theme in 'stop and search' interventions that disproportionately target them despite campaigns opposing these since the 1980s. William Hague, speaking to the Centre for Policy Studies as Tory Leader in 2001, attributed a 'rise in violent street crime in some areas to a drop in stop and searches of black people because police feared being called racist'. Home Office figures for January 2001 showed that the drop in stop and searches under Section 44(1) of the Terrorism Act 2000 was greatest for white suspects; black people in London were five times more likely to be stopped (Hearnden and Hough, 2004).

Society's usual concerns to maintain discipline, uphold 'law and order', punish those who transgress its norms, and mete out justice to the satisfaction of victims of crime have been complicated through the 'war on terror'. Its contentious nature was reflected in debates on the Prevention of Terrorism Bill 2005 in the House of Lords on 8 March 2005. This 'war' targets a new group of black people – 'Asian' Muslims – but impacts upon all citizens by shifting discourses from presumptions of innocence and habeas corpus into those of guilt until proven innocent; and detention without charge for specified periods. Terrorists have turned artefacts of everyday life practices (ELPs) into instruments of terror. The risk they pose to life and limb permeates daily routines and undermines people's sense of security and engagement with the social. Terrorists' threats to use concentrated hydrogen peroxide and TAPT to down transatlantic flights in August 2006 and the subsequent ban on liquids in carry-on luggage exemplify the entrenchment of terror in articles of ordinary daily life. Despite passengers' *in*capacity to alter any of their grievances, terrorists' actions indicate that they are preoccupied with issues of power and control over others, using insecurities to gain the upper-hand in an ideological struggle about peoples' places in the world.

Discourses of black people as a criminal class are affirmed by criminalisation of large numbers of 'black' people and are of grave concern as the talents of generations of black people are lost to the wider community. The question remains, what can social workers, probation officers and law enforcement agencies do to stem these trends? Below, I examine these issues and anti-racist approaches in the criminal justice system.

Reconfiguring deviancy: who are black offenders?

Who are black offenders? Inconsistencies in terminologies used to collect official statistics and the literature make it difficult to compare like with like (Powis and Walmsley, 2002). The choice of terms depends on what those collecting statistics aim to achieve. Debates over how to define black offenders to take account of diversities within the group have been inconclusive. The growth of postmodern discourses and greater acceptability in viewing identities as multiple and fragmented in public policy discourses have had an impact. Key terms to highlight differences between them have been black and Asian. Asians have been subdivided into Indian, Pakistani and Bangladeshi, formulations used in the 2001 Census (see Chapter 1).

Whilst acknowledging diversity of identities amongst offenders, this depiction is problematic. It affirms sloppy distinctions based on a binary of who is truly British and who is not. Some differentiation occurs on a skin colour binary: black and white. For example, Asian refers to people from a huge continent with a multiplicity of ethnicities and skin-colours; Indian, Pakistani and Bangladeshi refer to nationality more than ethnicity. People may be classified in this way even if born in the United Kingdom and as truly British as anyone else in a multicultural and multinational nation-state. Terminologies embedded in 'otherness' and 'foreignness' suggest that they 'do not belong here', a view endorsed by the state deporting residents who are not citizens after serving sentences or withdrawing citizenship and the right to enter from those considered a threat to 'national' security; for example, Oldham's imam Shafiq ur Rehman was deported as a terrorist for supporting struggles in Kashmir. The imam's activities were deemed dangerous, despite his claim of only providing money for welfare work. A further hysterical twist in media discourses revolves around special prisons for foreigners. Bullwood Hall in Essex and Canterbury Prison in Kent hold 154 and 284 of them respectively pending deportation proceedings at an annual cost of £40,478 per person, compared to £24,000 for local Category C prisoners. Personnel from the Borders and Immigration Agency work in each facility to address immigration issues including deportation (Taylor, 2007). Ignoring these extra staffing costs in the ensuing debates construes foreign prisoners as being too costly to maintain and can undermine rights to due process.

Images of black people as deviant offenders have impacted on public consciousness and the criminal justice system and contributed to their being discriminated against and receiving less fair treatment within it. One illustration of this discrimination involves the writing of Pre-Sentencing Reports (PSRs) that result in black offenders being less favourably treated than white ones. Probation officers' failure to incorporate the needs of black offenders in PSRs had been highlighted in the 1980s (Whitehouse, 1986), but reporting differentials persist with poorer outcomes for black offenders. Hudson and Bramhall (2002) revealed that white probation officers writing PSRs distanced themselves from black offenders, seeing those of Asian origins as having less remorse than white ones. This led to more black offenders on custodial sentences and community punishment orders (community service orders pre-April 2001) than on community rehabilitation orders (probation orders) and community punishment and rehabilitation orders (combination orders); and for longer. Such outcomes affirm images of black offenders as 'dangerous' or 'deviant' and in need of discipline and containment to reduce 'risks'. Discriminatory practices led a third (35 per cent) of them to favour probation officers matched for ethnicity (Calverley et al., 2004:). That the remainder did not register a preference shows the significance of ascertaining what an offender needs and tailoring responses to particular individuals by specific questions that eschew stereotypical reactions (Dominelli, 2002a).

The prison population has increased at an alarming rate in the past few years as magistrates make greater use of custodial sentences (Smart Justice, 2004). Within the overall rise, incarceration rates for black offenders rose eight times faster than for white ones (Smart Justice, 2004). Black offenders constitute 12 per cent of prison population but comprise 2 per cent of the United Kingdom's population. They are three times more likely to be arrested than white offenders. Differentiating amongst ethnic groups, the comparable figure for Asian offenders is 12 per cent. Young black offenders are less likely to get bail than young white offenders. Black offenders, like their white counterparts, are socially excluded and disadvantaged in many ways including having been in care: 19 per cent of all black offenders; 35 per cent of those of multiple heritages; and 3 per cent of Indian-origined ones (Calverley et al., 2004:48). Black offenders are more likely than white offenders to have been discriminated against in the job market, education system and housing (Calverley et al., 2004).

A BBC survey in 2002 showed that 51 per cent of black people and 46 per cent of Asians thought that the police and judiciary did not treat them equally. About 80 per cent of black and Asian respondents want the United Kingdom's ethnic diversity reflected in the criminal justice system (BBC News, 2002), findings affirmed by Calverley et al. (2004). The Esmeé Fairburn Foundation (EFF) (2004) mounted a critique of current approaches to crime and recommended fewer custodial sentences, especially for lower level crime, and the inclusion of family responsibilities when determining sentences, especially for women. This report recommended research to establish the causes of black people's over-representation in prison and disproportionate increase during the period discussed. These studies treat identity in each group as unitary.

Britain is not alone in having black people over-represented in penal establishments. Canada and the United States are in similar positions. The picture is more stark in the United States where half of all prisoners are young black men who constitute 12 per cent of the population (Beck and Mumola, 1999) and nearly all prisoners on Death Row are black (Dieter, 1998). In the USA, police brutality against Rodney King led to riots in Los Angeles in 1991; a police fusillade of 50 bullets killed an unarmed Sean Bell on his wedding morning, threatening social disorder in New York in 2006. O. J. Simpson's trial for the murder of his wife, Nicole Brown depicted a dangerous black man with a history of criminality based on acts of violence against her. His image as a violent black man was intensified by an alleged attempted armed robbery in 2007.

Media images of these men burden black masculinity with responsibility for lowering black people's moral standing in society while white people who fail to uphold 'justice' are simply fallible persons who cannot do their jobs properly. Gilroy (2000:212) claims that these events make black masculine integrity a signifier of contemporary 'blackness' and engender serious divides within black communities struggling for racial equality in American society. These include divisions amongst conservative black feminists, those creating new black 'street cultures', black Muslims comprising the Nation of Islam and autonomous black groups that draw on notions of solidarities across social divisions. African Americans now face extremely complex situations in uplifting the 'race'. Britain also has to address complexity in handling black offenders.

Racialised profiling of offenders in the 'war on terror'

Looking for the link between identity-based traits and criminality has a long history in forensic work dating back to Lombroso and Ferrara (1885). They dissected their way through countless imaginings, measuring and quantifying every aspect of the human body to ascertain the essence of criminality by body features, especially for women, without achieving their objective. Now, skin colour, accents, religious observances and dress act as identifiers for profiling offenders.

Sectarianism: profiling offenders of Irish descent

Racial profiling encompassing various groups has been evident in the United Kingdom for some time. As I lack space to examine all these, what follows is illustrative of processes involved in racial profiling. Peoples of Irish descent; Gypsies and Travellers; and Muslims have been badly affected. The 'troubles' in Northern Ireland began with the first signs of resistance to British occupation of the Emerald Isle, but are usually associated with developments since 1968. These events shifted discourses on 'law and order' towards a racial profiling that drew on culture and religion. Despite having white skin, their accents, religious and Celtic traits were racialised, creating stereotypes that all Irish Catholics in the UK, especially the men, were nationalist sympathisers and secret supporters of the Irish Republican Army (IRA).

The Irish were the most over-represented ethnic group in British prisons during the 1990s (Borland et al., 1995). Some, unfairly imprisoned in the drive to catch those who had bombed, murdered and maimed civilians on the British mainland, endured years of sustained campaigning to prove their innocence; for example, those accused of bombing Birmingham and Guildford. The danger of innocent people being labelled and treated as 'terrorists' persists, with lowered safeguards now in place to protect the British public from newly configured versions. This labelling has already been misapplied when the police killed Jean Charles de Menezes, raided the homes of Muslims in Forest Gate (Brittain, 2006) and arrested Helen John and Sylvia Boyers, feminists of Greenham Common vintage, for entering an American military location in the United Kingdom to protest the destruction of the environment and life on the planet (Morris and Brown, 2006). Preventing such incidents is crucial to maintaining public confidence in the criminal justice system.

Reactions to Irish bombers were not seen as part of racist dynamics, but of sectarianism. Their racial profiling was often missed because anti-racist discourses focused on people with dark skin. White Protestant Irish men and women were racialised differently from Catholic ones on the basis of religion. In Northern Ireland, territory was racialised on religious grounds. Until May 2007, loathing for those of a different religion continued in the pronouncements of Ian Paisley whose intransigence had been a main barrier to the full implementation of the Good Friday Agreement, even when the IRA promised to 'decommission its guns' and 'put them out of use forever'. By grafting together the political and military wings of the nationalist movement as Sien Fien/IRA, Paisley created a signifier of his unwillingness to consider Irish Catholics' desire for freedom as anything other than a criminal act to be resisted at all costs by dismissing and stereotyping those with such aspirations as 'terrorists'.

The 'war on terror', Islamophobia and configuring the 'Islamic terrorist'

'Who you are' continues to be significant in 'law and order' discourses. The racialisation of looks and space has been brought into the limelight by the shooting of Brazilian, Jean Charles de Menezes by the Metropolitan Police, because he 'looked like a terrorist' and was in a block of flats where a 'suspected terrorist' lived. Except for a darker skin tone and darker curlier hair than the average white Anglo-Saxon British citizen, he looked like the average person off to work on a sunny day. He died because those who bombed London's transport system on 7/7 were black people of Islamic faith. Fears of another atrocity together with racialised identities drew any dark man into the risk assessment frame as a 'potential hazard' that required action to minimise the perceived risk. Racial profiling racialises culture, religion and biological traits like skin colour and geographic space. It demonstrates a new racialisation of person and place, a terro-racism, if you will.

Racial profiling has been more researched in the United States where this phenomenon has dragged people of Middle Eastern features, Arabic names and Islamic faith into the law enforcement and immigration control nets in a way not done before 9/11 (Healy, 2007). Terrorism is a challenge for both law enforcement officers and society, not least because there is no way of identifying this type of murderer, any more than there is for any other kind of criminal. Like other violent acts, terrorism has to be tackled through due process of law, and murder treated as murder to avoid racial stereotyping.

Case study   The politics of racial profiling

Like Britain, Canada is taking the internal, homegrown threat to its security more seriously and combined this with racial profiling. Before the arrest of alleged terrorists in Toronto in June 2006, the Canadian Security Intelligence Service (CSIS) argued resource shortages prevented it from security vetting more than one in ten of 20,000 immigrants from the Afghanistan/Pakistan region entering Canada since 2001. Gordon (2006:A1) believes this claim aimed to bolster the CSIS' desire for more resources – a political motivation alongside security ones. The RCMP's (Royal Canadian Mounted Police) inability to pursue more than one-third of known organised criminals in the country was coupled to CSIS to substantiate arguments for more federal government finance. The alarmist racist configuration of the story was disputed by an immigration lawyer who argued that 'all applicants are heavily screened before they are given immigration visas' (Gordon, 2006:A1). The vice-chair of the Muslim Canadian Federation protested the profiling of people according to country of origin to ask: 'Why do you prejudge people? You are suggesting that the [people] of Pakistan are all crooks' (Gordon, 2006:A1).

The CSIS justified its stance by stating that 'Each individual identified [as a threat to Canada] had some connection to Afghanistan.' Its spokesman added that:

> threats from internal, 'homegrown' extremists are now on equal footing . . . [as] second- and third-generation extremists born and raised in Canada and able to easily blend into the population, is on the rise.
>
> (Gordon, 2006:A2)

This construction of extremists externalises racial profiling only to bring it back home giving a new focus for the 'You don't belong here' framing of racialised discourses in contradictory discourses about 'race'. These discourses co-exist alongside others, e.g., multi-cultural Canada celebrated 100 years of a 'fifth-generation' Indo-Canadian family living in BC (Bolan, 2006). As descendents of original immigrants from the Punjab had been 'denied voting and immigration rights for years', Sangha sought to establish rights for Indo-Canadian communities and make Canadian society better (Bolan, 2006:B4), indicating that discourses of not belonging – given they were 'fifth-generation immigrants', can converge with those of contributing to society.

How can there be second, third or other generations of 'immigrants' in a nation of immigrants? Is this necessary to justify new forms of racialisation that draw on old themes – the dichotomy between 'them' and 'us', outsiders and insiders, to justify treatment of outsiders as less than human, as beings with lesser rights? The above discourses show that these distinctions are blurring to the point of becoming meaningless; so new ways of shoring them up are being devised. Yet, the Canadian state deals with people convicted of offences overseas through due process to enable them to prove their 'innocence' and acquire the 'right to stay'. Lai Chingxing's case illustrates this response, despite having outstanding criminal convictions in China.

Case study   Due process

Lai Chingxing, his wife and three children arrived in Canada from Hong Kong in 1999 after learning that the Chinese government was investigating his businesses for people smuggling in Xiamen, Southern China, where he was accused of running a $10-billion people smuggling empire (Skelton, 2006a). Lai has been fighting to remain in Canada for years, having had his initial application for asylum during 2000 rejected. He appealed this outcome several times and reached the Canadian Supreme Court in 2005; the original decision was upheld. Following this ruling, Lai claimed the right not to be deported because it was 'unsafe for him to return' to China where he insists he will be 'tortured and killed'. Canada will stay deportation orders on human rights grounds if a person appeals, so Lai can remain in the country until all legal avenues with regards to this decision are exhausted.

A person facing a deportation order in Canada undergoes a 'pre-removal risk assessment' to determine whether any danger of torture or death exists. In Lai's case, the Canadian government deemed this non-existent as the Chinese government gave assurances he would face neither. Lai appealed this decision to the Federal Court as these could not be monitored, initiating a further stay of the deportation order until the Court determines whether this is so. Lai stated he is glad 'that Canada is providing protection to me' (Skelton, 2006a:A3). Lai divorced his wife. She faces her own deportation hearing while Lai lives under house arrest in Vancouver (Skelton, 2006a). Law enforcement that adheres to due process supports social workers seeking to ensure that people who transgress the social order are treated as human beings, even when condemning their behaviour. Acting within a moral framework is appropriate for social workers who lay claim to a moral profession. Such actions can also affirm public confidence in the criminal justice system.

The media's role in defining the direction of discourses on these issues is contentious. In the United Kingdom, the demand that 'terrorists' be denied the 'oxygen of publicity' began under Thatcher over the IRA. New Labour reframed this to prevent 'glorification of terrorism'. It impacts on what constitutes 'free speech', free press and the right to criticise government policies like the Anti-Terrorism Bill. Images of the terrorist have re-oriented debates on 'law and order' in ways that can be detrimental to liberal notions of justice. Angry responses to Danish cartoons deemed to disparage Islam by Muslims across the world exposed the contested nature of what constitutes acceptable behaviour amongst the different sides in these discourses.

The state, justice and institutional atrocities

Discourses about 'law and order' and identities are complex. Complications are more extensive if righting past wrongs that implicated the state. Fragmented, multiple identities can reduce collective action in righting violations of human rights to salami-slice social justice claims or despair if justice is denied. The state has to ensure that those convicted of offences, regardless of 'race' or other social division are punished. In a democracy, doing so while upholding the rule of law reflects critically on its capacity to prevent civil disorder and maintain public confidence in the law.

The South African Truth and Reconciliation Commission and Canadian state illustrate two paths to righting past wrongs. South Africa sought to reconcile white perpetrators of atrocities under apartheid with black victim-survivors through a process of telling the truth, apologising and being forgiven. Canada is embarking on a process of addressing wrongs practised against indigenous peoples and recognising traditional rights to land and resources. The process has been partly successful, but created its controversies; there are no easy answers. White Anglo-Canadians are contesting Canada's far from equitable solutions to secure fishing rights too. They argue against 'racial segregation' and for a colour-blind policy that treats 'all the same'. Those arguing for differentiated fishing access contend that preserving salmon stocks from extinction can draw all parties together for the good of all (O'Neil, 2006a:A1, A7).

The Canadian state apologised to Canadians of Japanese origins for atrocities committed during the Second World War – appropriating property and interning them – and awarded notional compensation to the person(s) concerned or their descendents. Other claims are off the radar. People of German and Italian origins await recognition of injustices perpetrated against them at the same time. Moore and Fedorowich (2005) recently began to document the stories of German and Italian prisoners of war in the United Kingdom, exposing the humiliating treatment and menial work undertaken, even after the Second World War ended, because they had been defined as 'enemies' who could legitimately be denied rights.

Other fronts are opening up and these are unlikely to be the last. Canadians of Sikh descent are claiming rectification of past wrongs. Chinese Canadians are seeking an apology and compensation for a $500 'head tax' charged at the end of the nineteenth and early twentieth centuries on each immigrant from China – cheap labour that built the railways. Britain, then in charge of Canadian policy-making, played a role in it. Responses to claims for compensation are not uncontested, even by Chinese Canadians. Terry O'Neill's comments are instructive:

If it's symbolism the claimants want, then give them the formal apology they deserve . . . the imposition of the $500 head tax (not to mention the subsequent banning for 24 years of all

Chinese immigration) was racist and unfair . . . a number of Chinese Canadians . . . said they don't want any money. Their grandparents and parents paid the head tax because they knew it was the key to opening a door of opportunity for future generations . . . to demand 'redress' would dishonour them . . . [Their descendants should] look past their hurt feelings and reject the too-easy allure of victimhood.

(O'Neill, 2006:A11)

The year 2007 marks the bi-centenary of the abolition of slavery in the United Kingdom. In 2006, Andrew Hawkins, a descendant of Sir John Hawkins who initiated the British transatlantic slave trade in 1562, apologised for his ancestor's behaviour and the suffering endured by African slaves. In late 2006, Prime Minister Tony Blair informally apologised for wrongs perpetrated under slavery. This leaves open the question of compensation, a long-standing claim of black activists to lay old ghosts to rest. These claims are contested not only in the United Kingdom, but also beyond. Difficulties in finding acceptable routes to reconciliation and compensation were exposed when the United States and Israel walked out of the Durban Conference or World Congress Against Racism and Zenophobia in 2000 as African-Americans demanded compensation for slavery and Palestinians for the atrocities that Israel had committed against them. Reparation for civilians' loss of homes, livelihoods, family and environmental security could arise from Israel's invasion of Lebanon in 2006. Who will compensate? Does compounding the issue with the genocide of Jewish people make resolving the Arab–Israeli dispute more difficult? Is it easier to reach agreement between perpetrators of injustice and victims if events are recent because evidence to make decisions is more readily accessed?

Each country will eventually have to respond to these concerns. Is compensation adequate for enslavement? Who should pay for it? Those who benefited directly? How far do people other than the white English who supported and profited from the slave trade become responsible for contributing to this compensation? Some of these no longer live in the United Kingdom. Other people currently living in Britain are recent arrivals and did not reside here to participate directly in its exploitative practices. Some have migrated to England from Africa within the last decade. How far back does society go in righting past wrongs? Who should compensate the Picts, Celts and Saxons whose homes were burnt, villages ransacked and women raped in acts of war that persisted for years? Raising other issues for consideration does not detract from the merit of any individual claim, it highlights the many instances of wrongdoing woven into the interstices of human history and threaded into daily life today. Social workers can help people deal with extensive pain, grief and loss these situations produce.

Other questions concern the point at which people become responsible for building their own futures and what the connections between past wrongs and current realities are. Valued added to economic infrastructures and social relations mean that Britain today is not what it might have been had the slave trade not occurred. At the time, Britons benefited differentially; some very little; many being forced off the land and sent to other countries to make their own way in the world. Would we do better if compensation today focused on: eradicating institutional and cultural racism; ending other forms of oppression; and freeing individual potential to maximum capacity? Would setting our sights on such possibilities enable us to see how the value added to society by slavery can be used to liberate both oppressors and oppressed? I have no easy answers. Each competing discourse substantiates its position by (re)configuring narratives differently. Little movement towards finding acceptable solutions will happen if the concerns of all are not addressed. Dialogue across differences to resolve these issues to the mutual satisfaction of those involved are necessary first steps. The state has obligations and responsibilities in facilitating this to happen. Social workers, skilled in non-violent conflict resolution techniques can assist in the process.

Employment in the criminal justice system

Despite improvements during the past few decades, black employees remain poorly represented at all levels of the criminal justice system. The HMIP (2000) found: little support for black staff; problems with their retention and promotion; and limited promotions at senior managerial levels including chief officer. Home Office (2002a) research concurred: 89 per cent of probation officers were white; 7 per cent were black and 2 per cent were Asian. The Home Office (2002a) is fast-tracking recruitment of black people to enhance progress. This has had some impact, but not at senior management levels. Other campaigns addressing this lack of representation were mounted by black officers in both probation and police services. Their initiatives included black empowerment and equal opportunities strategies based on actual social positioning (Jeffers, 1995). Some formed around specific identities. The Muslim Police Association raised concerns as a collective group; the Association of Black Probation Officers (ABPO), created in 1984, and the National Association of Asian Probation Staff (NAAPS), formed in 1987, did likewise in probation. NAAPS, formed when Asians differentiated themselves within other 'black organisations', highlighted the different needs of 'black' and 'Asian' personnel. For them, specific identities raised issues not covered by a symbolic unity in an anti-racist struggle for all.

The criminal justice system discriminates against black offenders

Flood-Page and colleagues (2000) suggest discrimination in employment and schooling places offenders of black, Pakistani and Bangladeshi origins at 'greater risk of offending'. Boys of African-Caribbean origins had the highest rates of school exclusions (Flood-Page, 1999). Those of Bangladeshi or Pakistani descent lived in the poorest communities, 60 per cent on low incomes (Pathak, 2000). Dichotomous 'othering' that ignores different aspects of identity by focusing on one trait reinforces their greater vulnerability. Racist dynamics are compounded by oppression derived from institutional racism in the criminal justice system (Macpherson, 1999). Labelling poor people as potential offenders, whether black or white, is unhelpful; most are not.

Caverley and colleagues (2004) indicated that the type of offence varied according to ethnicity – black offenders being primarily responsible for criminal damage; Asians for sex offences and fraud; and persons of multiple heritages for violence against the person. They showed that these offenders had lower assessed needs and lower scores on 'criminogenic' attitudes and beliefs, and proposed that probation officers focus on problems and disadvantage, not attitudes and beliefs. Black offenders have lower recidivism rates and are less likely to commit offences two years after completing their sentences than white ones (Powis and Walmsley, 2002). The use of 'criminogenic' attitudes as authoritative measures is problematic. They lump individual and structural forms of disadvantage together in assessing what individuals can do to become personally responsible for their plight even if structural inequalities and lack of opportunities contribute to their underachievement and unemployment.

Institutional racism in the British criminal justice system

Home Office Reports (2002a, 2004, 2006) conducted under Section 95 of the Criminal Justice Act 1991 have been worrying. The police were less likely to find perpetrators of homicides against black victims; charged black offenders more often; and asked for custodial sentences for black offenders more frequently than white ones. Given these trends, black offenders were more satisfied with their treatment from courts and probation services than white offenders; their positions were reversed for the police. More black offenders pleaded 'not guilty' and were more likely to be acquitted than white offenders. These responses indicate that the interface between black people and police is the most problematic in the criminal justice system, a finding affirmed by Macpherson (1999). Despite Macpherson raising hopes of eliminating institutional racism, little has changed in the intervening years. Macpherson recommended 'freedom of information' to subject the police to greater public control and more rights for victims of crime including racially motivated ones.

---

practice tips   defining a racist event

Macpherson (1999) defined a racist event as an 'incident which is perceived to be racist by the victim or any other person' and included those occurring in the home.

After Macpherson, a new Code of Practice was issued to record racist crimes. 'Double jeopardy' laws were changed to allow new prosecutions after acquittal if new viable evidence was produced. Police failing to perform these duties appropriately could be disciplined for at least five years after retirement. And, the Criminal Justice Act 2003 compelled magistrates to give reasons for sentencing practices. These measures produced greater awareness of racism's role in black offender outcomes but left the basic system intact.

> **Case study**   Black initiatives for younger men
>
> Black people have resisted racism and organised against the criminalisation of black youth. For example, the *National Black Boys Can Association* has a nationwide network to tackle underachievement amongst young black males at school. The *From Boyhood to Manhood Foundation* established in 1996 addresses the needs of young black boys excluded from school. And *Right Track Bristol* took up the issue of black people's over-representation in the prison system. *Reclaim* in Manchester provides black youths with black men as role models to curb gun crime and gang activity. Social workers and probation officers can link up with these organisations to improve services for black offenders or help create similar resources locally.

Provisions for black offenders

'Race', racism and anti-racism in the British criminal justice system had a less prominent profile during the mid-1990s. Even the Home Office's collection of statistics required under Section 95 of the Criminal Justice Act 1991, was compiled with missing information (Calverley et al., 2004), jeopardising decision-making. The Home Office's attempts to remedy this shortcoming include commissioning research through the Crime Reduction Programme and ensuring compliance with the Race Relations (Amendment) Act 2000 (RRA 2000) to promote harmonious race relations.

Black offenders on probation are concentrated in certain parts of the United Kingdom. London had 46 per cent in five probation services – Inner London, Middlesex, North East London, South East London and South West London – excluding West London (Powis and Walmsley, 2002). A further 12 areas had less than one per cent of offenders from minority ethnic groups, making it difficult to deliver services requiring large numbers of participants; for example, groupwork. Diversity within this population and divergent needs raise economic costs, negating group work options if numbers are small. Black staff running black offender programmes were poorly supported by management, received few referrals from other agencies and had limited resources, causing many to close.

Few group-based resources target minority ethnic groups specifically. Caddick's (1993) study of 1463 of these found only three for black and Asian offenders. Senior's (1993) research revealed that few offender groups differentiated between black, Asian and white offenders, with Asian ones less noticed. Powis and Walmsley (2002) survey of 54 probation services showed few provisions for black and Asian offenders in 2000. These they classified as: black empowerment groups; black empowerment within general offending programmes; black empowerment and reintegration programmes; and specific programmes for Asian offenders. Projects were gendered with men in the majority: seven out of ten projects catered mainly for men; three could include women, but in practice had mainly men. Provisions for black women offenders are scarce, a problem shared by white women (Walklate, 2004).

Mixed groups with one or two black offenders are not so effective. Offenders of Asian origins, often the only minority ethnic person in a group, seldom had their needs met and felt uncomfortable. Black and mixed groups failed to address the needs of multi-heritage offenders (ILPS, 1996). Powis and Walmsley (2002) revealed that black offenders who complete programmes in black groups have lower reconviction rates. Black offenders in all black groups liked: the positive role models offered by black staff; a focus on dealing with racism; and mentors of a similar ethnic background. They wanted groups to address typical offender issues like employment, education, training and integration back into the community after serving a sentence.

Authoritarian welfarism and punitive approaches to offenders

'Law and order' debates in Britain have converged around 'popular punitiveness' (Garland, 2001). These popularised a right-wing agenda on criminal justice amongst both Conservative and Labour voters. Under punitive welfarism (Dominelli, 2004), welfare concerns have become minimal with punishment rather than rehabilitation to handle offenders and protect the public (Duff, 2003). This approach seeks to change people's behaviour without the resources and environment necessary for reducing crime. Images of 'black people' as criminals have been aggravated by grafting discourses about 'terrorists' and broader global insecurities onto them. Ethnicity shapes the life chances of black offenders, but 'not everything is racism' (Ahmed, 1978). Identity is a fluid, multi-dimensional phenomenon, making black offenders more than 'black' and more than 'offenders'. Some of their needs converge, that is, common needs, with those of black people, black offenders, white people and white offenders; others diverge, that is, different needs, as their own specific needs as shown in Figure 6.1.

Figure 6.1   Convergent and divergent needs amongst offenders

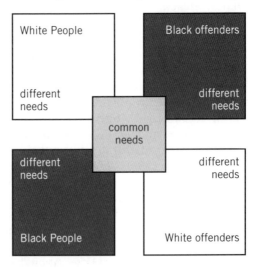

Half (49 per cent) of black offenders thought probation officers were unaware of their needs (Calverley et al., 2004:47). Above all, they wanted practical help, 'fairness', 'responding to individual needs' and learning about black history and racism. Probation officers could explore needs as convergent or common or overlapping and divergent or different ones, and engage in more effective practice with offenders by identifying these as varying according to individual specificities, including ethnicity, gender and age. Others are to be theirs as human rights, for example, education, health services, jobs, a home life. Popular authoritarianism and punishment paradigms dominate responses to young offenders. They are demonised in the media (Franklin and Franklin, 1996), 'rat boy' being a classic case of a young offender demonised as non-human. The United Nations criticised the punitive thrust of Britain's 1998 Crime and Disorder Act on young offenders and a sex offenders' register for young people (UNHCR, 2002). Young sex offenders on the register can be fast-tracked through Detention and Training Orders.

Case study   Local partnerships

Government promotes combined approaches to crime reduction by bringing together community players and professionals in Local Criminal Justice Boards (LCJBs). LCJBs bring together the police, Crown Prosecution Service (CPS), magistrates' courts, crown courts, youth offending teams, probation and prison service: 42 LCJBs co-ordinate and deliver justice in England and are crucial to this strategy. The Crime and Disorder Reduction Partnerships, formed under the 1998 Crime and Disorder Act, are responsible for community safety, tackling crime, and offenders complying with orders. There are 373 partnerships working on crime reduction strategies in England. The Home Office set up a Criminal Justice Race Unit in the Office for Criminal Justice Reform, Department of Constitutional Affairs and Crown Prosecution Service to develop a 'race self-assessment tool' that improves their interventions.

Returning offenders to society

Preparing offenders for inclusion in society, whether at the end of a probation order or prison sentence, is crucial for successful reintegration. Being employed in a secure well-paid job and living as good citizens are key to it. Probation officers and social workers can play proactive roles in developing links and networks between offenders and the communities to which they will return; and secure employment opportunities for them. Ex-offenders have difficulty securing employment post-sentence, a task that is more difficult for black offenders. Ex-offenders constitute one in three of the local population with numbers growing by 100,000 a year (Fletcher et al., 1998). Most (90 per cent) are unemployed, swelling these ranks by 2 to 3 per cent annually. Black offenders are under-represented in employment and training schemes; one-third are on benefit (Calverley et al., 2004:46). Fletcher and colleagues (1998) identified barriers to employing ex-offenders and criticised New Labour's New Deal for placing marginalised people in short-term work and using completions to measure a scheme's success, as this disadvantaged ex-offenders who left before it ended, often for breaching orders. Projects competing with each other for funds allocated according to successful completions would hesitate to employ them, adding to their exclusion. Fletcher and colleagues

(1998) suggested that using positive outcomes, not completions, to determine success could overcome this difficulty. Government ignored this advice. So, 'case management' techniques with quantifiable outcomes to control offenders and low-pay continue to exacerbate their exclusion.

Employers are unclear about the implications of the Rehabilitation of Offenders Act 1974 (Fletcher et al., 1998). Lack of clarity can jeopardise offenders' employability if employers are unaware of its requirements. This problem can intensify with police checks from the Criminal Records Bureau (CRB); a condition of employment for working with 'vulnerable' groups – children and older people. Employers might prefer to play safe and refuse to employ anyone with a record regardless of relevance to a specific job. The CRB requirement can complicate outreach work in finding employment for ex-offenders. Fletcher and colleagues' (1998) evaluation of schemes for black ex-offenders showed that 'negative labelling' and failure to address structural inequalities like racism had to be placed alongside their positive outcomes. Giving black communities a voice in designing and operating these could help meet individuals' specific needs and highlight structural problems.

Case study Youth Offending Teams (YOTs)

New Labour introduced a raft of initiatives to reduce and control crime. Many focus on young offenders, especially persistent ones responsible for the majority of recorded crime within this cohort. The 1998 Crime and Disorder Act initiated the Youth Justice System (YJS) and, under Section 37, Youth Offending Teams (YOTs) to cover offending by children and young people. YOTs are multi-professional teams that include the police, social workers, probation officers, and education and health care professionals. They are responsible for keeping young people out of trouble and follow an interventionist approach, particularly with persistent young offenders. Black professionals are in the minority in these (Hearnden and Hough, 2004). YOTs use risk assessments to determine the likelihood of offenders causing harm to themselves and others, including re-offending. Their capacity to accurately assess individual behaviour is questionable (Quinsey, 1995). Young black offenders are seriously disadvantaged by this approach (Kalunta-Crumpton, 2005).

The 1998 Crime and Disorder Act authorised the Action Plan Order (APO) as a YOT strategy for 10–17 year olds. APOs were to prevent re-offending through compliance with orders/action plans. Adherence to APOs was mandatory and strictly monitored by YOTs. Young people were breached (brought back to the courts for sentencing) for non-compliance. The Intensive Supervision and Surveillance Project (ISSP) aimed to reduce youth offending by mentoring each offender. Mentors are volunteers who offer the young person 25 hours per week of intensive support. They are less accountable than paid staff. ISSP involves the voluntary sector in the criminal justice system, a commitment of both Conservative and New Labour. New Labour's Crime Reduction Programme encompassed a range of measures including Pathfinder Projects, accredited by the Joint Prisons and Probation Accreditation Panel. Agencies that receive 'Pathfinder Status' follow evidence-based approaches to crime initiated in the 'what works' agenda begun by the Tories. They have to show a recognised change model and evidence that their interventions prevent re-offending.

Persistent failure in eradicating 'law and order' problems prompted New Labour to change the relationship between offenders and society with Anti-Social Behaviour Orders (ASBOs) created under the Anti-Social Behaviour Act 2003. This Act made individuals responsible for their behaviour by requiring them to desist from particular actions or absent themselves from specified geographic locales. Black offenders, receiving nearly a quarter of ASBOs, are over-represented (M. Ahmed, 2006). Most ASBOs target young offenders, can be combined with Parenting Orders, Reparation Orders and Referral Orders, and endorse a 'parental deficit' approach that holds parents accountable for children's actions. Young people on ASBOs may have poor relationships with their parents, avoid seeing them and reject their attempts at control. Making parents responsible for their offspring's behaviour aims to increase parental responsibility and control. Passing the buck onto parents absolves young people from responsibility and accountability for their actions and encourages the state to avoid tackling structural problems. Poor housing, low employment prospects, environmental degradation give young people the message of being irrelevant to society and alienate them. Creating a sense of belonging can help them understand their behaviour. Social workers can help them work on these issues.

Case study   Imprisoning Patricia Amos for her daughters' truancy

The daughters of Patricia Amos from Banbury were worried about a self-harming mother who misused drugs and truanted to look after her. This white lone mother was imprisoned for 60 days in 2002 for not sending her children to school. She promised to behave, but underlying issues of drug abuse, low income and isolation not tackled post-release exposed the limitation of punitive approaches (Gillan, 2002). Patricia and a daughter went to court in 2004 for more truanting offences. The original prison sentence had not acted as deterrent, but she was sentenced to 28 days once more.

The media made a 'cause célèbre' of this story, but ignored the plight of black people, more likely to be punished for truancy. This high-profile case illustrated New Labour's resolve in holding parents responsible for children regardless of outcome. Pathologising individuals won the day over structural analyses or addressing issues that underpin such behaviours. The government's approach to crime and disorder has become more punitive and controlling, often drawing on the private sector and new technologies in upholding individual culpability for what happens; for example, tagging. By targeting parents, popular authoritarianism gained a new site of operations; affirmed the role of ASBOs in regulating and controlling individual behaviour and neglected underlying structural inequalities underpinning it. Truancy Sweeps and ASBOs embody Foucault's (1988) 'technologies of self', whereby individuals discipline themselves to act in socially acceptable ways. Professionals are implicated in these 'technologies of the self' by monitoring activities. Opposition to ASBOs is limited. They have media value; practitioners refusing to use ASBOs face dismissal (Grier and Thomas, 2006).

The government has held professionals personally accountable for what they do without tackling structural inequalities. Developing capacities to do both is crucial in work with black offenders because black schoolchildren are over-represented in truanting statistics (Flood-Page, 1999) and suffer most from structural inequalities. That significant numbers of children and young people regularly truant from school (Smithers, 2002) suggests it is time to ask whether the school system is failing children. Society might achieve better results if it shifted professionals' energies to address structural inequalities rather than pathologising children. Making this move requires probation officers and social workers to respond holistically to offenders and examine links between different elements in their lives – barriers and opportunities; relationships with others (parents, family, peers); and social divisions (gender); 'race'; class; and disability. Besides not working, current methods adopted for handling truancy criminalise a group of people already disadvantaged in life. Rather than helping, this may simply exacerbate their difficulties in securing waged jobs (Garrett, 1999).

Institutional racism and offences of racial hatred

Black people experience increased levels of racial harassment and violence. The IRR estimated 25,000 racially aggravated offences between 2000 and 2001 (IRR, 2002). The highly publicised murder of black teenager Stephen Lawrence by white youths in London highlighted racial injustice at the centre of the criminal justice system's failure to convict white people who racially assault black people (Macpherson, 1999).

Case study   The murder of Stephen Lawrence

Stephen and his cousin Duwayne Brooks were attacked waiting for a bus in Eltham, London on 22 April 1993. Duwayne escaped and called for help. Without a prompt response from emergency services, Stephen bled to death on the pavement. Stephen's parents complained about police inaction, including a failure to collect appropriate evidence against the perpetrators when notified of the attack, and launched a campaign for justice for their dead son. Many people, black and white, joined a campaign they sustained for years. They demanded: justice; recognition of the severity of the offence; acknowledgement of the dignity, worth and humanity of black victims; and an end to the brutality of racist official responses to black people's quest for justice during stressful times.

Anti-racists and anti-fascist groups identified the British National Party (BNP) as an organisation that endorsed white supremacy and fanned racial hatred. The BNP, active in Eltham, had headquarters not far from where Stephen was murdered. Local protests endorsed anti-racists' demands that police shut down these offices. One occurred on 16 October 1993. Riot police tried to keep anti-racist supporters and BNP adherents apart, but it became violent, 41 demonstrators and 19 police were injured. Accusations and blame apportioning followed. Police asserted white anti-racists had specifically targeted black police officers. PC Leslie Turner, claimed white demonstrators had attacked him for 'being a traitor'.

The colour-blind position of the Metropolitan Police comes across in the assumption that a black officer should defend an organisation that opposed his presence as a black man in Britain (Gilroy, 2000). In 2006, PC Alexander Omar Basha, a Muslim officer requested exemption from protecting the Israeli Embassy in London, highlighting the increased personal dangers black police faced in such situations. Permission was granted. Despite following procedures including a risk assessment backing this claim, media furore suggested the approved request was grounds for dismissal.

The Macpherson (1999) Inquiry argued that the Lawrence case had been mishandled with institutional racism evident in police responses to being notified of the attack; neglecting its duty to care for the dying Stephen; and failing to uphold and maintain standards of justice for all London inhabitants. Macpherson's Report, hailed as a landmark in British race relations for its candour, acknowledged the reality of institutional racism at the heart of key British institutions. It produced 70 recommendations that led to changes in: Metropolitan Police procedures for handling complaints from black people; dealing with white people accused of racially motivated crimes; and amending the Race Relations Act to enable the Commission for Racial Equality to investigate public authorities including the police. The murders of black people since then, including Zahid Mubarek in Feltham Young Offenders Institution by a self-declared white racist and Anthony Walker in Liverpool in 2005, raise doubt as to the efficacy of these measures (CRE, 2003c; Dominelli, 2006b).

Rehabilitation or punishment

'Prison works' has been the mantra that has re-storied the role of social work and probation in the care and rehabilitation of offenders in favour of custodial sentences. In England and Wales, this has emphasised containment/control aspects of probation; reinforced its links to custodial arrangements; and removed it from social work training. Rooted in popular authoritarianism, this ideology is reflected in new structures for probation, the National Offenders Management Service (NOMS). NOMS was formed in 2004 to bring the probation and prison services together. Clearly proclaiming NOMS' role as managing offenders to complete orders and keep out of trouble, punishment rather than welfare is its overriding priority. Current dissatisfaction with probation officers' performance led government to propose more contracted out services and a larger role for the private sector by making probation bid for offender services and creating probation trusts (McCormack, 2006).

Constant changes in probation, as in social work more broadly, seem to be *the* government strategy for not resourcing adequately change initiatives or tackling structural inequalities. Imprisonment, its favoured option is also failing. Unprecedented prison numbers – exceeding 80,000 – place Britain amongst dictatorial regimes. Failure to re-orient offenders away from offending lifestyles once out of prison is exposed by 'repeat' offenders, with high rates of recidivism amongst those institutionalised by imprisonment and engaging in a revolving-door career of crime.

Privatisation is evident in the British prison service. Private prisons are designed, constructed and managed by the private sector under financial arrangements that last 25 years – the Private-Public Finance Initiative that authorises Private-Public Partnerships. Serco, G4S and Justice Services run 11 private prisons in the United Kingdom. Imprisonment costs £27,000 per offender a year and offers scope for significant profits, if costs can be curtailed in soft areas like staff wages and education for inmates. This outcome jeopardises inmates' reintegration efforts once out, but intensifies the search for alternatives.

Redistributive justice

Punitive authoritarianism with punishment to reduce crime and uncivil behaviour has been countered by alternatives that promote rehabilitation and support both offenders and victims. Discourses about retributive justice where punishment fits the crime is endorsed by government, and restorative justice with restitution to victims was addressed by the Truth and Reconciliation Commission of South Africa. By building partnerships for dialogue between offenders and victims, it aimed to establish mutual trust and allay deeply embedded feelings of being wronged in the hope of solving serious social problems. Social workers can facilitate these exchanges. Black people have developed alternatives to prison. Maoris in New Zealand/Aotearoa created the Family Group Conference (FGC) as alternatives to custody for their young people, over-represented in the criminal justice system. FGCs reintegrated those who had gone astray into the community with support networks and systems based on extended family and local community strengths. Their model was adopted for restorative justice in countries like the United Kingdom, Sweden and the United States to connect offenders with victims (Jackson and Nixon, 1999; Taylor, 1999). Restorative justice gives victims a voice and makes punishing offenders victim-focused.

International crime involving immigration violations, fraud, money laundering and Internet-related crime are lucrative organised gang activities. People smuggling is worth £10 billion a year. Drugs bring in £18 billion in dirty money. Half of crime in the United Kingdom is committed by 280,000 drug users (Serious Organised Crime Agency, 2006). Offenders and victims share community space. New approaches to crime reduction like restorative justice bring them together for frank discussions about the impact of crime upon victims' lives. Such encounters are unlikely to eradicate advantages conferred by crime that crosses borders, in an age when the local and the global spheres fuse together. Nor will simply improving cross-national co-operation amongst criminal justice agencies and communications across jurisdictional lines change local environments and social relationships that support lucrative and illegal income generation. Removing local support for such endeavours requires investment in people, particularly education and opportunities for long-term employment prospects as could be done for rural farmers growing poppies in Afghanistan.

Critiques of anti-racist approaches

Persistent racist behaviour within the British criminal justice system exposes the failure to tackle structural (institutional and cultural) racism. Either/or approaches to tackling racism have failed to address structural deficiencies and complexity and contributed to disillusionment with anti-racist struggles. Gilroy (2000) urges anti-racists to exercise reflexivity, while critiquing their positions for not considering the shifting nature of 'race' given the multiplicity of determinisms that confront them, including those of biology, nationalism, culture and scientific genometrics that root human difference in the genes. Gilroy claims that anti-racism has lost its way by focusing on biological traits that have outlived their useful-ness in the:

> barren terrain where work on 'race' is overshadowed by priva-tised, corporate multiculturalism and cultures of simulation in which racial alterity has acquired an important commercial value.
>
> (2000:52)

Gilroy (2000) shows how multiculturalist approaches have been appropriated by profit-making entrepreneurs who turn 'black chic' into highly sellable commodities ripe for exploitation. In arguing that biological attributes like skin colour, used to construct 'race' previously, have lost their saliency Gilroy ignores the racialisation of difference, namely, the politicisation of biological phenotypes to create new biosocial sites of oppression opened up by gene thera-pies and corporate multiculturalism. Nast and Pulido (2000) contend that multiculturalism has become an integral part of a corporate consumer culture where identity politics embody performance in time and space, leaving little room for transgressive or oppositional multiculturalism.

The commercialisation of racial alterity relies precisely on it being the *black* man or woman, that is, their *black bodies*, perform-ing in outstanding ways that makes them fit for commercial exploitation. Multicultural narratives enable white people to appropriate Michael Jordan's prowess and participate in the skills associated with this black player by wearing Nike shoes and buying the able-bodied dream of athleticism (Gilroy, 2000). This multicul-tural response improves their anti-racist credentials. In viewing racism as a despicable ideological practice, a token semblance of accepting a black person by paying lip service to multiculturalism is a small price to pay in generating greater profits. Older versions of racism were never simply biological or restricted only to the socio-political domain. Although not emphasised as much as they could be, they were rooted in everyday life practices (ELPs) as they are today. The specifics of these ELPs have changed/are changing. Slave-owners exploited the bodies of black slaves for commercial reasons: to make money through slave labour. Black women's bodies were also exploited in gender specific ways to produce and raise new generations of black labourers and sexually gratify the master (Weiner, 1997).

putting it into practice

The criminal justice system fails to meet black offenders' needs despite research indicating that black offenders suffer additional disadvantage because they are black. The state has played a key role in holding black offenders responsible for their behaviour without tackling the structural causes of crime that impact on it.

- Does being disadvantaged contribute to offending behaviour?
- How could the criminal justice system tackle structural inequalities?
- How can white practitioners become allies in the struggle for racial justice?

Further reading

Lewis, L., Raynor, P., Smith, D. and Wardak, A. (eds) (2006) *Race and Probation*. Cullompton: Willan.

Traynor, C. (1998) 'Social Work in a Sectarian Society', *Social Work and Social Change in Northern Ireland*. Belfast: CCETSW (NI).

7 | Anti-racist social work with (im)migrants, asylum-seekers and refugees

Introduction

The perpetration of racist dynamics and practices is a global issue. Immigration, embedded in new discourses around the internationalisation of social problems, reveals narratives of racialisation that are reproduced through everyday life practices. Racist discourses in the United Kingdom construct '(im)migrants' as problematic, betray a lack of acceptance, indicate that they are neither wanted nor belong here, and complicate entry by non-British nationals. The specific minority ethnic groups under fire in these hostile discourses alter as the socio-political and economic terrain changes. Over centuries, (im)migrants making East London home included Huguenots; Jews fleeing pogroms in Eastern Europe; black Commonwealth citizens employed in declining industries; and black and white asylum-seekers fleeing persecution, violence and fear.

Asylum seekers and refugees have become the latest racialised groups to evoke negative reactions from the residents of the United Kingdom. Denied acceptance as citizens, refugees pose difficult issues, depending on country of origin and reasons for departure. These include: trauma; fear that they or their families 'back home' will be killed; grief for loss of families, homes and livelihoods; isolation, if they do not speak English; poor health; communication difficulties in their own language if unable to read or write it; poor housing; unemployment; and subsistence incomes. Most refugees are located in Asia and Africa. Only 2 per cent come to the United Kingdom, mainly from Iraq, Zimbabwe, Afghanistan, Somalia and Sri Lanka.

Signatories to the Geneva Convention on the Status of Refugees (1951), like the United Kingdom, the United States and Canada, pledge to treat those claiming asylum in accordance with its provisions. The Convention defines a refugee as a person who:

> owing to a well-founded fear of being persecuted for reasons of race, religion, nationality, membership of a particular social group, or political opinion, is outside the country of his [sic] nationality, and is unable to or, owing to such fear, is unwilling to avail himself [sic] of the protection of that country.

The Convention is gendered and constructed in terms of protection and vulnerability linked to masculinity and nationality, with the nation-state responsible for its citizens.

Refugees and asylum-seekers expose a contemporary social problem that redefines racist policies and practices as territorial and cultural protectionism. In Europe, this state-led development ignores the blurring of national boundaries by globalisation, 'free' movement of people in the European Union (EU) tied into the 1986 Single Market Act and EU enlargement. The latter has altered the categorisation of asylum-seekers and refugees from Eastern Europe as people from ten countries that joined in 2004 enjoy freedom of movement, temporarily circumscribed to allay racist fears of being 'swamped' by Eastern Europeans entitled to live and work anywhere in the EU.

The position of (im)migrants is a shifting one. Initially planning temporary stays, circumstances in the country of origin or receiving country change and they become permanent settlers. Within this permanency, ties to relatives and friends overseas retained through periodic and sometimes lengthy trips back to the country of origin create and maintain 'transnational families'. Migration is not a fixed status, but combines elements of permanency with transiency to form new flexible and more adaptive relationships (Abye, 2007; Small, 2007). Transnational family relations carry implications for sending and receiving countries. Migrants contribute substantially to the economic well-being and cultural richness of the receiving country and create spaces of belonging, often in spatially segregated communities (Ehrkamp, 2005). Remittances 'home' contribute substantially to the economy and play a key role in the survival of extended family members overseas (Small, 2007).

In this chapter, I examine how social workers intervene in the lives of (im)migrants, asylum-seekers and refugees. Rooting this in case studies and research, I pay specific attention to problems encountered in receiving services and unaccompanied children (minors) seeking asylum. Inter-agency reactions are crucial in reducing the impact of the dispersal policy currently promoted by the British government via the National Asylum Support Service (NASS). These pitted their needs against those of poor populations already in receiving communities, to divide them when this need not be so. Who were the winners and losers of such policies? Isolation, inadequate housing and poor job prospects are serious problems for (im)migrants, asylum-seekers and refugees that social workers working with local communities address. Scarcity, lack of political will and low priority in repairing public service infrastructures to benefit existing and new claimants limit social workers' ability to meet the needs of all.

Shifting discourses on identity and immigration

Immigration status matters. It determines who gets in, what they can or cannot do and entitlement to benefits. Discourses concerned with who pays taxes for public welfare and costs of migration in a country of residence devalue (im)migrants' contributions to economic growth and the price borne by individual (im)migrants or families. Social workers are drawn into these when responding to unmet needs. Discourses about the entry of non-UK nationals are contextualised within a cultural norm of white Britons as racially tolerant people living in multiethnic and multicultural milieus that include the four original nations of the United Kingdom. Tolerance underpins notions of Britishness and appears in a 2002 survey of 'race' organised by BBC News Online. The CRE's study on Britishness affirming the relevance of 'race' over the last three general elections (Billig et al., 2006) tracks a move away from 'ethnic nationalism' to 'civic nationalism'. Civic nationalism, 'banally' reproduced, distances itself from 'old-style racism' under the umbrella of multiculturalism and shared values; and maintains distinctions between 'us' and 'them', the outsiders or foreigners (Billig et al., 2006:5).

This distinction between nationalisms is problematic. Old-style ethnic nationalism drew upon shared values, language and religion and invented uniformity in areas where these were lacking to forge a national identity. As long as identity is linked to the nation-state,

'Britishness', however defined, embraces the notion of a singular essentialised identity, even if composed of multicultural parts. Like civic nationalism, ethnic nationalism draws upon decontextualised or contentless details that are reproduced in everyday life alongside national institutions, symbols, linguistic practices, religious observances and cultural norms. Discourses about 'immigrants' in late 2007 focused on everyday life practices and competition over scarce public goods and discrepancies in the numbers entering Britain after EU enlargement. Defining these newcomers as 'outsiders' who put pressure on the existing welfare infrastructure and jobs, the Local Government Association (LGA) demanded that local authorities receive a further £250 million to respond to their needs for health, education and housing services.

Their treatment depicts how those inscribed as 'outsiders', and increasingly those of Islamic faiths and cultures, become excluded from 'civic nationalism', as they were from 'ethnic nationalism'. 'Civic nationalism' like 'ethnic nationalism' extols the dangers of (im)migration via 'scare' stories that overshadow those that celebrate the contributions of (im)migrants to British social, cultural and economic life; and thrives on the idea of a unitary identity. It is unable to deal with diversity in its midst, including differences that emerge around 'shared' values. People might share the value of equality in the abstract, but redefine it if asked to grant equality to different 'insiders'. For example, British nationals with a heterosexual orientation may 'forget' equality is a shared value with gays and lesbians to maintain heterosexual privileging. Current discourses about 'Britishness' accepting diversity within a unitary identity draw upon racial dichotomies that emphasise personal racism, othering processes and institutional racism. New discourses of diversities and commonalities are needed to achieve inclusivity in a society shared and shaped by many peoples living in a globalising world that is embedded in nation-states.

The nation-state with a singular national identity is being reinvented rather than destroyed under the impact of globalisation with increased migration, interpersonal relations among diverse peoples and transnationalities that transcend multiculturalism, to produce multiversity. Current multicultural discourses present diversities as parallel universes of spectacle. Lacking real engagement with difference, it is merely tolerated. As spectacle, it assumes passivity in the act of observing aspects of cultural life. The idea of multiversity overcomes this limitation by conceptualising difference as being created through intersecting universes of discourse.

Re-territorialising narratives of place and space

If human beings came out of Africa, most of the world's inhabitants have migrated in their ancestral past. Britain is a country of immigrants. The Phoenicians are alleged to have reached its shores. The Romans left their mark in people, culture, administrative structures and roads. With the Romans came black people from Africa. Followed by the Jutes, Angles and Saxons, Vikings, Normans and more recent others, they enrich its socio-political, economic and cultural life (Fryer, 1984). (Im)migration changed and continues to change Britain's ethnic mix. In the 1991 Census, the largest growing ethnic minority was the 'mixed' relationship involving a white and a black person; a position verified by the 2001 Census. Those in these relationships claim that they are more accepted in contemporary Britain than 30 years ago, with Londoners more tolerant than people in the provinces. This is due to a greater ethnic mix in London, although black people are located in specific boroughs (ONS, 2002; Dorsett, 2005:98). Concentration in 'ethnic enclaves' is greatest amongst Bangladeshi-origined communities and least amongst Chinese-origined ones. Clark and Drinkwater (2002:6–7) deem these enclaves 'a potentially important determinant of the welfare of ethnic groups' in urban areas in England and Wales and linked to higher unemployment and self-employment rates.

(Im)migrants, asylum-seekers and refugees are actively re-territorialising space, place and belonging by moving to different localities and insisting that they are treated as people with full human rights. Communities formed by (im)migrants in multicultural societies like the United Kingdom are depicted as failing to assimilate or integrate into white British culture, if they practise traditional customs or lead separate lives. These discourses have centred on dress codes, treatment of women, religion, language and food. The United Kingdom is not the only European country with negative perceptions of newcomers. Worryingly, it persists when 'newcomers' have become permanent settlers or citizens. Retaining links to countries of origin and maintaining traditional cultures are seen as 'visible markers [and] . . . expressions of immigrants' refusal to assimilate rather than the richness of transnationalism' (Çağlar in

Ehrkamp, 2005:346). Their tales affirm racialised narratives of exclusion. Racialisation imposes difficulties on peoples defined as not belonging to a place by converting their unwillingness to assimilate into personal pathology regardless of structural oppressions; poorly articulated intercultural relationships; or refusal of those already in a country to accept diversity in their midst.

Ehrkamp (2005) argues that these developments are better understood by unpacking 'the complexities of immigrants' transnational ties and multiple belongings' and not conceptualising their participation in more than one locality as mutually exclusive. Transnationality provides opportunities for belonging in several spaces and involves processes of transforming current places of residence by (re)creating local ties that engage both receiving and sending societies. These processes (re)configure identities and move them from fixed essentialist conceptualisations. Transnationality questions the term 'immigrant', reframes the issue of citizenship into one of belonging simultaneously to more than one place and enables those involved to engage in 'multiple public spheres across national borders in their social practices' (Ehrkamp and Leitner quoted in Ehrkamp, 2005:347). Dwyer (2000:475) suggests that transnationality 'cuts across fixed notions of belonging'. Scholars have rethought understandings of identity in the fluidity of time and space that transnationality represents. Anthias (1998, 2001) uses 'diaspora' to describe contemporary dispersals of people across the globe. Appaduri (1996) calls these movements 'ethnoscapes' that signify a *de*-territorialisation of belonging and prefigure new forms of identification to replace a singular nation-state.

Attempts to reconceptualise current trends remain problematic. They assume fixed points of belonging for a dominant group with established hegemony over a territory, but not others. This flies in the face of 'diasporic' positioning within human migratory movements. Since time immemorial, people have gone from territory to territory to establish belonging in other places. The history of human conquest is littered with examples of people who have been genocided out, displaced or assimilated by conquerors who then adopt land that once belonged to others. Imperialistic countries like the United Kingdom have original populations dispersed across the globe, making the British a diasporic nation. Would Australians, Canadians or Americans of British origins deny claims of belonging in their respective countries simply because their ancestors migrated during a period of settlement under colonial auspices? The struggles of aboriginal peoples in these countries to establish their rights to land suggest their answer is a firm 'no'.

White Rhodesians who left Zimbabwe for Britain after independence used British ancestry as entitlement to escape to the United Kingdom, despite being born in Zimbabwe and having family living there for generations. They left not because they felt they did not belong, but in fear of their safety. For many, the entire family, nuclear and extended, left; others retained interests and ties in the former colony. These are transnational ties, but are not considered such in the current transnational literature which focuses on the practices of minority ethnic peoples who have come over. The transnational ties of white entrants like these white Zimbabweans were different from other ethnic groups, especially black ones. Their place in the United Kingdom was unquestioned and they slipped into the country virtually unnoticed. These were white people with English roots. They looked English and spoke English. Responses to them highlight power relations expressed as racialised identities. Their entry was facilitated as they were not openly racialised, while benefiting from racialisation as white people. Unequal power relations and racialisation processes are more explicit for black peoples.

Some European countries actively encourage transnationality by offering dual nationality to the descendents of nationals who had emigrated previously. This has drawn new generations of 'white Europeans' into the mix who have had little or no contact with the country of ancestral origin. Many will not know the languages of their mothers or fathers, let alone be fluent in them, and may undermine Europe's future linguistic diversity. Their entry raises interesting questions about transnationality that complicate tax, immigration and welfare laws, the implications of which have not been thought out. Increasing population numbers by bringing in others like them is not foreseen to pose problems of integration. This assumption may be incorrect. They are unlikely to pose problems as long as they remain transient visitors. What happens if they decide to stay and participate in practices of permanency that transnationality allows for? What are the implications for the receiving state then? Does it not matter because white Europeans are facing declining birth-rates that threaten their sustainability on the continent?

What is occurring is not a *de*-territorialisation of place, but a *re*-territorialisation or redefining of land to include those who can demonstrate common ties and enable a broader sharing of specific territories. This process may involve one territory as in current treaties with First Nations peoples in Canada. The provincial government in British Columbia, negotiating ownership of parts of Vancouver Island with First Nations peoples, justifies allowing white Canadians to remain on the grounds that aboriginal culture always believed in sharing their territory with others. This is in a place where over centuries, white settlers took land from original inhabitants without treaty or permission and ignored aboriginal claims for its return or compensation.

The re-territorialisation process may involve several territories, for example, transnationality enjoyed by white British elders retiring to sunny Spain under treaties that allow pensions to be transferred over. They never lose the right to return to the United Kingdom; many do not become fluent Spanish speakers. Their elder care may occur on Spanish soil. This is creating problems in delivering services when many require medical or social care assistance in a context where none is publicly provided. Spaniards are questioning their entitlement to care as the number of retirees from other countries and associated costs of care rise substantially. Their government has requested reimbursement for elder care expenditures from Brussels. Mungo (2006) suggests that the current 600,000 Northern Europeans retiring in Southern Europe is set to rise to 2 million, straining the system further. However, private developers intend to build 'retirement communities' to meet their care needs. Their case indicates that while a transnational person's sense of belonging and entitlement is linked to particular territories through specific ties, they may participate fully in another until challenged. This development is likely to increase in the enlarged EU as place of birth becomes less crucial than place of residence. Another example illustrates a different facet of the re-territorialisation process. Persons of Pakistani origins living in Britain, as citizens of both the United Kingdom and Pakistan, are transnational with respect of these two countries. But unless they had family or other ties in Ethiopia, they would not claim their transnationality extended to it. Transnationality is configured around social relations linked to specific practices and relationships in particular locations.

Discourses about human smuggling have also shaped immigration discourses in the West. These are mainly negative and involve re-territorialising narratives of space without recognising their contributions to society. In the United Kingdom this covered 58 Chinese nationals who died being transported in a container and 22 cockle-pickers who drowned in Morecambe Bay performing illegal and poorly paid work. This activity is not confined to Europe: the 'mother of snakeheads' smuggled people from China to the United States via Canada from the mid-1970s until captured a couple of years ago. In 2005, Americans caught 22 Chinese nationals escaping from a container aboard a ship in Seattle in April; 12 South Koreans crossing the Canadian border in the Okanogan; and 7 escorted across Canada's border by a woman in December (Associated Press, 2006b). Attempts by Mexicans to cross the US southern boundary have been longstanding, causing hardship and loss of life. In 2006, Bush militarised this border by sending the National Guard to prevent its breach.

Case study   Citizenship rights for (im)migrants

Hispanics are the largest minority in the United States (Alberts, 2006). Americans estimate 12 million illegal workers, but exact numbers are not available. This is surprising given that the nation was formed through waves of (im)migration that unsettled the country's original inhabitants. In 2006, migrant workers launched widespread protests against injustices perpetrated by American immigration controls. Covering the entire United States, these culminated in 'A Day Without Immigrants'. 'Naturalized US citizens' marched alongside new entrants and others who supported them. Protestors aimed to demonstrate that without immigrant labour power, the United States would grind to a halt. The food production industry, e.g., Tyson Foods, Cargill and Swift, reliant on their labour had to shut down operations. The demonstrations and boycotts were called 'intimidation, and extortion' by Republican Senator Trent Lott, offended that 'illegal people come into this country, take jobs and wave foreign flags' (Alberts, 2006:A7).

Their actions were only partially successful. Illegal immigration remains a felony crime; and increased enforcement of deportation and construction of fences along the Mexican–American border (on lands once owned by Mexico) continues. The protests were supported elsewhere and linked migration, poverty and environmental degradation. Those in: Germany, Switzerland, Sweden, Russia, Mexico, Honduras and Nicaragua focused on globalisation's detrimental impact upon workers' lives, working conditions and income; Turkey targeted the IMF; Indonesia, the Philippines; and Bangladesh called for an improved quality of life, not profits.

Refugees and asylum-seekers endure racial harassment. Responses to asylum-seekers and refugees subject them to new narratives to re-territorialise space and violence including state and individual violence. Asylum-seekers and refugees are verbally or physically abused and murdered in the United Kingdom (Bridges et al., 2001), Canada and the United States and increase their feelings of vulnerability and non-belonging.

Case study   Racism makes asylum-seekers vulnerable

The Etibako family fled 'extreme violence' in the Congo (formerly Zaire), but were brutally murdered when their house was deliberately torched, killing five. Adela Etikako paid a smuggler $3000 to fly to the United States and went to Canada. Her claim for refugee status was denied and no official support was offered. They stayed because Canada does not deport failed asylum-seekers if 'dangerous conditions' exist in the country of origins, deemed to apply here. The family lived with the mother. Traumatised as refugees, they lived in poor conditions in a 'low-income complex where prostitution, domestic violence, drug use and aggression from others were normal' (Skelton, 2006:A4).

Without friendly neighbours such families are isolated and 'at risk' of racist attacks. Communities can become welcoming spaces. Had this occurred, the Etibakos' deaths might have been avoided. Social workers could assist in the task of creating these. Sadly, in Canada and the United Kingdom, social workers seldom work with asylum-seekers and refugees unless there are child protection concerns.

Language exclusion

The conditions for tolerating diversity cover a vast array of cultural signifiers like shared language. Speaking a language fluently facilitates communication, symbolises having attributes, values, traditions and ways of defining the world in common. Its lack becomes linguistically exclusionary. Minorities who speak different languages link up with those having a common heritage to create linguistic spaces of exclusivity and form safe spaces or sites of resistance that cannot be assailed by those speaking only majority languages. Such usage may be resented by majority communities because they feel left out and unable to participate. The number of languages involved may be high; for example, 300 in London.

People in majority language groups may respond to being so excluded by demanding that 'they' speak the majority language. Blunkett's requirement that immigrants applying for British citizenship speak English affirms this reaction. A common language that encourages discussion across racial divides is a good idea. Language fluency is a major means of communicating within a country. It is needed to contact official agencies, associated with social control and conveyed via bureaucratic means like letters that require language skills of a different order than conversations. As a condition of being accepted, language is problematic. It can exacerbate existing inequalities because language usage varies by ethnic group and gender that structure options according to social divisions. For example, older working-class women of Chinese descent are less likely to speak English than men. Cultural traditions, employment opportunities, lack of safe spaces for meeting others and an absence of shared activities impede black elders' encounters with wider society. A further question for society is: 'Why does a majority group not learn other languages?' Doing so could facilitate communications across language divides. The issue is not only about communication: unequal power relations, structural oppression and lack of equality matter too. These are not decontextualised factors without repercussions or consequences. Lazear (1999) claims that:

> shared language and culture improve group-specific opportunities for trade and many provide a 'protected market' for goods and services of religious or cultural significance.
> (Lazear quoted in Clark and Drinkwater, 2002:10–11)

Language exclusivity may be linked to a 'wage penalty' if a business only employs family. As a survival strategy in straightened circumstances, low-paid work in a family firm penalises women, but enables the group to survive. The migration of manufacturing jobs from the United Kingdom's metropolitan centres compels minority ethnic groups to adjust by increasing self-employment, a strategy favoured by those with low educational qualifications. Other variables include age, time in Britain and place of birth (Clark and Drinkwater, 2002).

Their position is not static. Change comes from within and outside a community in interactions and negotiations with others. Regentrification of cities is a movement that raises house prices. Poor black and white working-class individuals employed in the public sector, where many minority ethnic groups find jobs, become unable to purchase homes because wage levels do not keep pace with house prices (Clark and Drinkwater, 2002). Instead, they move further into suburbia, join commuter-land or live in overcrowded and deprived inner city areas with few public resources.

Racist practices, (im)migrants, asylum-seekers and refugees

Public expressions of personal racism

Personal racism comes out in disparaging comments about those settling in the United Kingdom. Racist attacks against people of African, Caribbean, Asian and Arabic origins have risen (IRR, 2000). Verbal abuse, emotional, physical and sexual violence against 'strangers', 'foreigners' or 'aliens' are associated with bigoted individuals who do not accept the multiversity of land deemed theirs by dint of birth. These attitudes persist, feed into and off institutional and cultural racism and reaffirm personal racism.

The BBC Multiculturalism Poll of 2005 shows that personal racism permeates public discourses and reinforces the idea that racism is an individual matter. The Poll poses decontextualised questions and highlights personal opinions that give insights into individual's views of multicultural Britain. The survey, conducted after 9/11, but before 7/7, distinguishes between a 'National' sample and a 'Muslim' one, indicating the crucial dichotomy was between Muslim and non-Muslim. This division does not make sense as the crucial signifier of identity in the Muslim category was a unitary one of religion that ignored diversity and different ethnicities within it. The National category submerges religion alongside other diversities to form a unitary entity that excludes Muslims. Religion as a key definer of cultural racism in contemporary Britain plays into hegemonic discourses that affirm narratives of exclusion for Muslims and presume a singular British way of life for all others. This division appears in statements like 'Parts of this country don't feel like Britain anymore because of immigration': 54 per cent of the National and 36 per cent of Muslim samples agreed without thinking it applied to the country overall: 86 per cent and 74 per cent respectively. Despite this, an overwhelming majority in both groups wanted to retain multiculturalism: 68 per cent of National and 74 per cent of Muslim samples.

Methodological and ontological difficulties notwithstanding, 'differences' between the two groups were not as great as might be anticipated. Questioned about Britain becoming a more or less tolerant society: 34 per cent of the National and 31 per cent of the Muslim group replied 'more'; 39 percent of the National and 31 per cent of the Muslim group said 'less'. Differences in opinion were greater amongst those who perceived multiculturalism as 'threatening the British way of life'. Unsurprisingly, 32 per cent of the National and 13 per cent of the Muslim group agreed with this statement. The question on what immigrants who wanted to become British citizens should do revealed striking levels of agreement between them indicating that language, loyalty to Britain, allegiance to the country's institutions, integration to British society and women's equality were crucial markers of living in the United Kingdom (BBC News, 2005). These findings can expose narratives of inclusion.

Britain is not alone in framing responses to (im)migrants in individualised terms applied to a collective group. Canada and the United States show similar trends. A 2006 briefing paper compiled by Ipos Reid for Citizenship and Immigration Canada (CIC) to track Canadian responses remarked 'Canadians have "generally positive" views on immigration'. Around 60 per cent of the national sample thought that the number of immigrants allowed entry was about right, having risen from 50 per cent in 2005. This compared with a drop from 48 per cent to 37 per cent in British Columbia during this period (O'Neil, 2006b:A19). The CIC briefing identified the two key immigration issues that worried Canadians as: the poor 'handling of refugee cases; and difficulty foreigners have in getting their professional credentials recognised' (O'Neil, 2006b:A19). This positive attitude, buried in the back pages, was negated by the front page headline, 'Refugee Crime

Fuels Immigration Concern' a view affirmed by Prime Minister Stephen Harper. He drew a link between his tough position on crime and immigration by referring to a car accident six years earlier when two young men of Asian descent killed a white woman by racing cars on city streets.

Describing them as 'permanent residents who hadn't become citizens and not failed refugee claimants', Harper's configuration othered these men by emphasising a link between (im)migrants and crime. This 'othering' created a dichotomy that suggested citizens, unlike others, would not commit offences, contributed to discourses that erode public confidence on immigration and built on notions stressing (im)migrant criminality since 2000, for example, Chinese migrants in rusty boats, the 9/11 terrorist attacks and 'failed refugee claimants who committed crimes in Canada [and] . . . challenged deportation after being convicted of offences (O'Neil, 2006b:A1,A19). These extracts reveal how personal, institutional and cultural racism combine in subtle and complicated configurations to reproduce racist discourses on immigration. A combination of personal, institutional and cultural racism strips individuals of dignity, worth and social justice to undermine their sense of self and belonging in a society.

Case study   Devalued overseas qualifications

Ahmed was a skilled engineer with an Iranian PhD who became a refugee in England after the Shah was deposed. Despite living and working in the United Kingdom for several decades, he remains a hospital porter in a large city hospital. He hides his shame in performing unskilled work from his parents in Tehran who receive regular remittances from him. They also do not know that his wife works as a nurse to make this possible. Ahmed refuses to let his children visit their grandparents in case they give the game away, and neither he nor his wife has returned to Iran since their fraught departure.

Institutional racism in immigration legislation

Immigration legislation is a potent source of institutional and cultural racism. Institutional racism is evident in immigration legislation that excludes people from other lands becoming part of a country or being accepted as settled immigrants who belong in a territory on the same basis as those already there. It is embedded in legislative provisions that have a differential impact upon each ethnic group and policies, regulations and practices of specific institutions. These endorse cultural racism with discourses and moral panics created and reinforced by media and political figures passing particular pieces of legislation as Harper's vignette above reveals.

I lack space for a detailed British history, but moral panics about people with African origins leading to their deportation trends can be traced from Elizabethan times (Fryer, 1984) to the present (Lahav, 2004). White British fears of being 'swamped' by foreigners produced the Aliens Act in 1905 to restrict the entry of Jews fleeing the Pogroms of Eastern Europe. The arrival of SS Empire Windrush at Tilbury docks on 22 June 1948 marks the beginning of 'mass migration' to the United Kingdom, but fewer than 500 people arrived. The key definer of difference was skin colour. They spoke English, were Christians, had had an English education in the West Indies as British subjects, and carried British passports that entitled entry without hindrance. Some were war veterans. Many were recruited to work in declining manufacturing industries and under-staffed public services, an issue resurfacing in health and social services. White Britons greeted the newcomers with curiosity, hostility or fear (Levy, 2004).

As immigrant numbers rose during the 1950s and 1960s, white people's fears led to racial violence in Birmingham, Nottingham and West London (Small, 2007). Moral panics about racial tensions and the ousting of *real* British people from the country were played out everywhere and exacerbated by leading politicians like Enoch Powell in his 'Rivers of Blood' speech of 1968. Orchestrated by the media, moral panics legitimated personal prejudices like refusing private housing to black people; denying black people jobs; restricting entry to high-quality educational institutions. Irish people facing other forms of discrimination and racial oppression also endured such acts.

Discrimination and social exclusion were outlawed; the re-education of white British people began in the 1960s; and legislation ended Commonwealth citizens' unhindered entry to the United Kingdom. Controlling racial tensions led to the Race Relations Act, 1965. It was amended in 1968, 1976 and 2000, the last under campaigns led by Stephen Lawrence's parents. Their allegation of institutional racism among the police was affirmed by Macpherson (1999). This legislation improved harmony across racial divides by promoting community links with multicultural festivals that celebrated ethnic foods and multicultural education. Integration and encouraging black people to learn English – resourced under Section 11 of the 1967 Local Authority Act – were key to this strategy. These discourses reproduced a racialised 'other' – a minority ethnic group incorporated into white British society by a multiculturalism that privileged Anglo-Saxon whiteness in judging 'the other' against their norms.

The notion of patriality in the 1971 Immigration Act carried the principle of the United Kingdom for white people to its ultimate conclusion and turned nationality into an immigration issue, advantaging people whose parents or grandparents had been born in the United Kingdom – mainly white people. Patriality allowed white 'Rhodesians' fleeing Zimbabwe to establish credentials to British passports while Ugandan Asians expelled by Idi Amin could not. A voucher system limiting the number of immigrants on work permits virtually halted permanent immigration, except for family reunifications. The 1981 Nationality Act continued to link citizenship to immigration. Patriality rules allowed white Americans, South Africans, Australians and New Zealanders to gain British passports without setting foot in the United Kingdom. Those born and living here with parents who paid taxes could not. Being born in the United Kingdom no longer gave an automatic right to be British. If applying for citizenship, one parent had to be a British passport holder born in the United Kingdom or the person had to live in the country for ten years after birth. The 1971 and 1981 Acts shifted immigration policy from an open-door to tightly regulated and controlled regime (Layton-Henry, 1985). Vouchers for professionals enabled South Asian men and women to staff crisis-ridden NHS facilities.

Sponsorship for family re-unification purposes is the main route for entering rich countries like the United Kingdom, Canada and Australia. Legislation requires entry requests for dependent family members to include guarantees of provision for their well-being for a specified period. This can become an open-ended commitment to pay for health, housing, education, food and other daily expenditures. Business people with money or those promising to create a business that offers jobs to existing residents do not encounter such restrictions. This suggests one law for the rich and another for the economy-class traveller, indicating a fracturing of racism by class. Immigration status defines entitlement to benefits. Disadvantaged Black Britain was acknowledged in the Scarman Inquiry that followed the riots of 1981 in London. Scarman (1981) recognised 'racial disadvantage [a]s a fact of current British life' but located its practice amongst a few racist people, including some in the British police force, and endorsed racism as personal prejudice. Its persistence led to serious racial tensions. These erupted in 2001, encompassing smaller towns not involved in earlier riots, for example, Oldham (Cantle, 2002) and indicated that institutional racism flourished.

Racism creates insiders as deserving claimants and outsiders as undeserving ones. Restricting outsiders' access to welfare benefits has been partially successful. The Gatecrashers scheme of 1979 and NHS Charges to Overseas Visitors in 1982 sought to limit medical services to those entitled to receive them. The government expected black overseas visitors to be abusing the NHS, but found Americans the largest group of non-British nationals using it. Yet, skin colour, accents and passports became key signifiers of difference in defining those subjected to stricter scrutiny.

During the 1990s, asylum became a hot immigration topic. Few immigrants could enter the United Kingdom through normal channels. Demands for asylum were fuelled by armed conflicts. A raft of legislation was passed, now linking asylum with nationality, citizenship and immigration. These included the Immigration and Asylum Act 1999, Nationality, Immigration and Asylum Act 2002, Asylum and Immigration (Treatment of Claimants) Act 2004 and Immigration, Asylum and Nationality Act 2006. These link immigration status to citizenship rights. Until John Major's government with Michael Howard as Home Secretary popularised the link, asylum did not make the headlines that it does now. Armed conflicts amongst tribes within fragmenting nation-states created by colonialism produced new waves of (im)migrants as people fled armed conflicts, political persecution and the devastation of homelands to seek better prospects elsewhere; for example, Sri Lanka, Zimbabwe, the former Yugoslavia. The Iraqi wars of 1991 and 2003 also produced refugees. Few of these are in Britain – 2.2 million are based in Syria and Jordan; 580 were registered in Britain compared to 9300 in Sweden last year. In the United

Kingdom, from 1998 to 2000, 45,000 people arrived from Africa; 22,700 from the Indian sub-continent; 25,000 from Asia and 12,000 from the Americas. In 2000, about 125,000 people settled in Britain, prompting demands to severely curtail numbers. Discourses about limiting asylum applications catapulted asylum-seekers into the target range of immigration policies driven by moral panics and hysteria in a country with a low birth rate and ageing population. Asylum applications running at 2000 a month have fallen to the lowest level since 1993; only 150 received refugee status (Frost, 2006:1). Those admitted as refugees have dropped over the past three years.

Legislative acts and immigration controls promulgated by New Labour have altered asylum-seekers' and refugees' entitlements. Government discourses demonised them and legitimated institutional and cultural racism whether racist or civic nationalism gained the upper hand. Media hysteria can be whipped up with small numbers. Chris Mullard (1973) identified the 'numbers game' in restricting black people's entry. Ludicrously, John Major argued that six white families from Bosnia were too many asylum-seekers for the United Kingdom. An unspoken taboo was that these families were Muslims seeking refuge from the brutality of the Milosevic regime that was destroying Muslim enclaves in the former Yugoslavia, like Bosnia-Herzegovina. Major's policy of creating safe havens for Muslims in their own country had led to Muslim men and boys being slaughtered in their thousands in Srebrenica in July 1995. Islamophobia entered the political landscape quietly through the back door before its association with terrorism. These discourses create 'ethnoscapes' that affirm Britain as a white Christian country (Appaduri, 1996). Popular and government discourses disregard reality in such cases to affirm narratives of non-belonging. In a BBC survey, two-thirds of respondents self-defined as Christian whether attending church or not and 75 per cent retained their Christian values (BBC News Online, 2006).

Explanations for movements of people include the reserve army of labour thesis that ties (im)migration to generating workers internally and externally by linking 'push' factors (joblessness) in sending countries to 'pull' factors (jobs) in receiving ones. Labour shortages call for (im)migrants even if governments are implicated in racist discourses about immigration, as is occurring in contemporary Britain where New Labour uses 'civic nationalism' to 'crack down' on asylum-seekers and refugees while extolling hiring (im)migrant labour under controlled conditions to keep the economy moving (Billig et al., 2006). A multiplicity of reasons causes people to cross borders and produce constant contradictions in migration patterns (Small, 2007; Abye, 2007).

The state becomes a formulator and enforcer of immigration policy, often farming out the internal policing of immigrants to a range of professionals outside the Immigration and Nationality Directorate (IND) and police force. The welfare state is caught up in policing internal borders as more and more public servants including social workers become unofficial immigration officers checking people's immigration status before providing services. Immigration controls then shift from those policing external borders at points of entry to internal controls. These mechanisms subject incoming black populations and settled ones to higher levels of surveillance and 'fishing expeditions' (Gordon, 1985). Internal surveillance is strengthened by links between government departments, for example, Home Office and IND. Hayes (2006) deems work with asylum-seekers and refugees the last in a line of control initiatives.

In Canada, the Immigration Services Society (ISS) that supports immigrants and refugees reports that 73 per cent had no family and 69 per cent knew no one in the area of arrival (ISS, 2006). In Vancouver, 25 per cent of refugees used food banks regularly and 64 per cent had no family member in paid work. Many of the 300 refugees settling there during the last three years originated in Afghanistan or Iran. ISS considers these 'high-risk' groups in an area that receives 12 per cent of the provincial intake because poverty and lack of services makes it harder to achieve integration. The challenge as ISS saw it was to 'build welcoming and inclusive communities' that were highly diverse. In 2005, British Columbians received 44,734 immigrant settlers, a 21 per cent increase from 2004. Social workers who build community cohesion inform families of services available and enrol children at school to learn English, including in English as a Second Language (ESL) classes. Briskman (2006) led an Australian social work initiative that identified appalling treatment of asylum-seekers by government and private firms. She argues that social work practitioners, educators and researchers could be more pro-active in highlighting their plight.

---

practice tips   entitlement to benefits

Social workers can help asylum-seekers and refugees receive the benefits to which they are entitled by:

- Treating others with dignity and respect.
- Informing them of their entitlements and human rights.
- Knowing the appropriate legislation.
- Assessing needs and linking these to research findings.
- Reducing competition for scarce social resources by arguing that the needs of all – asylum-seekers/refugees and locals are to be met.
- Advocating for policy changes.
- Mobilising community resources.
- Lobbying government.

Cultural racism shapes discourses of rejection

Cultural racism establishes norms for judging outsiders largely in negative terms and privileging insiders in the normalised category. It shapes public discourses that frame who immigrants are and how they are treated. Popular stereotypes of immigrants as uneducated rural dwellers have been weakened by new waves of highly qualified (im)migrants, asylum-seekers and refugees (Abye, 2007). Demonising asylum-seekers and casting them as burdens ignores their higher skills levels and educational qualifications than many British workers (Frost, 2006).

Images of (im)migrants, asylum-seekers and refugees are gendered as male. Women have struggled to get their specific oppressions recognised. These include being at the receiving end of systematic abuse as women through physical or sexual violence including rape during armed conflicts. Canada recognised the gendered nature of the Geneva Convention and accepted as legitimate women asylum-seekers' needs a while ago. Kassindja, escaping female genital mutilation (FGM) in Africa, had a lengthy struggle to establish these rights in the United States (Kassindja and Miller-Basher, 1998). Britain did so in 2006 when the House of Lords ruled Zainab Fornah could get asylum to escape FGM as one in a 'social group that feared persecution'. Social workers have been involved in campaigning for these rights and can ensure they are observed.

Redefining citizenship

Discourses about immigrants cast them as 'aliens' from another planet or non-human species. If they wish to become citizens of a land where they were not born, they have to be 'naturalised'. This perpetuates the idea they are 'alien' or 'abnormal'. Terminologies of 'naturalised citizens' promote discourses of otherness and lesser humanity. Why such distinctions? (Im)migrants are citizens in the countries of origin. Notions of citizenship linked to nation-states are exclusionary and create 'insiders' and 'outsiders' on several levels (Lister, 1997). Given what we know about the power of words and discourses to shape attitudes about or behaviours towards people, the terms 'acquired citizenship' or 'citizenship by acquisition' better describe the process of becoming a national of a country other than that of birth. This approach bares the social processes involved in becoming a 'citizen' of a territory, and exposes citizenship as an exclusionary category.

Citizenship by acquisition can be precarious, as the small print warns that citizenship can be withdrawn if a citizen is deemed to 'threaten national security'. As the definition relies on the state in question, this can give it enormous power over the individual. The potential risk of endangering one's status has convinced some not to become politically active or critical of government to not risk losing acquired citizenship (personal communication). This issue becomes extremely important in the post-9/11 world where protecting a given locality from terrorists can deprive innocent people of citizenship and stifle legitimate criticism and debate.

Immigrants can be deported, regardless of time spent in the United Kingdom, for behaviour deemed not 'conducive to the public good'. Hayes (2006) describes the case of a man, who was not an illegal immigrant, being deported on this ground after serving a prison sentence, although his wife and children had been born in the United Kingdom. Such actions expose ties between citizenship, immigration status and the nation-state; exclude people from entitlements to rights or benefits; and create a category of disenfranchised individuals. Citizens of another country can be denied human rights simply because they cross borders, even though they retain their earlier status. By international treaties, they are entitled to the same human rights (in their country of origin). Why can these be disregarded just because they cross borders, hold another nationality or have resided elsewhere?

Aggregation within the family or family dependency allows those who have not committed crimes to be punished. All members of a family including those born in Britain can be deported if incorrect information was given at the port of entry. This covers not having authenticated dates of birth in conditions where birth certificates might be lacking. In Canada, Joe Taylor, a 'third-generation Canadian' was denied citizenship because he was 'born out of wedlock' to a Canadian soldier and a British mother during the Second World War (McCulloch, 2006). The disregard of individual culpability appears to be spreading. Collective punishment of inno-cent civilians, including those rejected as citizens of a given nation-state is a defining feature of violent conflicts in Rwanda, Bosnia, Israel, Palestine, Lebanon, Iraq, Afghanistan or Sudan. National sovereignty can detract from the duty to observe human rights.

Restricting non-citizens or outsiders from accessing a country's resources preserves them for insiders. Excluding outsiders from welfare provisions emphasises discourses that cast asylum-seekers and refugees as abusers of welfare and endorse their being denied benefits. In the United Kingdom, asylum-seekers and refugees are excluded from claiming: income support; job seekers allowance, working family tax credit; housing benefit; council tax benefit; invalidity care allowance; and disability living allowance (Cohen, 2001:49). Exclusion from welfare benefits causes asylum-seekers and refugees great hardship (Frost, 2006). Cast as burdens on society, not as contributors, they are seen to undermine the contrib-utory principle that underpins the British welfare state (Hayes, 2006). Denying sponsored arrivals access to public funds passes welfare costs onto families. These practices are reflected in termi-nologies that reserve welfare for 'citizens', however defined. Globalisation, competition, privatisation and international market-based service providers favour those who can pay for services rather than those needing them. This disadvantages asylum-seekers and refugees who often enter a country without social and financial resources.

---

practice tips   maintaining human rights

Social workers can protect human rights from being endangered in the process of crossing borders by facilitating social cohesion initiatives for all.

➡

Given that every human being is a citizen of one country or other, they can question why citizenship rights are not linked to living on Planet Earth and inalienable regardless of place of residence or birth, especially in countries endorsing the Universal Declaration of Human Rights.

Citizenship rights have been associated with the nation-state but need not be. Global citizenship as a concept transcends national boundaries, but its realisation is a distant dream. Passports, a nineteenth-century invention, were not required until recently. No immigration officer held up a 'Grand Tour' of white British aristocrats on its way to Italy (Douglas, 1983). Claims to cosmopolitanism already enjoyed by wealthy people may revive such practices.

Wanted (im)migrants

Migrants have been welcomed to meet labour shortages in the welfare state. Externally trained overseas staff recruited to vacant posts instance privileged entry for health and social care workers to meet serious shortages (Devo, 2006). This solution causes complications for both receiving and sending countries. A receiving nation benefits from filling empty positions, but entry into skilled ranks is not guaranteed. Many (im)migrants are employed in positions below those warranted by their skills level or qualifications (Frost, 2006). The British Medical Association (BMA) warned that new rules regulating entry for overseas doctors from outside the EU were misinterpreted to exclude refugees from the Highly Skilled Migrant Programme, thus endangering the NHS' reputation as a fair employer. The BMA is consulting the CRE to determine if this action is discriminatory (Millar, 2006).

Case study   Overseas recruitment of social workers

Removing professionals from industrialising countries can damage the economy and service infrastructure in places that desperately need skills. At least 1.3 billion people across the globe lack access to basic health care because no health workers are available (Laurance, 2006). Similar problems arise in British social work. Serious shortages are being met by importing overseas expertise. Batty (2003) claims the majority of Zimbabwean social workers are in the United Kingdom. Birmingham has recruited 62 overseas

➡

social workers from Zimbabwe. These workers are poorly inducted into their new jobs and receive little assistance to settle, once they arrive (Devo, 2006). They are inadequately prepared for the different expectations, roles and skills needed here. These can differ considerably from those practised in the country of origins, despite transferable skills and a colonial past that makes them familiar with British institutions including the welfare state (Sewpaul and Hölscher, 2005; Devo, 2006). The recently formed Zimbabwean Network of Social Workers is taking up issues, demanding better induction for newly appointed practitioners from Zimbabwe (Devo, 2006). If a receiving country covers training costs, a sending country can offset losses from limited training budgets (Dominelli, 2004b). The UK Code of Practice for International Recruitment launched in 2006 does not address these specific criticisms. It emphasises rights for individual workers during recruitment.

Social work interventions with (im)migrants, asylum-seekers and refugees

Social workers receive little support or training to work with (im)migrants, asylum-seekers and refugees and often lack knowledge for doing so (Dominelli, 2004a). Legislation can restrict their capacities to work within social work values and ethics that promote social justice. Social workers are likely to act as gatekeepers rationing resources to those defined as 'deserving', reinforcing institutional racism in the process (Dominelli, 1997). Or, to quote Hayes (2006:192), social workers become involved in 'a culture of suspicion and blame to justify the unjustifiable'.

Similar trends are evident in other Western countries. Briskman (2005) names three converging discourses in the treatment of asylum-seekers and refugees in Australia: containing people-smuggling; controlling immigration; and protecting borders. She argues a conspiracy of silence about government's role in their maltreatment, including its culpability in the drowning of 353 asylum-seekers in 2001, exacerbates the likelihood of self-harm, despair and loss of hope as asylum-seekers' dignity and worth is removed in Detention Centres that contain them. Briskman (2006:27) claims a hospital was declared a detention centre when a mother gave birth so as to deny the child Australian citizenship, an act she terms 'organised and ritualised abuse'. Condemnation of such treatment closed the

Woomera Detention Centre. Briskman asks social workers to expose inhumane practices and support individual challenges.

Australian detention centres are run by private prison contractors who operate behind a wall of secrecy and use confidentiality to prevent access to information about what happens to those under their care. This highlights a new danger in privatisation that social workers ought to be aware of and address. Briskman (2006) suggests social work practitioners and educators promote the interests of refugees, even when subject to competing accountabilities, by exposing human rights abuses, breaches of international obligations and unethical practices while working alongside marginalised and oppressed people to present their views and solve problems.

Scarce welfare provisions

Scarcity and inadequate social provisions permeate the public service infrastructure and social policies covering education, health, housing or personal social services. Scarcity complicates entitlement claims already restricted by immigration status and citizenship. Public discourses on scarcity pit the needs of different groups against others – settled British citizens against those who are not. Margaret Hodge affirmed these dynamics in 2007 by suggesting that (im)migrants should be denied access to social housing. British citizens who spend considerable periods abroad may be caught out by regulations on immigration status, for example, exclusion from Child Benefit for British children living overseas and support for university tuition fees unless meeting a residential requirement.

With the fifth largest economy in the world, the United Kingdom is a wealthy country by any standards. It can pay for citizen entitlements. As a signatory to the UN Universal Declaration on Human Rights, the Convention on the Rights of the Child and numerous other UN instruments guiding state conduct in preserving the well-being of those living within its borders, the United Kingdom has a duty to meet the welfare needs of its peoples. The state's failure to provide public services to all residents is an issue about political choices and priorities. Social workers can advocate for change and ensure that all peoples' needs are met irrespective of immigration status by presenting evidence that challenges the premises on which political choices are made.

Services to asylum seekers and refugees

Housing, health and education, key resources needed by asylum-seekers and refugees, are difficult to access. The National Asylum Support Service (NASS) was developed in 2000 in response to local authorities like Kent and London claiming that they bore a disproportionate share of costs in servicing asylum-seekers and refugees. NASS used dispersal to reduce housing demand on 'overburdened' receiving communities. This created a separate and inferior system of support for asylum-seekers by placing claimants lacking support services in substandard housing on estates overwhelmed by multiple deprivation. Competition for non-existent resources increased tensions with local residents leading to violence against those seeking a safe place like Firsat Dag, a Kurdish refugee murdered in Glasgow. The city provided 2500 houses, but lacked funding to cover social care, health or education costs, which the Home Office refused to fund as these were considered local authority responsibilities, not theirs.

Refugee children's entitlement to schooling was undermined by Blunkett's demand that detention centres provide it. Private firms manage the centres that house distressed people pending decisions on asylum applications; for example, Group 4 at Harmondsworth. Detention centres as accommodation centres with education facilities were proposed in the Nationality, Immigration and Asylum Act 2002. The suggestion was fiercely opposed within Parliament and without (Travis, 2002). Opponents argued it undermined schools as sites for integrating young refugees into peer groups and broader society. Inferior provisions would further exclude and stigmatise asylum-seeking children, exacerbate their vulnerability and destitution and discourage social integration while enabling private providers to access 'soft' outlets for making profits in those institutions they managed.

Health provisions are problematic because asylum-seekers including children are excluded from services if subject to immigration controls (Frost, 2006). GPs impose limits on numbers that they accept on their lists. Their actions have been challenged in court. These ruled that local authorities have a duty of care, but are exempt from providing services if short of resources. Attempts to site detention centres in rural areas amongst affluent populations have encountered stiff resistance. Those proposed in Oxfordshire,

Cambridgeshire and Kent were withdrawn after hostile demonstrations. Asylum seekers got the message of being unwanted; their interests not mainstreamed. Hubbard (2005) argues this resistance signals a desire to maintain 'white privilege'.

Social workers may be part of an Asylum Team providing accommodation, money, vouchers (being phased out), GPs and school places. Those in local authorities lost the requirement to support asylum-seekers unless there are concerns about children. These responsibilities were also threatened when David Blunkett as Home Secretary sought to exclude these children from the 1989 Children Act and mainstream schools. Social workers' strategy of using Section 20 of the Act not Section 17 to secure more resources for unaccompanied children was affirmed by Save the Children's (2001) report. Child Protection Teams can support families in Immigration Tribunals and campaign for better treatment (Fell, 2004). The Asylum and Immigration (Treatment of Claimants) Act 2004 authorised social workers to reduce benefits to children of failed asylum-seekers. This undermines the 1989 Children Act, Convention on the Rights of the Child and 1998 Human Rights Act that protect rights to family life. Constantly changing legislation that curtails asylum-seekers' access to welfare benefits makes it difficult for social workers to intervene strategically on their behalf.

---

practice tips   supporting asylum seekers and local comunities

Social workers can support asylum-seekers in being accepted by local communities and retaining knowledge of and links to families and communities of origins by:

- Facilitating dialogue with existing local residents.
- Mobilising the community to get decent quality accommodation for all.
- Building networks to secure scarce social resources for disadvantaged people regardless of citizenship or immigration status.
- Arguing for good quality education as a right for all young people.
- Assisting the acquisition and skilful use of English.
- Establishing mentoring schemes to cover everyday life routines and activities.
- Promoting out-reach work.
- Arguing that the Children Act applies to all children.

- Re-establishing connections with families of origins where safe and advisable.
- Improving care by foster carers and preparing children to return 'home' when appropriate.
- Focusing on resilience and strengths alongside their vulnerable situations.
- Taking care of their psycho-social and emotional health and other needs.
- Securing benefits granted by the Geneva Convention and British legislation.
- Working with people in relevant communities to promote cultural links and connect to networks specifically tailored to a particular individual.
- Communicating appropriately with other agencies involved in asylum-seekers' lives and sharing good practice with them.

Unaccompanied minors, young refugees and asylum-seekers

Legislation reflects the latest political priorities and moral panics. It impacts on how those providing services access a given population, services they deliver and where. Unaccompanied minors remain under local authority care as determined by the Children (Leaving Care) Act 2000, but young people aged 18 or more are housed in accommodation centres while asylum applications are processed. In practice, this excludes young people under 18 who cannot prove their age because they lack the necessary documents and those supported by social services but not in care. Living in accommodation centres impacts negatively on their interactions with local people, sense of freedom and educational opportunities. Those in accommodation centres can leave after 6 months if their applications have not been processed. The likelihood of this is high as applications on average take 13 months to complete. A further 26 weeks can elapse for an appeal of the initial decision to be heard (Refugee Council, 2002a,b). The Immigration and Asylum Act 2002 withdrew the right to work granted in 1986. This reduces the young peoples' ability to retain their dignity, given that paid work facilitates self-support and contributes to society while voluntary work lacks the status of waged employment, however poorly paid.

Young people under 18 constitute 55 per cent of families seeking asylum in the United Kingdom. In 2000, there were 12,080 such children in England; 80 per cent living in London and the South

East (DH, 2001a). By 2002, this rose to 17,685 in London (LASC, 2003). Social services are responsible for providing services to these children. Following the establishment of NASS and a policy of dispersing asylum-seekers across the United Kingdom, numbers increased in Scotland. In 2001, one-third of Scottish asylum-cases were children (2042); 1029 of them attended schools, mainly in Glasgow (SASC, 2002).

These young people have been defined as 'vulnerable' and in need of 'rescuing' from long-term social exclusion, especially if they reached the United Kingdom alone. Chapman and colleagues (2003:7) interviewed 200 young refugees and identified key needs as 'guidance, friendship and financial support'. Their main aspirations were to be educated in Britain and contribute to society. Qualifications and language proficiency were essential for success, but 85 per cent had no UK-recognised educational qualifications; 52 per cent had an award from the country of origin. Most could not read or write English with confidence; 54 per cent could speak it satisfactorily. Most of the sample was young men; 59 per cent were Muslim. Families as crucial sources of support were often unavailable: 55 per cent travelled without family or people they knew.

Language difficulties, lack of family and friends and not having British educational qualifications were barriers to inclusion in British society. These young people were positive about their futures and 64 per cent wanted to settle in Britain, including raising families here. They wanted meaningful employment so they 'could earn the right to belong in Britain and become citizens on an equal footing' (Chapman, Calder and Danton, 2003:10). These requests were ignored; they did menial jobs. About 6 per cent lived with family or friends already settled in the United Kingdom, only two were in foster care. Despite dependence on NASS and local authorities for adequate housing, only 36 per cent lived in social housing; 21 per cent were in private rented accommodation, often a 'small dirty room' or 'friend's sofa' (Chapman, Calder and Danton, 2003:8). Those who became young parents enjoyed parental status but negative stereotypes about them intensified. Negative media coverage alleged they wanted 'everything for free' while living in highly deprived areas 'brought out the worst in people' (Chapman, Calder and Danton, 2003:10–11).

Nearly all (96 per cent) the sample rated the Refugee Council's Panel of Children Advisors helpful; 40 per cent chose NASS; and

31per cent Local Authority Social Services Departments (Chapman, Calder and Danton, 2003:13). One-third of young people living in accommodation provided by NASS did not rate it helpful. Racism impacted upon these young people, 55 per cent of whom felt that they were:

> disadvantage[d] because of their race . . . 'race' was defined as skin colour, language, religion, country of origin, and refugee status . . . non-white Britons were the most unwelcoming towards them.
>
> (Chapman, Calder and Danton, 2003:12)

The majority community should not assume that black peoples do not racialise different groups in their midst. They are compromised by racist frameworks that impact on their life chances. Black people may feel more vulnerable and subjected to racism because asylum-seekers are receiving bad press, as was the case for three Asians sentenced for stabbing asylum-seekers at a Glasgow school. It also illustrates that scarcity increases tensions amongst deprived groups.

---

putting it into practice

- How would you allocate scarce council housing in a rural area when a poor British Muslim family of two parents and three young children and a Somali refugee (i.e., one with permission or leave to remain in the United Kingdom) woman with four small children both request the one available unit on the grounds of being homeless?
- How would you protect the human rights of a 15 year-old unaccompanied child (no birth certificate) who refuses an immigration officer's demand for a dental x-ray?
- What is the significance of transnationality in work that social workers might undertake with asylum-seekers from the Democratic Republic of the Congo?

Further reading

Hayes, D. and Humphries, B. (eds) (2004) *Social Work, Immigration and Asylum: Debates, Dilemmas and Ethical Issues for Social Work and Social Care Practice*. Basingstoke: Palgrave Macmillan.

Roer-Strier, D., Strier, R., Este, D., Shimoni, R. and Clark, D. (2005) 'Fatherhood and Immigration: Challenging the Deficit Theory', *Child and Family Social Work*, 10:315–29.

8 | Anti-racist community work

Introduction

Communities are contested spaces whether formed on the basis of identity, interest or geography. Confined geographic areas with concentrations of minority ethnic people are called 'ethnic enclaves', 'ethnoscapes' or ethnically-based communities. Multi-cultural Britain's spatial segregation symbolises divisions between diverse communities that live side by side. Ethnoscapes occupied by black communities have higher levels of poor schooling, poor housing, poor health, poverty, unemployment and other social exclusions than white communities, even when class is considered (Clark and Drinkwater, 2002). Trevor Phillips, Chair of the CRE, warned that *de facto* segregation could undermine British multicul-turalism (Phillips, 2005b).

Communities inhabited by poor black and white people lack social resources to achieve decent standards of living and quality of life. Their physical environment is often run down, badly polluted and noisy. It envelopes lives in urban landscapes of poverty and scarcity. In poor communities, competition for scarce social resources is excessive; fear of the 'other' abounds. Negative state discourses of (im)migrants, asylum-seekers and refugees fan racial discord. Negative stereotypes contribute to the failure of different communities to interact effectively, or undertake action that bene-fits all. The state has to take significant steps to eradicate poverty from disadvantaged communities. The task cannot be left to philan-thropists like Bill Gates or Warren Buffet, who use personal priori-ties to decide causes worthy of support with private wealth.

Negative stereotyping of black communities produces antagonis-tic social relations between black and white residents living along-side each other and facilitates the unscrupulous exploitation of scarcity in social resourcing by perpetuating myths that black people acquire more than their share – a point exploited by overt extremists in the British National Party (BNP) and recently, by mainstream politicians. Their responses combine political power-lessness in deprived areas and poor 'race relations' to intensify pressures within and between different ethnic communities and can spill into violent confrontations. State indifference to their plight and failure to address class inequalities in *all* communities exacerbate these tensions. The BNP is becoming more active in local communities, recognising that escalating white working-class fear is a greater source of power than that gained via the ballot box. Its leader, Nick Griffin, expressed his use of this opening as: 'If we can't achieve anything in the parliamentary sense, we'll achieve it . . . by going into communities . . . it's easier than fighting elections' (Doward, 2006:13).

---

practice tips supporting asylum-seekers and local communities

The BNP is organising in favour of white 'indigenous Britons' by launching: the new Christian Council of Britain, a religious movement that opposes multiculturalism; Solidarity, a body that raises funds for the BNP; and Civil Liberty to train lawyers to fight for 'white rights' (Doward, 2006). It has a goal of 'de-Islamifying Europe' because Griffin asserts 'We have had enough of this ghastly multiracial experiment forced on us' (Doward, 2006:13). These discourses converge with those articulated by postmodern critics of multiculturalism and those linking Islam to terrorism.

Racist individuals are situated in communities. Racist policies and practices are elaborated in and through communities, enabling racist dynamics to pervade community structures. A 1997 poll conducted across various European countries revealed that one in three believed they were 'not at all racist' while an equal proportion confessed to 'quite' or 'very racist feelings'. These findings are similar to those collated by the BBC News Online for the United Kingdom in 2002. European research revealed that those admitting to being racist were dissatisfied with their lives. They feared losing their jobs; felt insecure about the future; and experienced deteriorating personal circumstances (Gearty, 1999). *These findings emphasise the centrality of tackling scarcity to promote social harmony and using social resources to reduce structural inequalities and redistribute power and resources in socially equitable ways.* Uncertainties about ameliorating one's status, limited future prospects, and lack of hope are key elements in social exclusion. Poverty can encourage black and white communities to become allies in removing structural inequalities.

Community workers as part of the social work profession engage with communities to resolve social problems; work with local people to identify unmet needs; plan their resolution; create alliances; undertake action; and network for that purpose. Community work initiated under diverse government initiatives to regenerate and energise disadvantaged urban communities has equal opportunities policies attached. Black people are under-represented in these schemes and get less of the monies. In this chapter, I examine community work's role in revitalising communities and its relevance for black and white ones. Stereotyping, environmental degradation, poverty, violence and crime shape perceptions of communities and the relative positioning of actors within them.

Social workers as advocates for harmonious pluralistic communities interacting in egalitarian frameworks have a major role in arguing for resources for those in need and standing against divisive policies and political parties that exploit difference to perpetuate structural inequalities and racist stereotyping. I look at these in light of various recent 'flashpoints' in community relations, for example, Oldham. Responses to these focused on bringing communities together rather than celebrating cultural differences, as did earlier ones in Brixton or Broadwater Farm in the 1980s.

(Re)configuring difference in poor communities

The term community is contested. It is typically conceptualised as the people who live in a locality and share a set of characteristics including language, religion, nationality, 'race', ethnicity and other social divisions (Abercrombie, Hill and Turner, 1994). Some think of community as a set of fixed, immutable attributes; others see it as a dynamic, fluid and changing entity formed through human interactions that bring people together on the basis of locality, identity and/or interests that define socially acceptable norms or 'givens' for a specific group as long as consent to maintain it exists. There are many different types of communities. Consensual 'givens' underpin social relations in a community as everyday life practices that are not questioned by its adherents (Dominelli, 2006b). Community formation is contextualised in particular ways. A specific community can be (re)defined differently if an existing definition is challenged or attributes normally submerged become prominent.

A community, however formed, integrates a number of different features together to define itself. People configure attributes in various combinations to meet specific ends like nation-formation; assign specified places to constituent groups; and establish community as a dyadic entity that brings together 'insiders' who oppose those cast as 'outsiders'. Binary dyads are constructed around different attributes defined in opposing pairs, for example, insider–outsider; black–white; men–women; adults–children; good–bad; assertive–submissive; faith-based–non-faith-based. These dyads establish communities based on shared attributes or sameness: similarity is valued, difference is not. This creates communities as simultaneously inclusive and exclusive.

Social relations within these dyads revolve around power relations based on zero-sum notions of power that conceptually and in practice configure the dominant part of a dyad as having power over the other element, affirming relations of domination in the process. These power relations value one attribute over others and underpin dynamics of oppression. In dyads that create racialised communities, one 'race' or ethnicity is produced as dominant by becoming accepted or defined as such. People within these communities or outside them can accept, accommodate or resist these definitions, setting in train motions that reproduce, reform or replace existing social relations. Neither identity nor community can be understood outside of power relations. They are created within and by power relations while (re)forming these at the same time.

Case study   Configuring and experiencing difference

A white middle-class, young English woman is configured differently from a white middle-class, older English woman. The position, status and opportunities accessible to each will be different although they may live in

➡

the same geographic community and share aspects of identity, resources and power. Because the defining difference is age, with old age being structurally devalued, the older woman will be cast in a socially subordinate position to the younger one, even if she challenges it as an individual. If she does so, this will be seen as unusual, perhaps deviant, because she will be questioning established norms that favour youth. In this interaction, she will be socially configured as old while she reconfigures herself as not old. Similar dynamics occur in relation to racist configurations of the black–white dyad. Black is structurally configured as inferior, so poorer positions, status and opportunities are allocated to black people who have to undermine these assumptions if they are to realise personal ambitions, individually and/or collectively. They utilise agency to challenge and transform broadly accepted social structures and norms.

Communities are simultaneously unified and fractured along different dimensions within one part of a dyad and between its two constituent parts. A community defined on the basis of ethnicity and 'race' interacts with other dyads that exist in the same space, for example, gender, age, disability, sexual orientation, so that a given community is configured differently within each social division or combination of them.

As communities are created in and through negotiated interactions with others, their formation is not a one-way imposition by the dominant group over the subordinate one. Traffic between them is two-way; each influences the other, even if one achieves dominance at the other's expense. Communities have permeable borders that can be shaped by others, adapted to and changed with different social, economic and political circumstances. What occurs in one community can impact upon another. Change can be significant and alter social relations in both communities. Cultural communities are vulnerable to such shifts and affected by cheap travel, information technologies and mass communications. A cultural community may be diffused across the globe while itself integrating elements from other cultures as in fusion cuisine or fashion.

People configure communities by bringing together different environmental factors, physical attributes, social forces and power relations to create various permutations of it. Focusing on one definition of community is a *political* choice guided by the desire to achieve certain objectives. A community defined primarily through ethnicity has to address diverse internal social divisions like gender, class, sexual orientation, age; and develop strategies to deal with the differences generated. These can create tensions in communities; for example, Christian communities refusing religious office to homosexuals or rejecting women priests. Dealing with change by hanging on to certainties in contexts of uncertainty is a major factor behind resistance to including others. Another is a refusal to cede privileges that go with higher status. Controlling and managing uncertainties is crucial for stable societies to enjoy a secure social order.

Communities sure of their place in the world give diversity space for self-defined roles within it. Those that feel threatened curtail space for self-expression to preserve culture and impose undifferentiated social unity. Communities have responded to the 'woman question' differently at various points in history. Liberal democracies under pressure from women and men compromised to create spaces for women to advance their concerns. In societies like Nazi Germany, white (Aryan) German women were reconfigured to deliver a pure ethnic race under restrictive definitions of motherhood that celebrated women as mothers while denying these rights to Jewish mothers. In slave-oriented societies like the eighteenth-century United States, African American women assumed traits that white America devolved onto black men to enable black families to survive slavery (Weiner, 1997).

Muslim women in traditional dress, as symbols of Islamic societies, have borne many Western attacks on their culture. In France, the banning of religious symbols included the 'headscarf' worn by Muslim women. Canadian newspaper coverage of suspected terrorists arrested in Toronto in 2006 focused on women relatives, none of whom were arrested, to emphasise difference as foreign or dangerous because they wore Muslim dress, the men did not. Jack Straw pushed this issue onto the British media in late 2006 by declaring that the niqab (full veil) prevented communication. His claim seems sexist, racist and disablist. Visually challenged people including Straw's colleague David Blunkett, communicate effectively without *seeing* anyone. Non-verbal communication, words, eyes and even dress can tell someone who is really listening more than is being articulated. By Straw's intervention, a private issue about dress and personal life-style choice became a signifier of not belonging in the United Kingdom and played into a highly charged political context where Islamic difference was defined as dangerous if not treasonous. Post-7/7, Muslim men and women, subjected to negative treatment, are portrayed as irrational or fanatic and entire communities configured as 'other'. These indicate that context and situation (re)configure attributes linked to ethnicity, 'race' and racism differently. Various ethnicities engage in constructing migrant communities, including those from sending and receiving countries.

Differing expressions of sexuality and the reproduction of successive generations complicate inter-communal relations. The West's growing liberalism around sexual orientation and marriage is being opposed in Christian and Muslim communities. This produces opportunities for new cleavages within and between communities; alliances between people who previously saw each other as enemies; and oppositional groups. Demographic restructuring of the population also impacts on inter-ethnic relations. For example, the age profile of ethnic groups in Oldham is changing. According to the 2001 Census, white people of working age in the city are expected to decline from 87 per cent in 2001 to 73.5 per cent by 2021; the black population will more than double from 11.5 percent to 23.8 per cent during this period (ONS, 2002a).

Community workers have learnt how the dynamics of racism operate in communities and in practice. The Gulbenkian Community Work Group's (1973) *Current Issues in Community Work* did not recognise racism as a key issue for white practitioners and treated communities as homogeneous and white. Even when acknowledged, racism was marginalised or deemed the problem of a few prejudiced people. A focus on personal racism occurs at the expense of institutional and cultural racism and linkages between the three. White people ignore interactive links between different types of racism; miss important targets of action; reinforce cultural, institutional and personal racism. As Ohri, Manning and Curno (1982:6) put it: 'Their neighbourhood is invariably one that excludes "the blacks" who live next door or over the road' and racism becomes a matter to be educated away with multicultural gatherings and food sharing. By the mid-1990s, community work competences took note of anti-racist practice (ACW/Mainframe, 1994). The Federation for Community Development Learning (FCDL) that sponsors the National Training Network of Black and Minority Ethnic Practitioners (UBUNTU) formed by black workers to foster their interests tackled these but the complexities of dealing with racism and its interactive dynamics remain in practice. Ledwith (2005) argues that addressing these in groups composed of black and white women requires careful and detailed work and the creation of trusting relationships.

Stereotyping communities: violence, crime and substitution strategies

Stereotypes are representations that apply a particular attribute to a whole community or social group, regardless of relevance. Individuality is lost by treating people as the same. They are embedded in unitary formulations of identity and frozen in time. Negative stereotypes depict people in harmful terms. Stereotypes link violence and crime to discourses about order and security at black people's expense. Since 9/11, people of Islamic faith and those of Arabic ethnicity have been demonised and cast as 'terrorists' who threaten liberal democracies. Underpinned by Islamophobia, 'stop and search' policies emphasise those who look 'Arabic' or Middle Eastern, indicating their religious faith has been racialised and ethnicised. Islam is now associated with danger and uncertainty, despite its associations with peace (Ahmed, 2003). This calls for 'Arabs' and Muslims to be controlled and to ensure safety for Western societies.

---

practice tips   substitution strategies

The stereotype of the Islamic terrorist does a grave injustice to the majority that observes this faith. The caricature would be obvious if the words 'Islamicists are terrorists' were substituted by 'Christians are terrorists'. I call this a substitution strategy. Substitution strategies assist bridge-building efforts across racialised ethnic and religious differences by highlighting logical absurdities and facilitate rethinking a situation.

Substitution strategies can help us appreciate the points at which prejudices and stereotypes replace thinking about the relationships between different social groups. They can promote harmonious relationships between ethnic groups, particularly at the individual level, by addressing personal racism. In these situations, being well-informed is a valuable tool. For example, knowing that Islam is a religion that promotes peace can reorient people's capacity to draw similarities between the situation they face and others like it. Knowing that Christianity has criminal elements whose misdeeds are addressed through the criminal justice system enables people to take a balanced view of the subject and not condemn all Christians as criminals. A substitution strategy would enable people to reassess their attitudes to Muslims. Taking specific individuals who commit offences through legal processes to be dealt with in a just and proportionate way would not condemn an entire community.

Case study   Networking

An awareness of a community's capacity to transcend national borders and create a wider community amongst its diasporic elements is evident in Muslims' formation of a global Islamic community the 'uemma'. Diasporic communities are formed through networks of identification, usually unitary ones; common communication, exchange mechanisms; and ties of support. These networks can cultivate cultural practices that promote peace and harmony between different social groups or create destruction and mayhem. The networks can be official, informal or illegal. Campaigns to end discrimination and social exclusion are sustained by such networks. To understand their allure and spread, it helps to place network formation within broader social contexts.

Failure to bridge different ethnic communities amidst security concerns can jeopardise innocent lives. The shooting of Brazilian Jean Charles de Menezes as a 'suspected terrorist' of 'Middle Eastern' appearance exposes a tragic stereotype that undermines community well-being. Many national, religious, cultural and ethnic communities get caught in the cross-fire of assaults committed against those not directly involved in a particular conflict, as lists of nationalities affected by New York's 9/11, the Madrid 3/11 and London's 7/7 reveal. Non-violent ways of resolving disagreements between different communities must become the norm if future atrocities are to be prevented. Social workers and community workers, skilled at promoting non-violent conflict resolution, can promote racial harmony if they direct their energies to 'dialogue across differences' (Dominelli, 2002a). No depth of regret can bring back lives lost by stereotyping Islamic, Christian or other communities and so their use is best avoided.

Resisting racial oppression, everyday life practices and social structures

Resistance to oppression is crucial to eradicating racism at personal and structural levels. Resistance takes place in everyday life practices (ELPs) alongside cataclysmic disruptions to the social order. The former occurs in daily interactions between oppressed peoples and those who oppress them. Resistance involves links with others through networks, campaigns and other forms of direct action to create circles of resistance at the personal, institutional and cultural levels. The binary dyad of oppressor and oppressed can be misleading and does not encompass the whole of a person's identity. An individual may oppress others on a single social division while themselves being oppressed on another; for example, a white woman oppressing a black woman. A person can oppress people on one dimension of their identity and be non-oppressive on others; for example, a man may act in sexist ways towards women but reject racism. Choosing whether or not to act in anti-racist directions is shaped by people's priorities and views about their own and other peoples' place in society. They may support the status quo by doing nothing. This act also involves the exercise of agency.

Conscientisation in changing personal and political behaviour

Individuals are more or less aware of the social relations guiding their realities. Changing perceptions of these involve complex and extensive processes that enable them to confront unacceptable parts of behaviour and to strengthen and develop those supporting egalitarian relationships with those different from them. These are deeply personal and political choices rooted in everyday life practices and social structures. Freire (1970) called the process of gaining awareness 'conscientisation'. Becoming conscious of personal racism as racist beliefs, attitudes and behaviours, and of structural racism in its institutional and cultural variants, is essential to becoming anti-racist. Conscientisation helps people understand themselves – who they are, their value system, and role, position and status in society. Making links between one's perception of the self and place in a community is central to using this knowledge in practice. White people's innermost concept of positive selfhood rests on a fragile sense of being non-oppressive. Being aware of processes whereby one personally colludes with institutional racism can make them extremely uncomfortable with, and dispirited by, the realisation that they oppress others. They are more likely to experience discomfort and feel guilty if oppressed along some other social division themselves.

Awareness of socially constructed roles enables people to improve situations by eradicating oppressive social relations between different community groups. Rooting social processes in biological attributes essentialises identity and casts it as immutable and disempowering both for people who oppress and those who are oppressed. People who consider racism a biological phenomenon can engage in avoidance strategies (Chapter 1) that facilitate collusion with structural racism. They will utilise strategies that minimise involvement in anti-racist behaviour while maintaining their image as liberal and tolerant. Provided that they see themselves as not racist, they will not enact anti-racist initiatives. Those who acknowledge and recognise racism in their own and others' behaviour will find it easier to engage with the deconstruction of all three forms of racism if they understand how it is socially configured through their actions, those of others and their embeddedness in social relations and structures.

Consciousness-raising endeavours, as part of the process of knowing oneself, link personal circumstances to social issues. These help people connect individual behaviour to structural constraints, including its institutional and cultural variations.

---

practice tips   knowing oneself

To know oneself, an individual has to deconstruct value systems, prejudices, identity traits, position in society and privileges that accrue on individual, group, community and national levels. This entails a holistic exploration of power relations in interactions that occur in different arenas. Some will be controlled by the person; others will not. Once they are aware of these complexities and the connections between different aspects of their realities, individuals can analyse their interactions with others and explore their self-concept as tolerant, decent human beings.

Understanding the processes whereby oppression is socially constructed enables people to acquire confidence in their ability to change social relations, alter their own behaviour and be held accountable for their actions. Undertaken in a way that allows people to explore fears without being humiliated or losing face through dignified, respectful processes strengthens their ability to engage with and continue change endeavours. If people cannot retain self-respect, they will feel disempowered and less willing to take the risks involved in initiating and consolidating personal and social change. The specific activities that help an individual undergo these sea-changes depend upon the person; position in the social structure; personal skills and knowledge; resources available; and constraints to be addressed. An individual may benefit as a member of a dominant group without directly creating these privileging structures. Institutional and cultural racism may involve and implicate white people indirectly in perpetuating racist social relations in ignorance of doing so.

> **Case study**   The priviledge of whiteness
>
> A white British person could benefit from racist dynamics that exploited black people under colonialism without being directly responsible for creating the edifices these privileges rested upon. For example, white slave traders who brought Africans to Liverpool developed Britain as an industrial superpower by using their labour and resources to give the country an advantage over other nations, i.e., as expropriated value added. Slave-labour facilitated a rise in living standards for all inhabitants at the time. It was differentially and unevenly distributed amongst residents with white upper classes gaining most.

That advantage has not been lost; but built upon. Those residing in Britain today continue to benefit from slavery. Having the fifth largest economy in the world is part of that legacy and locates Britain amongst richer more powerful states. Privileging remains unevenly distributed with some Britons profiting more than others. Significant disparities in wealth and status mar British communities, impacting negatively and primarily on black and minority ethnic groups. For example, Toxteth has had a settled black population for centuries. It remains disadvantaged compared to mainly white parts of Liverpool. Black and white working-class Liverpudlians are both disadvantaged vis-à-vis white upper-class ones. Knowledge of the dynamics of racism and their repercussions, critical reflexive approaches to equality for all and engaging in structural change can be self-empowering. It prepares people to act in more egalitarian ways and fosters cross-community involvement.

---

practice tips change processes

Change processes involve the following stages in no particular order:

- Exploring the contexts.
- Exploring the personal (knowing oneself).
- Exploring the structural (institutional and cultural) levels.
- Engaging in change processes and developing alliances to make this happen.
- Being reflexive.

Redistributive projects in tackling poverty

Poverty, a key form of social exclusion, blocks people from participating fully in economic, social and political structures, and exacerbates competition for scarce social resources. Poverty impacts differentially on black and white peoples and their communities. It is experienced differently by each community, ethnic group and other divisions within it. People of African-Caribbean descent are disproportionately represented amongst poor people; African-Caribbean women do better than men in this group in employment and education. Those of Bangladeshi and Pakistani origins remain amongst the poorest people in the United Kingdom. Employment prospects for those of Chinese and Indian descent have improved since the 1991 Census (ONS, 2002a).

The New Labour administrations under Tony Blair and Gordon Brown have placed tackling poverty and other social exclusions at the heart of the social agenda. The most significant initiative, the New Deal aims to eliminate structural poverty and inequalities through waged work. This programme is linked to neo-liberal strategies about individual self-sufficiency and personal achievements rather than social solidarity and social policies that *also tackle structural inequalities.* The focus on the personal causes of poverty, but not structural ones, makes it of limited impact in pulling people out of poverty. A nod in this direction, the minimum wage, did not eliminate wage poverty so that low-paid workers could genuinely break out of penury. Set at levels that would not lift people out of the poverty trap (£295 per week for a family of four at the time of writing), it reinforced structural inequalities, especially in de-industrialising communities. Structural labour market inequalities like workforce segregation and low pay were unaffected by the New Deal which also ignores contributions to community life from unpaid work provided largely by women (Dominelli, 2006a).

The government's concept of social justice rooted in state interventions, known as the 'Third Way', used social policy to ensure that people's behaviour in communities and workplaces was managed by the state (Giddens, 1998) and conformed with government expectations about a good society (Jordan, 2000). Thatcherite governments before 1997 had sought to achieve the same goals with 'economics as ideology' (Dominelli and Hoogvelt, 1996) and used economic incentives, primarily through severely curtailed welfare budgets, asset-stripping in the public sector, and contract government in the commercial and voluntary sectors to promote market-led welfare (Greer, 1994). Blair grafted Third Way politics onto this existing edifice and carried neo-liberal approaches over to social problems and welfare reform, calling the element relating to public services, 'modernisation'. This generated further opportunities for profit maximisation, but did little to promote the interests of disadvantaged communities and poor people. It also failed to address low pay in the public sector which, as a major location of women's employment, seriously damaged women's capacity to do better through paid work and retained existing gender inequalities in the workforce. Even in 2006, a pay gap of 17.2 per cent between men and women meant that women earned £330,000 less than men over their lifetime. Pakistani-origined women hold the lowest level jobs and earn least (EOC, 2006).

New Labour fostered 'Safer Cities' programmes to reintroduce civility in communities. This emphasised individual pathology over failing social organisations, inadequate community infrastructures, missing social resources and poor social arrangements. Declining communities did not see a promised uplift in material conditions.

Poverty and environmental degradation contributed to inter-communal strife by pitting the needs of one group against another's. The terrain on which racism was played out shifted onto communities of migrants, asylum-seekers and refugees facing poverty and structural restrictions on their entitlement to social resources and jobs, making it virtually impossible for them to tackle poverty while awaiting decisions on asylum applications (Chapter 7).

New Labour has taken limited, albeit important steps in creating less divisive communities. Enhancing equal opportunities came into vogue and people were enjoined to participate in a range of community initiatives that reaffirmed tolerance and decency. In the anti-racist arena, this included making 'incitement to racial hatred' a criminal offence and using anti-social behavioural orders (ASBOs) against people who were verbally or otherwise abusive to neighbours, black and white, in order to create peaceful and orderly communities. ASBOs have become an essential ingredient in ensuring community safety. If those on ASBOs breached conditions on their orders which could include injunctions, being denied access to a particular geographical area and refraining from offensive language, they could receive a custodial sentence. ASBOs focus on individual pathologies and behaviours and ignore the structural causes of crime embedded in structural inequalities like poverty. These are contributory factors in anti-social behaviour including racism as individual and communities assert claims to scarce resources.

Case study   Competing for social and human resources

Claims to resources are racialised according to territorial, ethnic, class, gender and other social divisions (Dominelli, 2000a). A young white working-class woman I interviewed highlighted the competitive nature of her relationship with others in space, jobs, political rights and intimate relationships by saying:

> These . . . [black people] don't belong in [place]. They come here and take our homes and jobs. The government gives them money, whatever they need. Me, I'm stuck here. No job. No prospects. Who's looking after me? And, my . . . girlfriend, she's taken off with one of them . . . She has no shame. One of my former boyfriends loves . . . shagging . . . [black] women. They're good at that. But me, I keep myself to myself.

She exposes her own isolation, along with her view that racism does not touch her life and lack of empathetic contact across racial divides. New Labour amended the Race Relations Act in 2000, drawing local authorities, public bodies and police in its remit to promote racial equality more actively. It excluded 'actions carried out by government officials in accordance with regulations or policies directly prescribed by the Secretary of State' (Chartist, 2000:2). This reduces its potential to hold government accountable for contributing to community disharmonies including its approach to asylum-seekers and refugees. Nor does the Act facilitate positive interactions between different communities. Exclusions intensify mistrust between black and white communities as state legislation, regulations and policies perpetuate institutional racism and legitimate moral panics around particular groups that occupy specific community spaces.

Social work interventions in communities

Community-based groups allied to struggles for racial equality include Rock Against Racism, Trades Union Council (TUC) and Anti-Nazi League (ANL). Each has attracted sizeable numbers to protest against state and police (in)action over racially motivated incidents and murders of black people. These take local action against organisations like the BNP that exacerbate antagonisms across racial divides. The BNP's activities indicate how deeply ingrained racism is amongst those who refuse to accept black people as a legitimate component of the British population. Of concern is that 50 per cent of racist incidents are perpetrated by young people under 16 (CRE, 2003a).

Inter-community tensions over scarce social resources can lead to communal violence. Their expression varies from incivilities and social disorder to civil war. Insufficient progress on eradicating racism from British society has caused serious social disorder in communities. Recent flashpoints flared up during the summer of 2001 in the Northern towns of Oldham, Burnley and Bradford (Cantle, 2002; Clarke, 2002; Denham, 2002). Ted Cantle was asked to investigate the reasons for violence in Oldham, Tony Clarke for Burnley; John Denham for Bradford. Community geographies in these towns contained ethnic enclaves that configured and divided residents along ethnic lines. The investigators' remit was to explore 'community cohesion' as this was thought to be lacking in the communities that resorted to violence.

These divisions discourage inter-community relationships because whether from majority or minority communities, people interacted primarily with those in their own ethnic space. For example, 13.9 per cent of the population in Oldham was black. They were concentrated in four wards that were amongst the most disadvantaged in the United Kingdom. Manningham in Bradford is populated largely by people of Asian descent. The same was true in Burnley. The white majority had limited interaction with them and usually applied racist stereotypes to their presence. Trevor Phillips' (2005a) prediction that separation perpetuates racist social relations and increases tensions between constituent parts in communities seems relevant in these locations.

Persistent poverty was one structural element to be addressed. Others included: celebrating visible differences; being a valued member of Britain; and contributing to well-being across racial divides. Cantle (2002), Denham (2002) and Clarke (2002) emphasised community cohesion and interacting with others to echo Parekh's Report (2000) *Multi-Ethnic Britain* and Ouseley's (2001) Report on Bradford. Both argued for an inclusive Britain where people used ethnic pride to find what they have in common and work towards a shared vision of a better future for all. Had Parekh's and Ouseley's suggestions not been ignored, the ensuing riots might have been avoided. Transcending racial divides remains a dream; its absence does not augur well for community harmony.

---

practice tips   barriers to social cohesion

Cantle's (2002) Report identified barriers to interactions between ethnic groups as:

- Limited interaction between people in different ethnic communities creating 'deep-rooted' segregation between them.
- Parallel worlds created by ethnic groups interacting with those like them.
- Fear about the 'other' pervading social relations between communities.
- Extremists exploiting ignorance and fear about the 'other'.
- Local leaders, national government and police failing these communities by not addressing racial divisions.

Cantle and colleagues (2006:25) recently evaluated progress in bringing black and white communities in Oldham together. Their report applauded the city for progress in:

- Moving from the thirty-eighth most deprived area in the United Kingdom in 2001 to forty-third by 2004.
- Raising the employment of black people from 2.6 per cent of the local authority workforce in 2001 to 7 per cent by the end of 2005.
- Forming forward-looking partnership arrangements with industry.
- Improving police–community relations through its Police Team (although the police lacked an Independent Advisory Group).
- Improving links between different schools and various ethnic communities.

---

practice tips overcoming inter-community antagonisms

Cantle and colleagues (2006) warn of long-term challenges. Inter-community relations have not reduced deep-seated antagonisms at the inter-faith and inter-ethnic levels. Key to transcending these limitations are: developing a long-term strategic vision that all residents own; improving the employment structure for city dwellers; and ensuring equal opportunities for all. Barriers to progress included fear of a 'white backlash' amongst those building bridges between communities in Oldham. Cohesion measures could be undermined if government injected new social resources into black communities while ignoring white ones. BNP activity in the area has highlighted such inconsistencies to keep its core vote stable (Cantle et al., 2006).

Arun Kundnani's (2002) critique of Cantle's Report suggested it sounded the 'death knell of multiculturalism'. Kundnani argues this is a turning point for black Britons because the multicultural myth of different communities living together has been exposed as empty rhetoric. To Kundnani, it was no accident that the Cantle Report was entitled 'Community Cohesion' and exposed Blair's aim of integrating these different communities into a unitary version of Britain that denied its ethnic and cultural diversity. Kundnani sums up this view as:

A set of core values is to put limits on multiculturalism and black people are required to develop 'a greater acceptance of the principal national institutions' ... Racism itself is to be understood as an outcome of cultural segregation, not its cause. And segregation is now seen as self-imposed. The ultimate problem is identified as 'cultural barriers', rather than institutional racism or deprivation.

(2002:4)

Under multiculturalism, black people and their cultures were solutions to earlier formulations of racism. Community cohesion now blames black people and their cultures for racist social relations by holding them culpable for failing to integrate and buy into the Great British myth of equal opportunities for all (Kundnani, 2001). Black people were defined as the disaffected 'enemy within', a depiction that resumed saliency after the London Bombings, and became associated with 'homegrown terrorists' and religious extremists preying on vulnerable youths. Such framings exacerbate views of communities as dangerous places, identified by cultural differences that emphasise language, religion and dress. Religious observance and rituals became signifiers in discourses of difference associated with danger and non-belonging. Kundnani (2001) claims that by measuring religious affiliation the 2001 Census could count the number of Muslims in the country for the first time. This move followed the Home Office's focus on the potential criminality of young people of Bangladeshi and Pakistani origins and racial profiling of British Muslims in police counter-terrorist operations.

The new cohesion agenda centres on notions of citizenship coupled to personal responsibilities and greater *external* policing of individuals. In this, Foucault's 'technology of the self' as imposing internal self-discipline has been found wanting. The proposed biometric identification (ID) card is a measure that will intensify social control of individuals. Intended as a 'passport' to benefits and identification, the card can provide the state with extensive details about individual lives. Potentially, there is no limit to what it can store and be linked to or with. The need for identity cards is contested. The state can already access an array of means of identification. British intelligence quickly identified the London Bombers without biometric ID. Compulsory ID cards did not prevent the Madrid Bombings. People's feelings of inclusion in the country that they live in are a better measure of their commitment to it and its institutions than ID cards.

The government could promote cohesive communities by diverting resources into ending inequalities expressed as alienation, not belonging, or lacking a *valued* place in society and ensuring that equal opportunities is about more than sharing low-paid jobs, poor housing, degraded physical environments and low status. In a democratic country, people believe they can criticise government policies without fear of imprisonment. Their civil liberties are essential elements in the democratic mix and should not be violated by a state ignoring due processes of law. Fair procedures are crucial in curtailing state powers and enhancing community confidence in its monitoring and surveillance functions. Denham's (2002) Report attempted to reconcile these difficulties by suggesting that a strong vision of cohesive communities would tackle discrimination and promote good relations between different groups.

---

practice tips   building social cohesion

Social workers can work to promote cohesive communities. Denham suggested this would involve creating:

- A common vision and sense of belonging.
- A positive valuing of diversity.
- Similar life opportunities regardless of community affiliation.
- Positive inter-ethnic relationships in schools, workplaces and neighbourhoods.

Denham's proposals can foster equality, but are insufficient as they do not address structural inequalities that require new injections of money and initiatives to build common ownership of a community. Poverty and exclusion obstruct this goal. Not reversing exclusion leaves a vacuum filled by those perpetrating inter-communal violence and racial antagonisms.

Social work interventions in instances of inter-communal strife

Bradford's 2001 riots took place in Manningham, causing injuries to people, including police officers, and extensive damage to property. A total of 177 individuals were charged: 137 with the serious charge of 'riot' and 40 with 'violent disorder'. The Institute of Race Relations (IRR) analysed 58 of the 115 convictions made in 2002 and found 'a huge discrepancy in the sentences imposed against the Manningham rioters, most of whom were of Pakistani descent' compared to those in other recent civil disturbances, for example, Belfast. They were also out of proportion to those meted out at the same time to the mainly white rioters on the Ravenscliffe Estate in Bradford. The IRR believes that the Manningham sentences aimed to discipline the entire community not the individuals concerned. The social context that fuelled the disorders was not presented to the courts, despite being cited as crucial to local disenchantment in the Ouseley Report earlier (IRR, 2002).

The IRR findings replicated those found during the Broadwater Farm disturbances of the mid-1980s. Poverty and extensive deprivation also featured on that estate. The disturbances illustrated the lack of mutually beneficial relationships between white and black people living in this poor part of London. However, in Broadwater, social workers and probation officers worked together to ensure that disproportionality in sentencing was reduced via concerted action at the time of the court appearances (Hutchinson-Reis, 1986) rather than relying on research to expose it after the fact as in Bradford. Lack of collective action among professionals in the Manningham situation reflects the split between social work and probation that took place in the 1990s; and reduced activism on social justice issues in practice in both professions.

Broadwater exposed white people's hope that the black community would control, manage and curtail rebelliousness amongst its youth (Hutchinson-Reis, 1986). This expectation remains and was highlighted in the 2001 disturbances and 2005 bombings when government ministers called on black leaders, especially those in Muslim communities, to prevent young people falling prey to extremists. Parents and community leaders in all communities are expected to serve as role models for children and teach young people how to become productive citizens. Ignoring the impact of racism on communities carries the danger of it being a 'dumping strategy' to hold them accountable for what goes wrong and putting it right. These processes involve the amplification of deviance so that anything that a young black person does is deemed outside 'usual' norms, as defined by white society, and more dangerous. Young black people's activities are considered more serious or grave than similar acts committed by young white people. This is because a young black person is configured within notions of 'dangerousness' and membership of deviant communities. Institutional racism, embedded in such definitions, subjects black communities to tighter regimes of police surveillance and control, as indicated by 'sus' laws in the past (Young, 1999) and 'stop and search' today (IRR, 2002).

Young black people are clientised by social workers and probation officers and subjected to the heavy end of sentencing tariffs for being considered 'dangerous' and 'out of control'. This configuration makes it difficult for social workers and probation officers to uphold social justice and human rights (Hutchinson-Reis, 1986) when supporting them as victim-survivors of inter-communal violence and white racism.

Case study   Community social work

Hutchinson-Reis, a social worker on the Broadwater Farm Estate, expressed concern over these problems and argued that it was imperative for social workers to ensure that young black people are treated fairly by police and courts. He said:

> Juveniles were often intimidated by the thought of murder or affray charges being brought against them if they did not co-operate with the police investigation.
>
> (Hutchinson-Reis, 1986:76)

In Broadwater, black and white social workers aiming to maintain client rights on a case by case basis were 'severely obstructed' and 'denied the opportunity to perform that function' (Hutchinson-Reis, 1986:76). Black workers were adversely affected by institutional racism that compromised and negated their racial and political integrity (Hutchinson-Reis, 1986:79). Black and white workers got together to empower themselves and deliver more appropriate services to those who had been charged. Hutchinson-Reis (1986) called this 'community social work' as it was based on community action principles. Weekly meetings were created to discuss issues, share information about individual cases, uncover patterns in the responses to them and consider how to handle subsequent interventions.

Given the large number of young people who had been arrested, detained, charged, remanded into care and needing placements, community social work proved an effective intervention (Hutchinson-Reis, 1986:77). Through their actions, black and white social workers were able to better defend their clients, undermine institutionalised racism and support each other. This model of working could be applied in today's context, especially where black communities fear adverse labelling of residents after social disturbances. It is also a model that promotes organisational change at the level of routine practices in professional social work.

Black parents worry about the lack of safe community space for young black people. Given the rise in black on black crime, they are correct to worry. The murder of 10-year-old Damilola Taylor in Peckham in 2000 was one such instance replicated since. Differing from Stephen Lawrence's murder in exemplifying black-on-black crime, it shook black and white communities. As in the Lawrence case, the police reacted inadequately to capturing and charging the culprits (Stevens, 2002). Social workers' responses to assist those living in this community were notable by their absence.

Implicating personal lives in adverse constructions of communities

The themes of 'arranged marriages as bogus marriages' and young people as involved in 'inter-generational conflict' with parents and elders leave an imprint on how white people view black communities. The acceptability of these traditions can be better understood if placed within specific cultural contexts, accompanied by the values of treating people with respect and dignity and not basing conclusions on stereotypes. White families have had 'arranged marriages' in the past and some would argue that marriages within the royal family, for example, Prince Charles and Lady Diana Spencer, show that this custom is not dead within certain white communities. 'Arranged' marriages should not be confused with 'forced' marriages. Understanding the differences between them is essential if the gap between those compelled and those doing the compelling is to be addressed and for any necessary intervention to be handled in ways that do not endanger the lives of the women involved.

The questioning of parental authority by teenagers is acceptable in the development of white young people and not deemed inter-generational conflict or community breakdown. Why should young people in black families be denied the privileges of testing authority and developing their own responses to key milestones? Ahmed (1984) asked white practitioners not to interpret disagreements between young people and parents as a rupture with their culture or community. This message is important as Asian culture develops, alters and fuses through exchanges with other communities and cultures to produce new and vibrant cultural practices that other people, including white ones, assume; for example, Madonna adopting the bindi. Cultures transcend community boundaries and influence each other through the porous borders of cultural practices to produce cultural change.

---

putting it into practice

- Communities are sites of inclusion and exclusion that constantly change. Inter-community relations are affected by a range of factors, including the demographic make-up of communities, interactions across communities, and distribution of social resources. Growing inequalities and exclusions like racism exacerbate tensions between community groups, pit one ethnic group against another and produce social disorder. Social and community workers can prevent conflict and rebuild torn communities by contributing to tackling personal and structural racism at individual and community levels. Consider how you might become involved in this.
- How would you support a British Muslim woman of Omani descent who is worried that her family might kill her for wanting to marry someone outside her particular ethnic group?
- Discuss the importance of women in maintaining national constructs based on ethnicity.

Further reading

Dwyer, P. (2000) *Welfare Rights and Responsibilities: Contesting Social Citizenship*. Bristol: Policy Press.

Etzioni, A. (1997) *The New Golden Rule: Community and Morality in a Democratic Society*. London: Profile Books.

9 | Conclusions: towards practice in a racially equal society

Introduction

Racial inequality continues to bedevil society. Deeply embedded forms of racism trouble our planet, whether perpetrated by white people or not. Changing social relations under globalisation, including the increasing role of private firms like private equity firms in provisions for children and older people, will create new challenges for anti-racist social work. Global pressures could become especially problematic when profit-maximisation drives practices within these establishments to determine whether they will support egalitarian measures, or even remain open for service. And, they may set standards which are below those endorsed by players in the public arena and voluntary sectors. The struggle to establish egalitarian social relations amongst people is a source of optimism, but setbacks like the failure of the Durban Summit to shift racism make it seem intractable. I conclude by calling for an egalitarian world that people work towards by transforming practices and forming racially equal and just societies wherever they live. I identify policies and resources to assist anti-racist work in the profession and broader society, and offer guidelines for practice. Anti-racist social work aims to change the behaviour of those who benefit from inequalities *and* those disadvantaged by them.

Social workers' contributions to realising an egalitarian, life-affirming world occur through relieving misery and oppression in and through practice. Meeting this aspiration involves them in re-envisioning the profession – its theories, training and practice, and engaging with the following tasks:

- Developing social work agencies that respond to peoples' specific needs.

- Creating egalitarian working relations and workplaces.
- Transforming professional practice to deliver person-centred services and engage with people who access services in empowering, strengths-based ways.
- Sustaining anti-racist social interactions in all communities.
- Working for the creation of egalitarian social relations between people in everyday life routines.

Transforming social work theories and practice

Social work educators and practitioners face ongoing challenges in eradicating racism in the field and academy. They can contribute to socially just, egalitarian social relations that accord each individual dignity and worth and retain self-concepts as humane and tolerant beings by taking action to eliminate racism. Whether a person is black or white, acting as an oppressor or being oppressed, responding will be differently contextualised and contingent on structural location, personal attributes, knowledge, skills and resources. Action takes place in all aspects of life: the personal and social domains; workplaces; political arenas; economy; and interpersonal interactions.

---

practice tips   transforming social work theory and practice

The goal of transforming social work policies and practices to create an anti-racist, socially just profession calls for programmes of action that:

- Espouse equality for all;
- Involve those who access services in their formation;
- Develop people-centred provisions rather than ration resources unfairly;
- Decline to divide people into 'deserving' and 'undeserving' clients; and
- Promote a caring and inclusive professionalism.

Some activities require government interventions – legislative changes around citizenship and immigration; poverty alleviation initiatives; sustainable economies; and environmental protection. Collaborative rather than competitive relationships among professionals can create allies for social workers seeking anti-racist policies and legislation to underpin practice and enable practitioners to: develop capacity to work across racial divides with all client groups; be empathetic in resolving differences between black and white people; and celebrate diversity.

---

practice tips   taking action

Eradicating racism involves social workers in transforming the profession's theories, practices, routines, policies, legislation and cultures at societal and organisational levels. These will impact on personal and structural racism in the profession and broader society. Social workers can build on foundations like the Race Relations (Amendment) Act 2000 to ensure that public authorities promote good race relations and use its provisions to improve social relations between different ethnic groups, encourage discussions about local communities and facilitate processes of egalitarian interaction between diverse ethnic groups. Activities cover education; advocacy; and direct action campaigns and networks. They can: clarify and agree common objectives; recognise diversity amongst participants who bring different issues and skills to the bargaining table and have different views about what should be done, how, and when; and end the conspiracy of silence around racist practices.

Anti-racist social work needs broader social change

The Macpherson (1999) Report identified the need for institutional change. To achieve organisational and social change social workers have to:

- Formulate immigration legislation that resists the demonisation of (im)migrants, asylum-seekers and refugees.
- Reconfigure social relations to promote equality across all social divisions.
- Encourage open and honest debates about how anti-racist policies and practices best meet the needs of individuals, groups and organisations.
- Implement equal opportunities policies in workplaces and ensure that responsibility for eradicating racism does not fall on black employees or short-change their career progression and inclusion as workers.
- Establish machinery to monitor progress on the realisation of anti-racist policies and practices across social work agencies and society more generally.

Transforming social work and the structures that connect it to the broader society involves social workers in forming alliances with other professionals, the lay public, professional associations, trade unions, supportive councillors and politicians. Embarking on social change can be risky. Opposition carries consequences for supporters and opponents. Employees seeking to change a workplace might endanger existing friendships, livelihoods or promotion prospects. Networks of support amongst professional associations and community members can minimise some of these outcomes. Having sufficient allies and being well-rooted in communities can safeguard one's position and mitigate risk of dismissal. Community support and belief in each other can create a sense of security and ownership that maintains continuity of effort acceptable to those involved. Moves that are endorsed by the local and central state are likely to endure longer. *Change is a constant process of evolution and evaluation, not a one-off event.* Thus, the task may be unending.

Ending a 'conspiracy of silence' (Lorde, 1984) on racism in social work exposed the fragility of progressive action. Attacks against anti-racist social work peaked in 1993 and undermined its progress (see Phillips, 1993; Pinker, 1993). Opinion-formers in the media and government objected to making visible the racist dynamics of social work practice and declared that highlighting gaps between racist realities and anti-racist ideals was extreme 'political correctness'. This stance obscured more than it revealed. Calling the eradication of racist practices 'politically correct' deflects attention from and trivialises serious messages about improving social relations (Dominelli, 2004b). But it revealed a crucial weakness: anti-racists' lack of friends amongst government and powerful opinion-formers, an issue that remains to be addressed. Acting in anti-racist directions involves practitioners and educators in:

- Using research to evidence the varied forms of racism in social work.
- Standing against racist behaviour, theories, policies and practices.
- Working individually and collectively for anti-racist policies and practices.
- Forming alliances across society to eradicate structural inequalities.

Abolishing racial oppression in social work needs holistic change (Dominelli, 2002b). Reaching this goal requires allies for support and to maintain morale in tough times.

---

practice tips   practical questions

Practitioners should answer questions like:

- What needs doing, who should do it and why?
- What allies/alliances are necessary?
- How will these alliances be formed and what targets need to be set?
- What blockages will be encountered?
- How can such barriers be overcome?
- Who will evaluate the success (or its lack) of an action and how?

In thinking through these questions, social workers cannot assume that black communities are homogenous, stick together or help each other. In black and white communities, caring relationships are divided across a number of social divisions that produce unequal power relations and tensions in some and solidarity in others. *Each is to be contextualised, thought about, interrogated and addressed in specific terms.*

National professional activities to secure change can draw upon and contribute to international ones, creating allies in the process. Social work as a profession has international associations that can create alliances and collaborations to promote well-being. Endeavours to work in anti-racist and egalitarian ways across differences has featured in the activities of the International Association of Schools of Social Work (IASSW) and International Federation of Schools of Social Work (IFSW) at the Durban Summit; in collaborations to jointly define social work; provide an ethics document for the profession; and agree global qualifying standards. Each document is based on the idea that social work is a profession rooted in the values of social justice and equality and that education and practice should embody these in what is taught and how; in relationships between those who provide services and those receiving them; and in employment practices. Their public statements and endeavours in the United Nations through a global civil society movement show that political priorities, legislation, professional ethics, allocation and management of resources can endorse action to improve the lives of the world's poorest peoples, most of whom are black.

---

practice tips anti-racist social work guidelines

Anti-racist social work tackles personal, institutional and cultural racism by introducing change at both personal and structural levels. Individual conduct in interpersonal relations and the allocation of power and resources in society have to be transformed to eradicate racism. Engaging white people in activities that promote and sustain it will embed anti-racist social work firmly in the social fabric. The guidelines below (in no particular order) can help anti-racist practitioners and educators and apply to other forms of oppression not just racial oppression. Promoting anti-racist practice is good practice of relevance to all. It enables practitioners to:

1. Create new narratives to establish equality across differences in social divisions like 'race', gender, disability, age, class, sexual orientation.
2. Redefine the social work task as one of rendering oppression visible and engaging in action that eradicates it.
3. Deconstruct the 'objectivity' embedded in a professionalism that ignores the lived in day-to-day reality of racial oppression and people's strengths in resisting it.
4. Alter the power imbalance between people who access services and workers
5. Value expertise contained in the subjugated knowledges of oppressed people.
6. Affirm service users' right to participate as equals in determining what welfare provisions are appropriate for them.
7. Refuse to treat individual and group welfare as a commodity that is rationed to exclude people, but seek to enhance personal fulfilment and social well-being.
8. Change the ontological and epistemological foundations of training from those that assume neutrality on major social and ethical issues to make explicit the profession's value base and moral and political stance against oppression.
9. Think of the world as organised holistically with interdependent social relations that bring people together according to agreed shared objectives that acknowledge differences rather than work in binary dyads rooted in relations of superiority and inferiority that submerge differences.

10. Allocate power and resources to promote justice and equality for all.
11. End the theoretical separation between social work and (a) other key elements of the state, especially welfare sectors like housing, education, health, social security; and (b) the 'law and order' apparatus including probation, the police, courts, Home Office, and Immigration and Nationality Directorate.
12. Make visible the connections between these organisations and the social control of people at the expense of their well-being.
13. Expose linkages between policy and practice to avoid the split between theory, practice and policy-making.
14. Form alliances across racial divides, working to establish common ground and ensure that differences are considered.
15. Advocate for political commitment to ending racial inequalities.

Conclusion

From the variety of changes envisaged, anti-racist social work confronts racism in the profession, and exposes and contributes to eradicating racial inequalities in wider society alongside tackling other forms of oppression that intersect and interact with racial oppression. Anti-racist social work creates forms of practice relevant to all ethnic groups, but relevance has to be established in specific contexts. Creating a racially equal society does not begin or end with anti-racist social work. Black and white practitioners can engage in empowering practices to develop a society in which 'race' is not a basis for exclusion and really does not matter (Gilroy, 2000). Forming egalitarian relationships across racial divides requires equal power, equal access to resources, equal opportunities and prospects, and acknowledging work of equal value. Ultimately, black and white social workers will be skilled in working with all clients, regardless of 'race', ethnicity or other social division, and deliver services fit for that person.

Transforming social work in anti-racist directions for both black and white people entails using resources effectively to meet human need. This should be underpinned by involving service users fully in designing, creating and delivering services within an egalitarian framework that rests on solidarity and collective responsibility in caring for others. The focus is not social exclusion and control, but significant improvements in the life chances and well-being of individuals and communities, regardless of 'race', ethnicity, gender, class, age, physical or intellectual abilities, sexual orientation, religious affiliation or linguistic capabilities. Anti-racist social work bridges a racist society and non-racist one to endorse universal entitlements for all.

Bibliography

Abercrombie, N., Hill, S. and Turner, B. (1994) 'Community', *The Penguin Dictionary of Sociology*. Harmondsworth: Penguin.

Abye, T. (2001) 'Ethnicity and Universalism' in Dominelli, L., Lorenz, W. and Soydan, H. (eds) *Ethnicities in Social Work*. Aldershot: Ashgate.

Abye, T. (2007) 'Ethiopian Migration: Challenging Traditional Explanatory Theories' in Dominelli, L. (ed.) *Revitalising Communities in a Globalising World*. Aldershot: Ashgate.

Adams, R., Dominelli, L., and Payne, M. (eds) (2002) *Social Work: Critical Themes, Issues and Debates*. Basingstoke: Palgrave Macmillan.

Ahmad, B. (1990) *Black Perspectives in Social Work*. Birmingham: Venture Press.

Ahmed, A. S. (2003) *Islam Under Siege: Living Dangerously in a Post-Honor World*. Oxford and Malden, MA: Polity Press and Blackwell.

Ahmed, E. (2006) 'Money in Mind', *The Guardian*, 25 November.

Ahmed, K. and Hinsliff, G. (2002) 'Race Row as Blunkett Backs "Snoopers Charter", *The Observer*, 20 June.

Ahmed, M. (2006) 'Ethnic Minority Young People Are Over-Represented in ASBO Numbers', *Community Care*, 2–8 November, p. 6.

Ahmed, S. (1978) 'Asian Girls and Cultural Conflicts', *Social Work Today*, 8 August, pp. 14–15.

Ahmed, S. (1984) *Social Work with Ethnic Minorities*. Paper given at BASW Annual Conference, Nene College, April.

Alba, R., Schmidt, P. and Wasmer, M. (1995) *Germans or Foreigners: Attitudes to Ethnic Minorities in Post-Reunification Germany*. Basingstoke: Palgrave Macmillan.

Alberts, S. (2006) 'Foreign Workers Rally to Protest Proposed US Law', *The Vancouver Sun*, 2 May, p. A7.

Ali, A. A. (2006) *The Caged Virgin*. New York: Simon & Schuster.

Alibhai Brown, Y. (2001a) *Mixed Feelings: The Complex Lives of Mixed Race Britons*. London: The Women's Press.

Alibhai-Brown, Y. (2001b) 'After Multiculturalism', *Political Quarterly*, 72(3), pp. 47–56.

Amnesty International (2004) *Stolen Sisters: A Human Rights Response to Discipline and Violence Against Indigenous Women in Canada*. Ottawa: Amnesty International Canada.

Anthias, F. (1998) 'Evaluating "Diaspora": Beyond Ethnicity', *Sociology*, 32(3):557–81.

Anthias, F. (2001) 'New Hybridities, Old Concepts: The Limits of "Culture"', *Ethnic and Racial Studies*, 24(4):619–41.

Anthias, F. and Yuval-Davis, N. (1993) *Racialized Boundaries: Race, Nation, Gender, Colour and Class and the Anti-Racist Struggle*. London: Routledge.

Appaduri, A. (1996) *Modernity at Large: Cultural Dimensions of Globalization*. Minneapolis: University of Minnesota Press.

Asante, M. (1987) *The Africentric Idea*. Philadelphi: Temple University Press.

Askham, J. (1995) *Social and Health Authority Services for Elderly People from Black and Minority Ethnic Communities*. London: HMSO.

Associated Press (2006a) 'Governor-General: Mother's Day in her Motherland', *The Province*, 14 May, p. A16.

Associated Press (2006b) '4 Women, 18 Men Arrive in Container', *The Vancouver Sun*, 6 April, p. A12.

Associated Press (2006c) 'Canadian Held on Suspicion of Human Smuggling', *The Vancouver Sun*, 6 April, p. A12.

Audit Commission (2003) *Human Rights: Improving Public Service Delivery*. London: Audit Commission.

Ayotte, W. and Williamson, L. (2001) *Separated Children in the UK: An Overview of the Current Situation*. London: Save the Children.

Back, L. (1996) *New Ethnicities and Urban Culture: Racism and Multiculture in Young Lives*. London: University College London Press.

Bagley, C. and Young, L. (1982) 'Policy Dilemmas and the Adoption of Black Children' in Cheetam, J. (ed.) *Social Work Education and Ethnicity*. London: Allen & Unwin.

Banks, N. (2003) 'What is a Black Identity?' in Dwivedi, K. N. (ed.)

Meeting the Needs of Black Children: Including Refugee, Black and Mixed Parentage Children: A Handbook for Professionals. London: Jessica Kingsley Publishers.

Barker, H. (1986) 'Recapturing Sisterhood: A Critical Look at "Process" in Feminist Organisations and Community Action', *Critical Social Policy*, 16:80–90, Summer.

Barker, M. (1981) *The New Racism: Conservatives and the Ideology of the Tribe.* London: Junction Books.

Barn, R., Ladino, C. and Rogers, B. (2006) *Parenting in Multi-Racial Britain.* London: NCH.

Barnes, D., Carpenter, J. and Dickinson, C. (2000) 'Interprofessional Education for A Common MA: Attitudes to Community Care and Professional Stereotypes', *Social Work Education*, 19(6):565–83, December.

Barrow, C. (1996) *Family in the Caribbean: Themes and Perspectives.* Oxford: James Currey.

Batty, D. (2003) 'Crippled by Ambition: Exodus from Zimbabwe Highlights Winners and Losers' in *The Guardian*, Wednesday, 19 February available from http://society.guardian.co.uk/careers/story/0,7916,898167,00.html accessed 1 March 2004.

Bauman, Z. (1993) *Mortality, Immortality and Other Life Strategies.* Cambridge: Polity Press.

Baxter, H. (2000) 'What are the 'Needs' of Cancer Patients and the Main Carers?', *Disability Review*, 5(1), pp. 2–3.

BBC News (2001) *Ethnic Birth Rate Climbs* from www.news.bbc.co.uk accessed 23 May 2005.

BBC News (2002) http://news.bbc.co.uk/1/hi/in_depth/uk/2002/race/1998159.stm accessed 23 May 2005.

BBC News (2005) *UK Majority Back Multiculturalism*, 10 August. www.news.bbc.co.uk/1/hi/UK/4137990.stm accessed 23 October 2007.

BBC News (2006) *Reid discusses EU Prisoners Deal*, 6 Oct. www.news.bbc.co.uk accessed 13 May 2007.

Beck, J. and Mumola, C. (1999) 'Prisoners in 1998', *Bureau of Justice Statistics Bulletin.* Washington, DC: Bureau of Justice.

Beck, U. (1992) *Risk Society: Towards a New Modernity.* London: Sage.

Beck, U. (1999) *World Risk Society.* Cambridge: Polity Press.

Begum, N., Hill, M. and Stevens, A. (1993) *Reflections: The Views of Black Disabled People on Their Lives and on Community Care.* London: CCETSW.

Bennett, W. and Reese, B. (1999) 'Power and Prejudice' in *Socialist Review*, 229, pp. 1–3, website.

Berridge, D. and Brodie, I. (1996) 'Residential Child Care in England and Wales: The Inquiries and After' in Hill, M. and Aldgate, J. (eds) *Child Welfare Services: Developments in Law, Policy and Practice*. London: Jessica Kingsley.

Berthoud, R. (2005) 'Family Formation in Multicultural Britain: Diversity and Change' in Lowry, G., Modood, T. and Teles, S. (eds) *Ethnicity, Social Mobility and Public Policy*. Cambridge: Cambridge University Press.

Berthoud, R. and Modood, T. (1997) *The Fourth National Survey*. London: PSI.

Bhat, A., Carr-Hill, R. and Ohri, S. (1988) *Britain's Black Population*. Aldershot: Gower.

Biggs, S., Phillipson, C. and Kingston, P. (1995) *Elder Abuse in Perspective*. Buckingham: The Open University.

Billig, M., Downey, J., Richarson, J., Deacon, D. and Golding, P. (2006) *'Britishness' in the Last Three General Elections: From Ethnic to Civic Nationalism*. London: CRE and Loughborough University, Centre for Communication Research.

Binnema, T. and Hutchings, K. (2005) 'The Emigrant and the Noble Savage: Sir Francis Bond Head's Approach to Aboriginal Policy in Upper Canada, 1836–38', *Journal of Canadian Studies*, 39(1):115–35, Winter.

Bhatti-Sinclair, K. (1994) 'Asian Women and Domestic Violence from Male Partners' in Lupton, C. and Gillespie, T. (eds) *Working with Violence*. London: BASW/Macmillan.

Bhavani, K. K. (1993) 'Talking Racism and the Editing of Women's Studies' in Richardson, D. and Robinson, V. (eds) *Introduction to Women's Studies*. Basingstoke: Macmillan.

Biggs, S., Phillipson, C. and Kingston, P. (1995) *Elder Abuse in Perspective*. Buckingham: Open University Press.

Bignall, T. and Butt, J. (2000) 'Young, Black and Disabled', *Black Information Link* on www.blink.org.uk/disab/young.htm accessed on 21 March 2002.

Billig, M. (1997) 'From Codes to Utterances: Rhetoric and Ideology in Conversation', *Analysis, Discourse and Society*, 10(4), pp. 543–58.

Bishop, A. (2001) *On Becoming an Ally: Breaking The Cycle of Oppression in People*. London: Zed Press. First published in 1992.

Black, R., Collyer, M., Skeldon, R. and Waddington, C. (2005) *A Survey of the Illegally Resident Population in Detention in the UK: Findings*. London: Home Office. Available at www.homeoffice.gov.uk as Home Office Report Online accessed 20 May 2005.

Blackaby, D. and Frank, J. (2000) '*Ethnic and Other Minority Representation in UK Academic Economics*' in *The Economics Journal*, 110(464), pp. 293–311.

Blakemore, K. and Boneham, M. (1994) *Age, Race and Ethnicity: A Comparative Approach*. Buckingham: Open University Press.

Bloch, A. (2000) 'A New Era or More of the Same: Asylum Policy in the UK', *Journal of Refugee Studies*, 13(1):29–42.

Bloch, A. (2004) *Making It Work: Refugee Employment in the UK*. London: Institute for Public Policy Research.

Blom-Cooper, L. (1986) *A Child in Trust: The Report of the Panel of Inquiry into the Circumstances Surrounding the Death of Jasmine Beckford*. London Borough of Brent: Kingwood Press.

Boateng, J. (1999) 'Foreword by the Chair of the Ethnic Minorities Steering Group', *Ageing Matters: Ethnic Concerns*, ed. Patel, N. London: PRIAE.

Bolan, K. (2006) 'Indo-Canadian Pioneers Honoured' in *The Vancouver Sun*, 29 May, p. B4.

Bolger, S., Corrigan, P., Dorking, J., and Frost, N. (1981) *Towards a Socialist Welfare Work*. Basingstoke: Macmillan.

Booth, T., McConnell, D. and Booth, W. (2006) 'Temporal Discrimination and Parents with Learning Difficulties in the Child Protection System', *British Journal of Social Work*, 36(6):997–1016.

Borger, J. (2006) 'New York on Edge as Police Kill Unarmed Man in Hail of 50 Bullets on His Wedding Day', *The Guardian*, 27 November, p. 3.

Borland, J., King, R. and McDermott, K. (1995) 'The Irish in Prison: A Tighter Nick for the Micks', *British Journal of Sociology*, 46(3), 371–94.

Bowlby, J. (1983) *Attachment*. New York: Brunner-Routledge.

Bowling, B .and Phillips, C. (2002) *Racism, Crime and Justice*. London: Longman.

Braidwood, J. (2003) 'Nationality, Identity and Minorities in the UK and Ireland', *European Integration Studies*, 2(2):29–38.

Branney, J. (2003) 'Pensioners Fightback Against an Unfair Tax', *Social Work Online*. 4 October.

Bridges, L., Pierce, G., Netter, F., Sivanandan, A., Athwal, H., Bourne, J., Fekete, L. and Kundnani, A. (2001) *The Three Faces of British Racism*. London: IRR.

Brinkworth, L. (2005) 'What Happened to the Babies Who Wouldn't Cry' in *REAL*, 9–23 December, pp. 14–18.

Briscoe, C. (2006) *Ugly: The True Story of a Loveless Childhood*. London: Hodder & Stoughton.

Briskman, L. (2005) 'Pushing Ethical Boundaries for Children and Families: Confidentiality, Transparency and Transformation' in Adams, R., Dominelli, L. and Payne, M. (eds) *Social Work Futures: Crossing Boundaries, Transforming Practice*. Basingstoke: Palgrave Macmillan.

Briskman, L. (2006) *Asylum Seekers and Social Work Educators*, Paper for the IFSW Conference 'Social Work: Makes a World of Difference' in Munich, 27 July.

Briskman, L. and Cemlyn, S. (2004) 'Reclaiming Humanity for Asylum-Seekers: A Social Work Response', *International Social Work*, 48(6):714–24.

Brittain, V. (2006) 'It Didn't End at Forest Gate', *The Guardian*, 25 November.

Brixton Black Women's Group (BBWG) (1984) 'Black Women Organizing', *Feminist Review*, 17, pp. 84–9, July.

Brook, E. and Davis, A. (1985) *Women, the Family and Social Work*. London: Tavistock.

Brook, K. (2004) *Labour Market Data for Local Areas by Ethnicity*. London: ONS.

Brown, J. (2006) 'The New Face of Terrorism', *The Independent*, 6 April.

Brown, L., Callahan, M., McKenzie, P. and Whittington, B. (2002) *Grandmothers Caring for their Grandchildren: From Practice to Policy*. Victoria: School of Social Work.

Brugher, T., Brugher, D., Jenkins, R., Farrell, M., Lewis, G. and Singleton, N. (2002) *Ethnic Differences in Prisoners*. London: Home Office.

Butler, I. and Drakeford, M. (2003) *Social Policy, Social Welfare and Scandal: How British Public Policy is Made*. Basingstoke: Palgrave Macmillan.

Butler, J. (1990) *Feminisms and the Subversion*. London: Routledge.

Caddick, B. (1993) 'Using Groups in Working with Offenders: A

Survey of Groupwork in the Probation Services in England and Wales' in Brown, A. and Caddick, B. (eds) *Groupwork with Offenders*. London: Whiting & Birch.

Çağlar, A. S. (2001) 'Constraining Metaphors and the Transnationalisation of Spaces in Berlin', *Journal of Ethnic and Migration Studies*, 27(4):601–13.

Calverley, A., Cole, B., Kaur, G., Lewis, S., Sadeghi, S., Smith, D., Raynor, P., Vanstone, M. and Wardak, A. (2004) *Black and Asian Offenders on Probation*. Home Office Research Report 277. London: Home Office Research, Development and Statistics Directorate.

Canter, D. (2006) 'The Samson Syndrome', *Journal of the Academy of Social Sciences*, 1(2):107–28.

Cantle, T. (2002) *Community Cohesion: Report of the Independent Review Team*. London: Home Office.

Cantle, T., Kaur, D., Athar, M., Dallison, C., Wiggans, A. and Joshua, H. (2006) *Challenging Local Communities to Change Oldham: Final Report*. Coventry: Coventry University, Institute of Community Cohesion.

Carlberg, C. (2006) *A Better Life is Possible: On Empowerment and Social Mobilisation*. Stockholm: Swedish ESF Council and EU EQUAL Programme.

Carlisle, D. (1997) 'The Voice of Experience', *Community Care*, 16–22 October, pp. 16–17.

Cashmore, E. and McLaughlin, E. (1991) *Out of Order? Policing Black People*. London: Routledge.

Chakraborti, N. and Garland, J. (2004) *Rural Racism*. Cullumpton: Willan.

Chapman, R., Calder, A. and Danton, K. (2003) *Starting Over: Young Refugees Talk About Life in Britain*. London: Prince's Trust and Diana, Princess of Wales Memorial Fund.

Chartist (2000) 'Corporate Racism: Words and Reality' in *Chartist: For a Democratic Socialism*. London: Chartist Publications, March/April. Website.

Cheetham, J. (1972) *Social Work with Immigrants*. London: Routledge.

Cheetham, J. (1982) *Social Work Services for Ethnic Minorities in Britain and the USA*. London: DHSS.

Chrisafis, A. (2007) 'French Families Tell of Motives for Signing Up with Agency at Centre of Chad Abduction Inquiry', *The Guardian*, 1 November, pp. 1–3.

Churchill, W. (1998) *A Littler Matter of Genocide*. Winnipeg: Arbeiter Ring.

Clark, K. and Drinkwater, S. (2002) 'Enclaves, Neighbourhood Effects and Employment Outcomes: Ethnic Minorities in England and Wales', *Journal of Population Economics*, 15:5–29.

Clarke, H. (1998) *Preliminary Analysis on Attitudes Towards Funding and Provision of Care in Old Age*. London: NCCSU.

Clarke, T. (2002) *Report of the Burnley Task Force*. London: Home Office.

Coard, B. (1971) *How West Indian Children are Made Educationally Sub-Normal*. London: New Beacon.

Cohen, P. (1986) *The Perversions of Inheritance*. Unpublished Paper from the Institute of Education, London.

Cohen, S. (2001) *Immigration Controls, the Family and the Welfare State*. London: Jessica Kingsley.

Cohen, S., Humphries, B. and Mynott, E. (eds) (2001) *From Immigration Controls to Welfare Control*. London: Routledge.

Coid, J., Petruchevitch, A. and Bebbington, P. (2002) 'Ethnic Differences and Mental Disorders', *British Journal of Psychiatry*, 181(1), pp. 473–480, December.

Commission on Racial Equality (CRE) (1997) *Discrimination and the Irish Community in Britain*. London: CRE.

Commission on Racial Equality (CRE) (2003a) *Racial Attacks*. London: CRE.

Commission on Racial Equality (CRE) (2003b) *Racial Equality in Prisons*. London: CRE.

Commission on Racial Equality (CRE) (2003c) *Report on Zahid Mubarek*. London: CRE.

Commission on Racial Equality (CRE) (2006a) *Common Ground: Equality, Good Race Relations and Sites for Gypsies and Irish Travellers: Report of a CRE Inquiry in England and Wales*. London: CRE.

Commission on Racial Equality (CRE) (2006b) *Fact File 1: Employment and Ethnicity*. London: CRE. On www.cre.gov.uk/duty/reia/statistics_labour.html accessed 25 May 2005.

Connell, W. (1995) *Masculinities*. Cambridge: Polity Press.

Coombe, V. and Little, A. (1986) *Race and Social Work: A Guide to Training*. London: Tavistock.

Coplan, D. B. (2006) '"I've Worked Longer Than I've Lived": Lesotho Migrants' Songs as Maps of Experience', *Journal of Ethnic and Migration Studies*, 32(2):223–41.

Cowgill, D. O. and Holmes, L. (1972) *Aging and Modernization.* New York: Appleton-Century-Crofts.

Crick, B. (2003) *The New and the Old: The Report of the Life in the UK Advisory Group.* London: Home Office.

Cross, W. E. (1992) *Black Identity: Theory and Research.* Philadelphia: Temple University Press.

Curtis, P. (2006) 'Black Students Failing to Get into Top Universities', *The Guardian,* 3 January.

Dai, D. and Thiara, R. (1997) *Re-Defining Spaces: The Needs of Black Women and Children and Black Workers in Women's Aid.* London: Women's Aid Federation, England.

Dalmage, H. (2003) *Tripping the Color Line: Black-White Multiracial Families in a Racially Divided World.* Piscataway, NJ: Rutgers University Press.

Davis, G. and Cocayne, D. (2006) 'Peer Support in Child Protection Practice' in *JCN*, 20(6):1–10.

Dearden, C. and Becker, S. (1998) *Young Carers in the UK: A Profile.* London: Carers National Association.

Delight, S. and McGuire, J. (2002) *Problem Solving Skills Training (PSST).* Congleton: Delight Training Services.

Demirbag, M. and Aldridge, M. (2003) 'Minority Elderly Care in the United Kingdom' in Patel, N. (ed) *Minority Elderly Care in Europe.* Leeds: PRIAE.

Denham, J. (2002) *Building Community Cohesion. A Report of the Ministerial Group on Public Order and Community Cohesion.* London: Home Office.

Department of Education and Skills (DfES) (2003) *The Children Act Report, 2002.* Nottingham: DfES.

Department of Education and Skills (DfES) (2004) *Every Child Matters.* Norwich: The Stationery Office.

Department of Education and Skills (DfES) (2005) *Aiming Higher: Understanding the Educational Needs of Minority Ethnic Pupils in Mainly White Schools.* Norwich: The Stationery Office.

Department of Education and Skills (DfES) (2006) *Care Matters: Transforming the Lives of Children and Young People in Care:* London: DfES.

Department of Health (DH) (2001a) *Children in Need in England.* London: DH.

Department of Health (DH) (2001b) *Valuing People.* London: DH.

Department of Health (DH) (2006) *Care Matters: Transforming*

the Lives of Children in Care: Equality Impact Assessment.
London: DH.

Department of Work and Pensions (2002) *Simplicity, Security and Choice: Working and Saving for Retirement.* London: TSO.

De Souza, P. (1991) 'Black Students', *One Step Towards Racial Justice.* London: CCETSW.

Devo, J. (2006) 'Out of Africa into Birmingham: Zimbabwean Social Workers Talk to Professional Social Work' in *Professional Social Work,* 1 August, pp. 12–13.

Dieter, R. (1998) *The Death Penalty in Black and White: Who Lives? Who Dies? Who Decides?* Washington, DC: The Death Penalty Information Center.

Dixon, J. (2007) 'Housing Project will Help At-Risk First Nations Youth', *Times Colonist,* 31 March, p. 31.

Dodd, V. (2007) 'Only 1 in 400 Anti-Terror Stop and Searches Leads to Arrest', *The Guardian,* 31 October, p. 7.

Dominelli, L. (1983) *Women in Focus: Community Service Orders and Female Offenders.* Coventry: Warwick University.

Dominelli, L. (1986) 'The Power of the Powerless: Prostitution and the Enforcement of Submissive Femininity', *Sociological Review,* Spring, pp. 65–92.

Dominelli, L. (1988, 1997) *Anti-Racist Social Work.* Basingstoke: BASW/Macmillan.

Dominelli, L. (1991) '"Race", Gender and Social Work' in Davis, M. (ed.) *The Sociology of Social Work.* London: Routledge.

Dominelli, L. (1996) 'Deprofessionalising Social Work: Equal Opportunities, Competence and Postmodernism', *British Journal of Social Work,* 26:153–75.

Dominelli, L. (1997) *Sociology for Social Work.* Basingstoke: Macmillan – now Palgrave Macmillan.

Dominelli, L. (2002a) *Anti-Oppressive Social Work Theory and Practice.* Basingstoke: Palgrave Macmillan.

Dominelli, L. (2002b) *Feminist Social Work Theory and Practice.* Basingstoke: Palgrave Macmillan.

Dominelli, L. (2003) 'Culturally Competent Social Work: A Way Towards International Anti-Racist Social Work?' in Guttierez, L., Zuniga, M. and Lum, D. (eds) *Education for Multicultural Social Work Practice.* Alexandria, VA.: Council on Social Work Education, pp. 281–94.

Dominelli, L. (2004a) 'Practising Social Work in a Globalising

World' in Tan, T. and Rowlands, A. (eds) *Social Work Around the World III*. Berne: IFSW.

Dominelli, L. (2004b) *Social Work: Theory and Practice for a Changing Profession*. Cambridge: Polity Press.

Dominelli, L. (2006a) *Women and Community Action*. Bristol: Policy Press, 2nd edn.

Dominelli, L. (2006b) 'Racialised Identities: New Challenges for Social Work Education' in Lyons, K. and Lawrence, S. (eds) *Social Work Education for a Changing Europe*. Birmingham: Venture Press/IASSW.

Dominelli, L. (2006c) 'Dangerous Constructions: Black Offenders in the Criminal Justice System' in Gorman, K, Gregory, M, Hayles, M and Parton, N (eds) *Constructive Work with Offenders*. London: Jessica Kingsley.

Dominelli, L. and Hoogvelt, A. (1996) 'Globalisation and the Technocratisation of Social Work', *Critical Social Policy*, 16(2):45–62.

Dominelli, L., Callahan, M., Rutman, D. and Strega, S. (2005) 'Endangered Children: The State as Parent and Grandparent' in *British Journal of Social Work*, 35(7):1123–44, October.

Dorsett, R. (1998) *Ethnic Minorities in the Inner City*. Bristol: The Policy Press and JRF.

Douglas, N. (1983) *Old Calabria*. London: Century Books.

Doward, J. (2006) 'BNP Link to New Campaign Groups' in the *Observer*, 16 April, p. 13.

Duff, A. (2003) 'Probation, Punishment and Restorative Justice', *Howard Journal of Criminal Justice*, 42(2):181–97.

Dunant, S. (ed.) (1994) *War of the Words: The Political Correctness Debate*. London: Random House.

Dwyer, C. (2000) 'Patterns of Belonging and Citizenship', *International Journal of Population Geography*, 10(5), pp. 357–60.

Eaton, L. (1997) 'New Order: The European Convention on Human Rights', *Community Care*, 3–9 July, pp. 18–19.

Ehrkamp, P. (2005) 'Placing Identities: Transnational Practices and Local Attachments of Turkish Immigrants in Germany', *Journal of Ethnic and Migration Studies*, 31(2):345–64.

Ely, P. and Denny, D. (1987) *Social Work in a Multi-Racial Society*. Aldershot: Gower.

Equal Opportunities Commission (EOC) (2006) *The Gender Gap: Women's Pay*. Manchester: EOC.

Erickson, E. H. (1959) 'Identity and the Life Cycle', *Psychological Issues*, 1(1):151–71.

Esmeé Fairburn Foundation (EFB) (2004) *Crime, Courts and Punishment: A Report of an Independent Inquiry into Alternatives to Prison*. London: The Stationery Office.

Essed, P. (1991) *Understanding Everyday Racism: An Interdisciplinary Theory*. London: Sage.

Estes, C. L. (1989) 'Ageing, Health and Social Policy: Crisis and Crossroads' in *Journal of Aging and Social Policy*, 1(1/2):17–32.

European Commission (2003) *Report on the Ageing Population in Europe*. Brussels: EC.

European Monitoring Centre on Racism and Xenophobia (EUMC) (2005) *Report on Racism and Xenophobia in Europe*. Brussels: EUMC.

Fanon, F. (1968) *Black Skins, White Masks*. London: MacGibbon & Kee.

Fathers Direct (2005) 'Finding Black Fathers' in *Families in Working with Fathers: A Guide for Practitioners*. Available from www.fathersdirect, accessed 11 November 2006.

Fekete, L. (2001) 'The Emergence of Xeno-Racism' in *The Three Faces of British Racism: A Special Report*. London: IRR.

Fell, P. (2004) 'And Now it has Started to Rain: Support and Advocacy with Adult Asylum Seekers in the Voluntary Sector' in Hays, D. and Humphries, B. (eds) *Social Work, Immigration and Asylum*. London: Jessica Kingsley.

Fernando, S. (1999) 'Ethnicity and Mental Health' in Ulas, M. and Connor, A. (eds) *Mental Health and Social Work*. London: Jessica Kingsley.

Fletcher, D. L., Woodhill, D. and Herrington, A. (1998) *Building Bridges into Employment for Ex-Offenders*. York: York Publishing Services.

Fletchman-Smith, B. (1984) 'Effects of Race on Fostering and Adoptions', *International Journal of Social Psychiatry*, 30:121–28.

Flood-Page, C. (1999) *The Changing Lives of Young Men*. Unpublished Report. London: Cabinet Office.

Flood-Page, C., Campbell, S., Harrington, V. and Miller, J. (2000) *Youth Crime. Findings from the 1998/99 Youth Lifestyles Survey*. Home Office Research Study 209. London: Home Office.

Foster, J. (1997) *Women in Social Services: Maximising the Potential of the Workforce*. London: SSI.

Foster, P. (2006) 'The Dark Side of India's Success', *The Vancouver Sun*, 2 May, p. A9.

Foucault, M. (1983) 'The Subject and Power', in the 'Afterword' to Dreyfus, H. and Rabinow, P. (eds) *Michel Foucault: Beyond Structuralism and Hermeneutics*. Chicago. Chicago University Press.

Foucault, M. (1991) 'Technologies of the Self' in Martin, L., Gutman, H. and Hutton, P. (eds) *'Technologies of the Self': A Seminar with Michel Foucault*. London: Tavistock.

Frankenburg, R. (1997) *The Myth of Whiteness: Essays in Social and Cultural Criticism*. London: Duke University Press.

Franklin, A. and Franklin, B. (1996) 'Growing Pains: The Developing Children's Rights Movement in the UK' in Pilcher, J. and Wagg, S. (eds) *Thatcher's Children? Politics, Childhood and Society in the 1980s and 1990s*. London: Falmer Press.

Franklin, J. (ed.) (1998) *The Politics of Risk Society*. Cambridge: Polity Press.

Freeman, R. B. (1992) 'People Flows under Globalisation', *Journal of Economic Perspectives*, 20(2), pp. 145–70.

Freire, P. (1970) *The Pedagogy of the Oppressed*. Harmondsworth: Penguin.

Frost, V. (2006) 'False Starts and Fresh Beginnings', *The Guardian*, 25 November.

Fryer, P. (1984) *Staying Power: The History of Black People in Britain*. London: Pluto.

Garland, D. (2001) *The Culture of Control: Crime and Social Order in Contemporary Society*. Oxford: Oxford University Press.

Garrett, P. M. (1999) 'Producing the "Moral" Citizen: The "Looked After" Children System and Regulation of Children and Young People in Public Care', *Critical Social Policy*, 19(3):291–311.

Gearty, C. (1999) 'Racism's Bigger Picture' in *The Tablet*, 6 March from www.TheTablet.co.uk accessed 25 November 2006.

General Social Care Council (GSCC) (2002) *Regulations for the New Award in Social Work*. London: GSCC.

General Social Care Council (GSCC) (2006) *Social Work Education and Training Statistics: Data Pack, 2004–2005*. London: GSCC.

George, M. (1997) 'The Workforce Taking the Strain', *Community Care*, 9–15 October, pp. 20–1.

Giddens, A. (1998) *The Third Way: The Renewal of Social Democracy*. London and Cambridge: Polity Press.

Gilbert, S. (2001) 'Social Work with Indigenous Australians' in Alston, M. and McKinnon, J. (eds) *Social Work: Fields of Practice*. Victoria: Oxford University Press.

Gilder, G. (1981) *Wealth and Poverty*. New York: Bell Books.

Gillan, A. (2002) '"Prison Worked" says Truants' Mother' in the *Guardian*, 27 May.

Gilroy, P. (1982) 'The Organic Crisis of British Capitalism and Race' in Centre for Contemporary Culture Studies, *The Empire Strikes Back*. Birmingham: CCCS.

Gilroy, P. (1987) *There Ain't No Black in the Union Jack*. London: Hutchinson.

Gilroy, P. (2000) *Against Race: Imagining Political Culture Beyond the Color Line*. Cambridge, MA: The Belknap Press and Harvard University Press.

Gilroy, P. (2005) 'Multiculture, Double Consciousness, the "War on Terror"', *Patterns of Prejudice*, 39(4):431–43.

Gitterman, A. and Schaeffer, A. (1972) 'The White Professional and the Black Client' in *Social Casework*, May:280–91.

Gobineau, J. (1953) *Essai sur l'Inégalité des Races Humains*. Paris: Firmin et Didot, 4th edn.

Goffman, E. (1961) *Asylums*. Harmondsworth: Penguin.

Goldane, M., Davidson, J. and Lambert, T. (2004) *Country of Training and Ethnic Origins of UK Doctors: Database and Survey Studies*. Oxford: Oxford University, Department of Public Health.

Goldsmith, B. (2002) 'Asserting Cultural and Social Regulatory Principles in Converging Media Systems' in Raborg, M (ed.) *Global Media Policy in the New Millennium*. Luton: University of Luton.

Goldsmith, O. (2000) 'Culturally Competent Health Care', *The Permanente Medical Journal*, 4(1), pp. 1–4.

Gordon, P. (1985) *Policing Immigration: Britain's Internal Controls*. London: Junction Books.

Gordon, H. (2006) 'Homegrown Threat to Security', *The Vancouver Sun*, 28 June, p. A1–A2.

Gore, C. (1998) 'Inequality, Ethnicity and Educational Achievement' in Lavelette, M., Penketh, L. and Jones, C. (eds) *Anti-Racism and Social Welfare*. Aldershot: Ashgate.

Gouldbourne, H. (1999) *Caribbean Transnational Families*. London: Pluto Press.

Graham, J. (2006) 'Tory Bill would Make it Easier to Adopt Foreign Kids', *The Vancouver Sun*, 13 May, p. A3.

Graham, M. (2002) *Social Work and African-Centred World Views*. Birmingham: Venture Press.

Greer, P. (1994) *Transforming Central Government: The Next Steps Initiatives*. Buckingham: Open University Press.

Grier, A. and Thomas, T. (2006) 'Troubled and in Trouble: Young People, Truancy and Offending' in Adams, R., Dominelli, L. and Payne, M. (eds) *Social Work Futures: Crossing Boundaries, Transforming Practice*. Basingstoke: Palgrave Macmillan.

Guardian, The (2001) 'Breaking the Chains', Leader, 4 September.

Gulbenkian Community Work Group (1973) *Current Issues in Community Work*. London: Gulbenkian (Calouste) Foundation.

Gutierrez, L. and Lewis, E. (1999) *Empowering Women of Color*. New York: Columbia University Press.

Haig-Brown, C. (1988) *Resistance and Renewal: Surviving the Indian Residential School*. Vancouver: Tillicum Library/Arsenal Pulp Press.

Hall, C. (1997) *Social Work as Narratives: Storytelling and Persuasion in Professional Texts*. Aldershot: Ashgate.

Hall, S. (1980) 'Race, Articulation and Societies Structured in Dominance' in UNESCO (ed.) *Sociological Theories: Race and Colonialism*. New York: UNESCO, pp. 305–45.

Hall, S. (1992) 'The Question of Cultural Identity' in Hall, S., Held, D. and McGrew, T. (eds) *Modernity and its Futures*. Cambridge: Polity Press.

Hall, S, Critcher, C, Jefferson, T, Clarke, J and Roberts, B (1978) *Policing the Crisis: Mugging, the State and Law and Order*. London: Macmillan.

Harding, J. (2000) *The Uninvited: Refugees at the Rich Man's Gate*. London: Profile Books.

Hayes, D. (2006) 'Social Work with Asylum Seekers and Others Subject to Immigration Control' in Adams, R., Dominelli, L. and Payne, M. (eds) *Social Work Futures: Crossing Boundaries, Transforming Practice*. Basingstoke: Palgrave Macmillan.

Hayes, D. and Humphries, B. (eds) (2004) *Social Work, Immigration and Asylum: Debates, Dilemmas and Ethical Issues for Social Work and Social Care Practice*. London: Jessica Kingsley.

Hayter, T. (2000) *Open Borders: The Case Against Immigration Controls*. London: Pluto Press.

Healy, L. (2007) 'Retheorising International Social Work for the Global Professional Community' in Dominelli, L. (ed.) *Revitalising Communities in a Globalising World*. Aldershot: Ashgate.

Hearnden, I. and Hough, M. (2004) *Race and the Criminal Justice System: An Overview to the Complete Statistics 2002/3. Report Under Section 95, Criminal Justice Act, 1991*. London: Kings College, Institute of Criminal Policy Research.

Help the Aged (2006) *Elder Abuse*. London: Help the Aged.

Her Majesty's Inspectorate of Prisons (HMIP) (2000) *Thematic Inspection Report: Towards Race Equality*. London: Home Office.

Hernstein, R. and Murray, C. (1994) *The Bell Curve: Intelligence and Class Structure in American Life*. New York: Free Press.

Hessle, S. and Zavirsék, D. (eds) (2005) *Sustainable? Development in Social Work – The Case of a Regional Network in the Balkans*. Stockholm: SIDA and the University of Stockholm.

Higgins, J. (1989) 'Caring for the Carers', *Journal of Social Administration*, Summer, pp. 382–99.

Hill, A. (2000) 'First Nations Child Welfare' in Callahan, M., Hessle, S. and Strega, S. (eds) *Valuing the Field: Child Welfare in International Perspectives*. Aldershot: Ashgate.

Hill-Collins, P. (2000) *Black Feminist Thought: Knowledge, Consciousness and the Politics of Empowerment*. London: Routledge. First published in 1990.

Hocking, J. (2006) 'Forced Marriage: Whose Shame?' *Community Care*, 16–22 November, pp. 28–30.

Home Office (1994) 'The Ethnic Origins of Prisoners', *Home Office Statistical Bulletin*, 21(94). London: HMSO.

Home Office (1996) *Exchange of Information with the IND of the Home Office* in Circular IMG/96 1176/1193/23.

Home Office (2002a) *Race and the Criminal Justice System 2001. A Home Office Publication under Section 95 of the Criminal Justice Act, 1991*. London: Home Office.

Home Office (2002b) *Secure Borders: Safe Havens, Integration within Diversity*. London: TSO.

Home Office (2004) *Race Self-Assessment Tool*. London: Home Office, CPS and Department of Constitutional Affairs.

Home Office (2006) *Race and the Criminal Justice System: An Overview to the Complete Statistics, 2004–05 under Section 95 of the Criminal Justice Act, 1991*. London: Home Office.

Hood, R., Shute, S. and Seemungal, F. (2003) *Ethnic Minorities in the Criminal Courts: Perceptions of Fairness and Equality.* London: Lord Chancellor's Department.

Hubbard, P. (2005) 'Accommodating Otherness: Anti-Asylum Centres Protests and the Maintenance of White Privilege', *The Transcription of the Institute of British Geographers,* 30(1):52–65.

Husband, C. (1980) 'Notes on Racism in Social Work Practice', *Multi-Racial Social Work,* 1, pp. 5–15.

Hudson, B. and Bramhall, G. (2002) *Race Equality and Criminal Justice: A Study of Pre-Sentence Reports for the National Probation Service.* Unpublished paper.

Hughes, B. (1995) *Older People and Community Care: Critical Theory and Practice.* Buckingham: Open University Press.

Hume, S. (2006) '$1.36 a Day Proves to be a Bit Low for Island Band', *The Vancouver Sun,* 26 April, p. A19.

Humphries, S. (1997) *The Lost Children.* Sydney: Hale & Iremonger.

Hunter, M (2006) 'Doing It for the Money?' *Community Care,* 12–18 October, pp. 28–31.

Hutchinson-Reis, M. (1986) 'After the Uprising – Social Work on the Broadwater Estate', *Critical Social Policy,* 17:70–80, Autumn.

Immigration Services Society (ISS) (2006) *Resettlement Patterns in the Greater Vancouver Regional District 2003 to 2005.* Vancouver: ISS.

Ingleby, E. (2006) *Applied Pyschology for Social Work.* Exeter: Learning Matters.

Inner London Probation Service (ILPS) (1996) *Black and Ethnic Minority Offenders' Experience of the Probation Service: June 1995.* London: ILPS.

Institute of Race Relations (IRR) (2002) *IRR Expresses Concern over Excessive Sentencing of Bradford Rioters,* 5 July.

Jackson, S. and Nixon, P. (1999) 'Family Group Conferences' in Dominelli, L. (ed.) *Community Approaches to Child Welfare.* Aldershot: Ashgate.

Jeffers, S. (1995) *'Black' and Ethnic Minorities' Experience of Probation.* Report produced for the School of Advanced Urban Studies. Bristol: Bristol University.

Jenkins, R. (1996) *Social Identity: Key Ideas.* London: Routledge.

John-Baptiste, A. (2001) 'Africentric Social Work' in Dominelli, L., Lorenz, W. and Soydan, H. (eds) *Beyond Racial Divides: Ethnicities in Social Work*. London: Routledge.

John, C. (2002) *Mixed Race: Britain's Fastest Growing Minority* from www.bbc.co.uk/hi/english/static/in_depth/uk/2002/race/mixed_race.stm accessed 23 May 2006.

Jordan, W. (2000) *Social Work and the Third Way: Tough Love as Social Policy*. London: Sage.

Kalunta-Crumpton, A. (2005) 'Race, Crime and Youth Justice' in Bateman, T. and Pitts, J. (eds) *The RHP Companion to Youth Justice*. Lyme Regis: Russell House.

Kam Yu, W. (2000) *Chinese Older People: A Need for Social Inclusion in Two Communities*. Bristol: Policy Press and JRF.

Kassindja, F. and Miller-Basher, L. (1998) *Do They Hear You When You Cry?* New York: Delacourt Press.

Kaufman, G. (1998) 'When All Else Fails', *International Security*, 23(2):120–56.

Keida, R. P. (1994) *Black on Black Crime: Facing Facts, Challenging Fiction*. New York: Wyndham Hall Press.

Keith, B. (2006) *The Report of the Zahid Mubarek Inquiry*. London: The Stationery Office.

Khan, P. and Dominelli, L. (2000) 'Globalisation, Privatisation and Social Work Practice', Paper presented at the *Rethinking Social Work Seminar*, 30 November – 2 December. Southampton: Southampton University.

Khan, V. (ed.) (1979) *Support and Stress: Minority Families in Britain*. London: Macmillan.

Khan, Z. (2000) 'Muslim Presence in Europe: The British Dimension – Identity Integration and Community Activism', *Current Sociology*, 48(4):29–43.

Knijn, T. and Ungerson, C. (1997) 'Introduction: Care Work and Gender in Welfare Regimes', *Social Politics*, Fall, pp. 323–7.

Kohli, R. K. S. (2006) 'The Sound of Silence: Listening to What Unaccompanied Asylum-Seeking Children Say and Do Not Say', *British Journal of Social Work*, 36(5):707–22.

Kohn, M. (2006) 'Made in Savannastan', *New Scientist*, 191(2558):34–9, 1 July.

Kundnani, A. (2001) 'From Oldham to Bradford: The Violence of the Violated' in the 'Three Faces of British Racism' in *Race and Class*, 43(2), pp. 41–60.

Kundnani, A. (2002) 'The Death of Multiculturalism' in *IRR (Independent Race and Refugee News Network) News*, 1 April, pp. 1–6.

Kuyek, J. N. (1990) *Fighting for Hope: Organizing to Realize Our Dreams*. Montreal: Black Rose Books.

Lahav, G. (2004) *Immigration and Politics in the New Europe: Reinventing Borders*. Cambridge: Cambridge University Press.

Lambeth Social Services (Lambeth) (1987) *Whose Child? The Report of the Public Inquiry into the Death of Tyra Henry*. London: London Borough of Lambeth.

Laming, H. (2003) *The Inquiry into Victoria Climbié*. London: Stationery Office.

Laurance, J. (2006) 'WHO Asks Britain to Stop Poaching Foreign Doctors' in the *Independent*, 7 April.

Lavernex, S. (1999) *Safe Third Countries: Extending EU Asylum and Immigration Policies to East and Central Europe*. Budapest: Central European Press.

Layton-Henry, Z. (1985) *The Politics of Race in Britain*. London: Allen & Unwin.

Lazear, E. (1999) 'Culture and Language', *Journal of Political Economy*, 107:95–126.

Ledwith, M. (2005) *Community Development: A Critical Approach*. Bristol: Policy Press. First published 1997.

Ledwith, M. and Asgill, P. (2007) 'Feminist, Anti-Racist Community Development: Critical Alliance, Local to Global' in Dominelli, L. (ed.) *Revitalising Communities in a Globalising World*. Aldershot: Ashgate.

Levy, A. (2004) *Small Island*. London: Headline Books.

Lewis, S., Raynor, P., Smith, D. and Wardak, A. (2006) *Race and Probation*. Cullompton: Willan.

Littlewood, R. and Lipsedge, M. (1992) *The Aliens and the Alienists: Ethnic Minorities and Psychiatry*. Harmonsworth: Penguin.

Lister, R. (1997) *Citizenship: Feminist Perspectives*. Basingstoke: Macmillan – now Palgrave Macmillan.

Lombroso, C. and Ferraro, O. W. (1895) *The Female Offender*. London: Fisher & Unwin.

London Asylum Seekers Consortium (LASC) (2003) *London Boroughs at December 2002*. London: LASC.

Lorde, A. (1984) *Sister Outsider*. New York: The Crossing Press.

Lorenz, W. (1994) *Social Work in a Changing Europe*. London: Routledge.

Lorenz, W. (2006) *Perspectives on European Social Work: From the Birth of the Nation-State to the Impact of Globalisation*. Leverkusen Opladen: Barbara Budrich.

Lum, D. (2000) *Culturally Competent Practice*. Belmont, CA: Brooks/Cole.

Lyons, K. and Lawrence, S. (eds) (2006) *Social Work Education for a Changing Europe*. Birmingham: Venture Press.

Mac an Ghaill, M. (2000) 'The Irish in Britain: The Invisibility of Ethnicity and Anti-Irish Racism', *Journal of Ethnic and Migration Studies*, 26(1):137–47.

MacKay, F. (2006) 'Black Managers in Further Education: Career Hopes and Hesitations', *Educational Management, Administration and Leadership*, 34(1):9–25.

Macpherson of Cluny, Sir William (1999) *A Report into the Death of Stephen Lawrence*. London: HMSO.

Mama, A. (1989) *The Hidden Struggle: Statutory and Voluntary Responses to Violence Against Black Women in the Home*. London: Race and Housing Unit.

Maxime, J. (1986) 'Some Psychological Models of Black Self-Concept' in Ahmed, S., Cheetham, J. and Small, J. (eds) *Social Work with Black Children and Their Families*. London: Batsford.

McConkey, W., Balloch, S. and Andrew T. (1997) *The Northern Ireland Social Services Workforce in Transition*. London: NISW.

McCormack, H. (2006) 'Probation Board Shake-Up Looms', *Community Care*, 16–22 November, p. 18.

McCulloch, J. (2006) '3rd Generation Canadian Can't Get Citizenship', *Times Colonist*, 23 October, p. B2.

McLeod, T. (1997) 'Work Stress Among Community Psychiatric Nurses' in *British Journal of Nursing*, 6:569–74.

McQuire, J. (ed.) (2002) *What Works: Reducing Re-Offending*. London: Wiley.

McVeigh, T. and Hill, A. (2005) 'Racists Axe Black Teenager to Death', *The Observer*, 31 July, p. 15.

Memmi, A. (1959) *Dependency: A Sketch for a Portrait of the Dependent*. Boston, MA: Beacon Press. Republished 1984.

Millar, M. (2006) 'BMA Warns NHS Trusts May be Discriminating Against Foreign Doctors' in www.Personneltoday.com accessed 10 June 2006.

Modood, T., Berthoud, R., Lakey, J., Nazroo, J., Smith, P., Virdee, S. and Beishon, S. (1997) *Ethnic Minorities in Britain: Diversity and Disadvantage*. London: Policy Studies Institute.

Moffat, P. and Thoburn, J. (2001) 'Outcomes of Permanent Family Placement for Children of Minority Ethnic Origins', *Child and Family Social Work*, 6(1):13–22.

Moore, B. and Fedorowich, K. (2005) *Prisoners of War: British Empire and Its Italian Prisoners of War, 1940–47*. Oxford: Berg.

MORI (2005) *BBC Multiculturalism Poll*. 10 August.

Morris, L. (1995) *Dangerous Classes: The Underclass and Social Citizenship*. London: Routledge.

Morris, N. and Brown, J. (2006) 'The New Face of Terrorism', *The Independent*, 6 April.

Morrison, T. (1986) *The Bluest Eye*. New York: Alfred A Knopf.

Moulds, J. and Weale, N. (2007) 'Scandal of the Care Home "Robbers"', *The Daily Express*, 18 October, pp. 30–1.

Moynihan, D. (1965) *The Negro Family: The Case for National Action*. Washington, DC: US Department of Labor.

Muncie, J. (2004) *Youth and Crime*. London: Sage.

Mungo, P. (2006) 'Spain: Retirement Centre for Europe', *World Business*, 24 October, pp. 14–18.

Murray, C. (1994) *Underclass: The Crisis Deepens*. London: Institute of Economic Affairs.

Murray, U. and Brown, D. (1998) *They Look After Their Own, Don't They?* London: DoH/SSI.

Naples, N. A. (ed) (1998) *Community Activism and Feminist Politics: Organizing Across Race, Class and Gender*. London: Routledge.

Nast, J. H. and Pulido, L. (2000) 'Marketing Ethnicity: Resisting a Consumer Corporate Culture', *Professional Geographer*, 52(4):722–37.

National Institute for Social Work (NISW) (1994) *The Black Students' Handbook*. London: NISW.

Netter, K. and Fekete, L. (2001) 'The Emergence of Xeno-Racism', *Race and Class*, 43(2), pp. 1–56.

Nolan, S. (2006) 'Out of Africa: A Trickle of Orphans', *The Vancouver Sun*, 24 May, p. A3.

Norford, L., Rashid, S. and Thoburn, J. (2000) *Improving Outcomes in Family Placements: Explorations and Experiences*. London: Jessica Kingsley.

Norman, A. (2006) 'Rights that Can Wrong', *Professional Social Work*, October, pp. 12–13.

Office of the Deputy Prime Minister (ODPM) (2003) *Preparing Older People's Strategies: Linking Housing to Health, Social Care and Other Strategies*. London: ODPM.

Office for National Statistics (ONS) (2000) *Population Trends, 2000*. London: ONS.

Office for National Statistics (ONS) (2002a) *Census 2001. Facts and Figures*. Accessed on www.statistics.gov.uk on 16 Oct 2004.

Office for National Statistics (ONS) (2002b) *Minority Ethnic Groups in the UK* from www.statistics.gov.uk/releases accessed 23 May 2005.

Office for National Statistics (ONS) (2004) *Population Estimates for Older People*. London: ONS.

Ohri, A., Manning, B. and Curno, P. (1982) *Community Work and Racism*. London: Routledge.

Oldfield, S. and Stokke, K. (2004) *Building Unity in Diversity: Social Movement Activism in the Western Cape Anti-Eviction Campaign*. Durban: CCS, University of KwaZulu-Natal.

O'Neil, P. (2006a) 'Native Fishery Deal would End 14-Year Battle' in *The Vancouver Sun*, 30 May, pp. A1, A7.

O'Neill, T. (2006b) 'Heartfelt Gov't Apology Enough' in *Tri-City News*, 4 June, p. A11, A19.

Ore, K. with Yu, J. (2005) *Song of the Azalea: Memoir of a Chinese Son*. Toronto: Penguin Group Canada.

Orphanides, K. (1986) 'The Cypriot Community in Britain' in Coombe, V. and Little, A. (eds) *Race and Social Work: A Guide to Training*. London: Tavistock.

Ouseley, H. (2001) *The Ouseley Report – Community Pride, Not Prejudice: Making Diversity Work in Bradford*. Bradford: Bradford Vision.

Palmer-Hunt, S. (2003) *Response to the Laming Report: A Community and Multi-Faith Perspective*. Hull: Hull Social Services and ADSS.

Parker, J. (ed.) (2005) *Aspects of Social Work and Palliative Care*. London: Quay Books.

Parekh, B. (2000) *Parekh Report: The Future of Multi-Ethnic Britain*. London: Runnymede Trust.

Patel, K. (2006) *Count Me In: The National Mental Health and Ethnicity Census 2005: Service User Survey* from www.mhac.org.uk accessed 25 November.

Patel, N. (1990) *Race Against Time: Ethnic Elders*. London: Runnymede Trust.

Patel, N. (1999a) 'Black and Minority Ethnic Elderly: Perspectives on Long-Term Care' in Patel, N. (ed.) *With Respect to Old Age*, Volume 1. London: HMSO.

Patel, N. (1999b) *Ageing Matters: Ethnic Concerns*. London: Age Concern.

Patel, N. and Lim, S. P. (2004) *Proposal for a Chinese Extra Care Home in London*. London: PRIAE.

Patel, N. and Mirza, N. (1998) *CNEOPSA Study: Dementia and Minority Ethnic Older People: Managing Care in the UK, Denmark and France*. Lyme Regis: Russell House.

Patel, N., Naik, D., and Humphries, B. (1999) 'Visions of Reality: Religion and Ethnicity in Social Work', *Race and Class*, 40(2), pp. 102–3.

Patel, N., Watson, K., Abye, T., Voutlainen, P., Quiras, M. A. M., Bolzman, C., Teng, B., Schuijtlucassen, N., Kislter, E., Orsó, E. and Baráth, A. (2004) *Minority Elderly Heath and Social Care in Europe: PRIAE Research Briefing*. London: PRIAE.

Pathak, S. (2000) *Race Research for the Future: Ethnicity in Education, Training and the Labour Market*. London: DfEE.

Phillips, M. (1993) 'An Oppressive Urge to End Oppression', *The Observer*, 1 August.

Phillips, T. (2005a) 'Equality in Our Lifetime: Talking About a Revolution', *CRE Newsletter*, 28 October. London: CRE.

Phillips, T. (2005b) 'Sleep Walking into Segregation', in the *Guardian*, 22 September.

Phillipson, C. (1998) *Reconstructing Old Age: New Agendas in Social Theory and Practice*. London: Sage.

Pincus, A. and Minahan, A. (1973) *Social Work Practice: Model and Method*. Itasca, IL: F. E. Peabody.

Pinker, R. (1993) 'A Lethal Kind of Looniness', *Times Higher Educational Supplement*, 10 September.

Pittaway, E. (1995) *Services for Older Canadians*. Victoria, BC: Ministry of Health/Ministry Responsible for Seniors.

Platt, L. (2006) *Pay Gaps: The Position of Ethnic Minority Women and Men*. Colchester: University of Essex.

Powis, B. and Walmsley, R. (2002) *Programmes for Black and Asian Offenders on Probation: Lessons for Developing Practice*. London: Home Office Research, Development and Statistics Directorate.

Pratt, H. J. (1993) *Gray Agendas: Interest Groups and Public Pensions in Canada, Britain and the United States*. Ann Arbor: University of Michigan Press.

Putnam, R. (2002) *Democracies in Flux: The Evolution of Social Capital in Contemporary Society*. Oxford: Oxford University Press.

Quereshi, T., Berridge, D. and Wenman, H. (2000) *Where to Turn? Family Support for South Asian Communities*. London: NCH.

Quinsey, V. (1995) 'Predicting Sexual Offences: Assessing Dangerousness', Campbell, J. (ed.) *Violence by Sexual Offenders, Batterers and Child Abusers*. London: Sage.

Ramazanoglu, C. (1989) *Feminism and the Contradictions of Oppression*. London: Routledge.

Randerson, J. (2006) 'DNA of 37 per cent of Black Men Held by Police', *The Guardian*, 5 January.

Ratcliffe, P. (ed.) (1996) *Race, Ethnicity and Nation: International Perspectives on Social Conflicts*. London: Routledge.

Raynor, D., Smith, D., and Lewis, S. (2005) 'The Irish on Probation in Northwest England', *Probation Journal*, 52(3), pp. 293–5.

Read, N. (2006) 'Young and Muslim in BC', *The Vancouver Sun*, 10 June, pp. A1, A6.

Refugee Council (2002a) *The Nationality, Immigration and Asylum Act, 2002: Changes to the Asylum System in the UK*. London: Refugee Council.

Refugee Council (2002b) *Starting Over: Young Refugees Talk About Life in Britain*. London: Refugee Council.

Richards, A. (2001) *Second Time Round: A Survey of Grandparents Raising their Grandchildren*. London: Family Rights Group.

Riley, J. (1985) *The Unbelonging*. London: The Women's Press.

Robb, P. (2006) 'Okay, So Here's How We All Can Just Get Along', *The Vancouver Sun*, 20 April, p. A19.

Robinson, L. (2002) 'Social Work through the Life-Course' in Adams, R., Dominelli, L. and Payne, M. (eds) *Social Work: Themes, Issues and Debates*. Basingstoke: Palgrave Macmillan.

Robinson, L. (2007) *Cross-Cultural Child Development for Social Workers: An Introduction*. Basingstoke: Palgrave Macmillan.

Rose, P. (2002) *The Education Fast Track Initiative*. Brighton: University of Sussex: Centre for International Education.

Sale, A. U. (2006) 'Just Making You Aware', *Community Care*, 12–18 October, pp. 32–3.

Sargeant, H. (2006) *Handle with Care*. London: Centre for Policy Studies.

Saunt, C. (2006) *Black, White and Indian: Race and the Unmaking of an American Family*. Oxford: Oxford University Press.

Scarman, L. (1981) *The Brixton Report, 10–12 April 1981 – The Report of An Inquiry*. London: HMSO.

Scarpino, S. (1992) *Tutti a casa, terroni*. Milan: Leonardo Paperback.

Scottish Asylum Seekers Consortium (SASC) (2002) *Asylum Seekers*. Glasgow: SASC.

Scruton, S. (1989) *Counselling Older People: A Creative Response to Ageing*. London: Edward Arnold.

Senior, P. (1993) 'Groupwork in the Probation Service: Care or Control in the 1990's' in Brown, A. and Caddick, B. (eds) *Groupwork with Offenders*. London: Whiting & Birch.

Sensoy, O. (2006) 'Asian Heritage Month Not Just for Asians' in *The Vancouver Sun*, 17 May, p. A17.

Selwyn, J., Frazer, L. and Fitzgerald, A. (2004) *Finding Adoptive Families for Black, Asian and Black Mixed-Parentage Children: Agency Policy and Practice*. London: NCH.

Serious Organised Crime Agency (2004) *One Step Ahead: A 21st Century Strategy to Defeat Organised Crime*. London: Home Office.

Sewpaul, V. and Hölscher, D. (2005) *Social Work and Neo-Liberalism*. Pretoria: Van Shaik.

Siltanen, J., Jarman, J. and Blackburn, R. (1995) *Gender Inequality in the Labour Market*. Geneva: ILO.

Sivanandan, A. (2000) 'Macpherson and After: Comment' in *IRR (Independent Race and Refugee News Network) News*, 19 February.

Shah, R. and Hatton, C. (1999) *Caring Alone: Young Carers in South Asian Communities*. London: Bernardo's.

Shakib, S. (2002) *Afghanistan: Where God Only Comes to Weep: A Woman's Story of Courage, Struggle and Determination*. London: Century.

Skelton, C. (2006a) 'Fugitive's Deportation Stayed' in *The Vancouver Sun*, 2 June, p. A3.

Skelton, C. (2006b) 'Slain Family Fled Brutal Regime', *The Vancouver Sun*, 17 May, pp. A1–4.

Small, J. (1987) 'Transracial Placements: Conflicts and Contradictions' in Ahmed, S., Cheetham, J. and Small, J. (eds)

Social Work with Black Children and their Families. London: Batsford.

Small, J. (2007) 'Caribbean Migration' in Dominelli, L. (ed.) *Revitalising Communities in a Globalising World*. Aldershot: Ashgate.

Small, S. (1994) *Racialised Barriers: The Black Experience in the US and Britain*. London: Routledge.

Smart Justice (2004) *The Racial Justice Gap: Race and the Prison Population Briefing*. London: Smart Justice.

Smith, G. D., Harding, S., Chaturvedi, N., Nazroo, J., and Williams, R. (2000) 'Health Inequalities in the UK', *Critical Public Health*, 10(4):377–408.

Smithers, R. (2002) 'Truancy Sweep Catches 12,000' in *The Guardian*, 19 June.

Soyei, A. (2006) 'More "Safeguards" Against Refugee Confusion', *Professional Social Work*, October, pp. 18–19.

Staples, R. (1988) *Black Masculinity: The Black Male's Role in American Society*. San Francisco: Black Scholar Press.

Stevens, J. (2002) *The Damilola Taylor Murder Investigation Review: The Report of the Oversight Panel*. London: The Stationery Office.

Stone, K. (1997) 'The Body Political', *Community Care*, 9–15 October, pp. 18–19.

Tait-Rolleston, W. and Pehi-Barlow, S. (2001) 'A Maori Social Work Construct' in Dominelli, L., Lorenz, W. and Soydan, H. (eds) *Beyond Racial Divides: Ethnicities in Social Work*. Aldershot: Ashgate.

Taylor, A. (2006) 'Churches Need "Eternal Vigilance"', *Community Care*, 23–29 November, p. 16.

Taylor, J. (2007) 'British Jails for Foreigners Only', *Metro*, 24 October, p. 1.

Taylor, M. (1999) 'Family Group Conferences: A Coordinator's Perspective' in Dominelli, L. (ed.) *Community Approaches to Child Welfare: International Perspectives*. Aldershot: Ashgate.

Taylor, M. (2006) 'BNP Tries to Polish its Image at Blackpool', *The Guardian*, 25 November.

Thiara, R. and Breslin, R. (2006) 'Message is Loud and Clear', *Community Care*, 2–8 November, pp. 32–3.

Thomas, R. and Green, J. (2007) 'Learning through Our Children, Healing for Our Children' in Dominelli, L. (ed.) *Revitalising Communities in a Globalising World*. Aldershot: Ashgate.

Thompson, A. (1997a) 'Black Power', *Community Care*, 24–30 July, pp.18–19.

Thompson, A. (1997b) 'A Woman's Liberation', *Community Care*, 4–10 December, pp. 18–19.

Thompson, N. (2006) *Anti-Discriminatory Practice*. Basingstoke: Palgrave Macmillan.

Thorpe, L (2005) *Race for Health: A Transformational Change Programme*. Bradford: Bradford City PCT.

Tizard, B. and Phoenix, A. (2002) *Black, White or Mixed Race? Race and Racism in the Lives of Young People of Mixed Parentage*. London: Routledge.

Transracial Adoption (2006) *Transracial Adoption: The Preferred Choice*. From www.intermix.org.uk/news-031005-0.1asp accessed on 29 October 2006.

Travis, A. (2002) 'Charities and Unions Attack Asylum Proposals', *Guardian*, 11 June.

Turney, D (1996) *The Language of Anti-Racism in Social Work: Towards a Deconstructive Reading*. London: University of London, Goldsmith.

Turton, J., De Maio, F. and Lane, P. (2003) *Interpretation and Translation Services in the Public Sector: Findings Summary*. London: Home Office.

UK Labour Code of Practice for International Recruitment (2006) from www.sccir.org.uk/download.asp accessed 12 March 2007.

UNHCR (United Nations Human Rights Commission) (2002) *Report of the Committee on the Rights of the Child: Review of the United Kingdom*. Geneva: UNHCR.

UNICEF (2006) *Progress for Children: A Report Card on Malnutrition*. Paris: UNICEF.

Undergown, A. (2002) '"I'm Growing Up Too Fast": Messages from Young Carers', *Children and Society*, 16(1), pp. 57–60.

Van Aken, M. (2006) 'Dancing Belonging: Contesting Dabkeh in Jordan Valley, Jordan', *Journal of Ethnic and Migration Studies*, 32(2), pp. 203–22.

Walker, A. (1990) 'The "Economic" Burden of Ageing and the Prospect of Intergenerational Conflict', *Ageing and Society*, 10(1), pp. 377–96.

Walklate, S. (2004) *Gender, Crime and Criminal Justice*. Culompton: Willan.

Walvin, J. (1992) *Slaves and Slavery: The British Colonial Experience*. Manchester: Manchester University Press.

Worrall, A. (1990) *Women Offending: Female Lawbreakers and the Criminal Justice System*. London: Routledge & Kegan Paul.

Weatherburn, D., Fitzgerald, J. and Hua, J. (2003) 'Reducing Aboriginal Over-Representation in Prison', *Australian Journal of Public Administration*, 62(3), pp. 65–73.

Weiner, F. (1997) *Mistresses and Slaves: Plantation Women in South Carolina, 1830–80*. Chicago: University of Illinois Press.

Wheeler, B. (2006) 'Will BNP Election Gains Last?' in *BBC News*, www.news.bbc.co.uk/2/hi/uk-news/politics/4974870.stm accessed 11 November 2006.

Williams, A. (1978) *Finding a Voice*. London: Virago.

Williams, C. (2003) 'Anti-Oppressive Practice?' *British Journal of Social Work*.

Williams, C., Soydan, H., and Batty, D. (2005) 'When and How Does Ethnicity Matter? A Cross-National Study of Social Work Responses to Ethnicity in Child Protection Cases', *British Journal of Social Work*, 35(6), pp. 901–20.

Williams, C., Evans, N and O'Leary, P. (2006) *A Tolerant Nation? Exploring Ethnic Diversity in Wales*. Cardiff: University of Wales Press.

Williams, L (2007) 'Home Alone' in Dominelli, L (ed) *Revitalising Communities in a Globalising World*. Aldershot: Ashgate.

Wilson, M. (1993) *Crossing the Boundary: Black Women Survive Incest*. London: Virago.

Winkelman, M. (2005) *Cultural Awareness, Sensitivity and Competence*. Peosta, IA: Eddie Bowers.

Winter, P. (2006) 'Blair Fights Shy of Full Apology for Slave Trade', *The Guardian*, 27 November.

Whitehouse, P. (1986) 'Race and the Criminal Justice System' in Coombe, V. and Little, A. (eds) *Race and Social Work*. London: Tavistock.

Young, J. (1999) *The Exclusive Society*. London: Sage.

Yuval-Davis, N. (1992) 'Fundamentalism, Multiculturalism and Women in Britain' in Donald, J. and Rattansi, A. (eds) *'Race', Culture and Difference*. London: Sage.

Author Index

Subject Index